William S. Cleveland

Visualizing Data

AT&T Bell Laboratories, Murray Hill, New Jersey

To Lisa, Bob, and Marylyn

Acknowledgements

To Jon Bentley, for numerous discussions of content and writing that had a remarkable effect on the outcome.

To Sue Pope, for the exceptional skills that were needed to produce the text.

To Estelle McKittrick, for meticulous proofreading of the manuscript.

To Rich Drechsler, Paul Glick, and Howard Trickey, whose solutions to difficult software problems were vital to the typesetting of the book.

To Sandy Persaud, for the efficient administration that the book required.

To Jerome Shepheard, for a high level of quality control in producing camera-ready output.

To Gerard Gorman, for many good ideas on color production.

To Rick Becker and Ming Shyu for our collaboration on software for visualizing statistical data.

To Eric Grosse, for our collaboration on fitting curves and surfaces to data.

To several who commented on the manuscript, providing important feedback — Rick Becker, Jon Bentley, Nick Fisher, Eric Grosse, David James, Colin Mallows, and Ted Walenius.

To Allan Wilks for inventing the path-breaking graphics system Pictor.

To many colleagues at Bell Labs, for creating an optimal environment to study visualization.

Published by Hobart Press, Summit, New Jersey

Copyright ©1993 AT&T. All rights reserved.

Printed in the United States of America

ISBN 0-9634884-0-6   CLOTH

LIBRARY OF CONGRESS CATALOG CARD NUMBER: 92-075077

PUBLISHER'S CATALOGING IN PUBLICATION
Cleveland, William S., 1943–
    Visualizing data / by William S. Cleveland.
    p. cm.
    Includes bibliographical references and index.

    1. Graphic methods.   2. Mathematical statistics–Graphic
    methods.   I. Title.

QA90.C549 1993   511'.5
                                     QBI93-693

Contents

Preface

Visualization is critical to data analysis. It provides a front line of attack, revealing intricate structure in data that cannot be absorbed in any other way. We discover unimagined effects, and we challenge imagined ones.

Tools

Tools matter. There are exceptionally powerful visualization tools, and there are others, some well known, that rarely outperform the best ones. The data analyst needs to be hard-boiled in evaluating the efficacy of a visualization tool. It is easy to be dazzled by a display of data, especially if it is rendered with color or depth. Our tendency is to be misled into thinking we are absorbing relevant information when we see a lot. But the success of a visualization tool should be based solely on the amount we learn about the phenomenon under study. Some tools in the book are new and some are old, but all have a proven record of success in the analysis of common types of statistical data that arise in science and technology.

Graphing and Fitting

There are two components to visualizing the structure of statistical data — graphing and fitting. Graphs are needed, of course, because visualization implies a process in which information is encoded on visual displays. Fitting mathematical functions to data is needed too. Just graphing raw data, without fitting them and without graphing the fits and residuals, often leaves important aspects of data undiscovered. The visualization tools in this book consist of methods for graphing and methods for fitting.

Applications

The book is organized around applications of the visualization tools to data sets from scientific studies. This shows the role each tool plays in data analysis, and the class of problems it solves. It also demonstrates the power of visualization; for many of the data sets, the tools reveal that effects were missed in the original analyses or incorrect assumptions were made about the behavior of the data. And the applications convey the excitement of discovery that visualization brings to data analysis.

The Legacy of the Past

The visualization of statistical data has always existed in one form or another in science and technology. For example, diagrams are the first methods presented in R. A. Fisher's *Statistical Methods for Research Workers*, the 1925 book that brought statistics to many in the scientific and technical community [38]. But with the appearance of John Tukey's pioneering 1977 book, *Exploratory Data Analysis*, visualization became far more concrete and effective [76]. Since 1977, changes in computer systems have changed how we carry out visualization, but not its goals.

Display Methods

When a graph is made, quantitative and categorical information is encoded by a display method. Then the information is visually decoded. This visual perception is a vital link. No matter how clever the choice of the information, and no matter how technologically impressive the encoding, a visualization fails if the decoding fails. Some display methods lead to efficient, accurate decoding, and others lead to inefficient, inaccurate decoding. It is only through scientific study of visual perception that informed judgments can be made about display methods. Display methods are the main topic of *The Elements of Graphing Data* [20]. The visualization methods described here make heavy use of the results of *Elements* and other work in graphical perception.

Prerequisites

The reader should be familiar with basic statistics and the least-squares method of fitting equations to data. For example, an introductory course in statistics that included the fundamentals of regression analysis would be sufficient.

How to Read the Book

For most purposes, the chapters need to be read in order. Material in later chapters uses tools and ideas introduced in earlier chapters. There are two exceptions to this general rule. Chapter 6, which is about multiway data, does not use material beyond Section 4.6 in Chapter 4. Also, sections of the book labeled "For the Record" contain details that are not necessary for understanding and using the visualization tools. The details are meant for those who want to experiment with alterations of the methods, or want to implement the methods, or simply like to take in all of the detail.

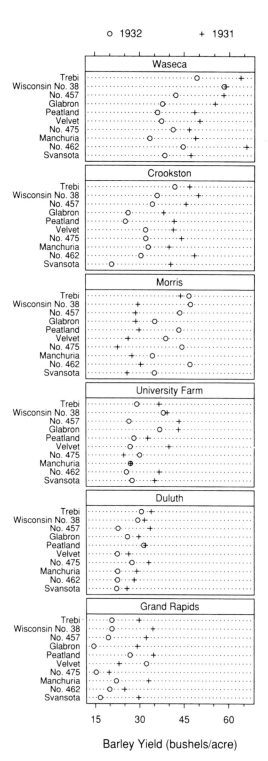

1.1 A multiway dot plot graphs data from a barley experiment run in the 1930s. This visualization reveals an anomaly in the data that was missed by the experimenters and by others who subsequently analyzed the data.

1 Introduction

Visualization is an approach to data analysis that stresses a penetrating look at the structure of data. No other approach conveys as much information. As W. Edwards Deming puts it, visualization "retains the information in the data" [33]. Conclusions spring from data when this information is combined with the prior knowledge of the subject under investigation. An important discovery springs from Figure 1.1. It attests to the power of visualization.

In the early 1930s, agronomists in Minnesota ran a field trial to study the crop barley [55]. At six sites in Minnesota, ten varieties of barley were grown in each of two years. The data are the yields for all combinations of site, variety, and year, so there are $6 \times 10 \times 2 = 120$ observations. In Figure 1.1, each panel displays the 20 yields at a single site.

The barley data have been analyzed and re-analyzed for decades. Their first analysis appeared in a 1934 report published by the experimenters. The statistician and geneticist R. A. Fisher, who established the modern foundations of statistics, presented the data for five of the sites in his book, *The Design of Experiments* [39]. Francis J. Anscombe [3, 4] and Cuthbert Daniel [29], pioneers of diagnostic methods for determining when statistical models fit data, also analyzed them.

Now, the visualization of Figure 1.1 reveals an anomaly that was missed in these previous analyses. It occurs at Morris. For all other sites, 1931 produced a significantly higher overall yield than 1932. The reverse is true at Morris. But most importantly, the amount by which 1932 exceeds 1931 at Morris is similar to the amounts by which 1931 exceeds 1932 at the other sites. Thus we have a mystery. Either an extraordinary natural event, such as disease or a local weather anomaly, produced a strange coincidence, or the years for Morris were inadvertently reversed. The mystery is investigated at the end of the book; the conclusion will be revealed there, not here, to retain the suspense of the full story, which is complicated.

1.1   Tools and Data Types

Tools matter. The Morris anomaly is revealed in Figure 1.1 because the tool used to display the data, a *multiway dot plot,* is an effective one. In the analyses of the past, the methods were insufficient. Even the most adroit data analyst cannot divine effects in data. The critical revelation in Figure 1.1 is not simply that the year effects at Morris are reversed — that was noted in the past. The revelation is that at Morris, the 1932 yields minus the 1931 yields have about the same overall level as the 1931 yields minus the 1932 yields at the other sites. This observation triggers the thought that the years might have been reversed. As Chapter 6 will show, important aspects of the display method of the multiway dot plot contribute to this revelation and other revelations of importance in solving the mystery. Tools matter indeed.

The tools of this book are organized by type of data. Each chapter treats a different data type: univariate, bivariate, trivariate, hypervariate, and multiway.

Univariate Data

Figure 1.2 uses histograms to graph heights of singers in the New York Choral Society [16]. The singers are divided into eight voice parts, shown by the panel labels in the figure. Starting from the lower left panel of the display, and then going from left to right and from bottom to top, the pitch intervals of the voice parts increase. For example, the second basses sing lower pitches than the first basses, who in turn sing lower pitches than the second tenors. The goal of the analysis of the singer data is to determine if the heights tend to decrease as the pitch interval increases. The heights are univariate data: measurements of a single quantitative variable. In this case the variable is broken up into groups by the categorical variable, voice part. The visualization of univariate data is treated in Chapter 2.

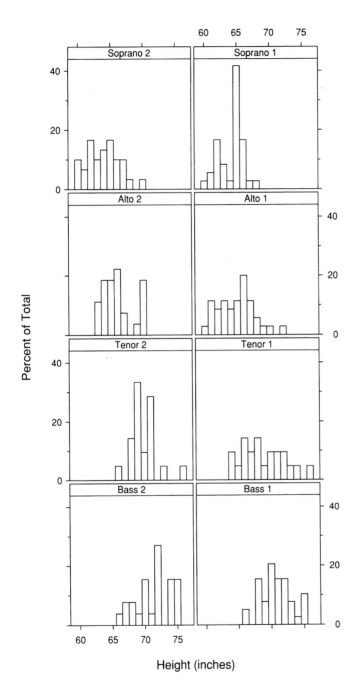

1.2 Histograms graph the singer heights by voice part. The interval width is one inch.

The histogram is a widely used graphical method that is at least a century old. But maturity and ubiquity do not guarantee the efficacy of a tool. The histogram is a poor method for comparing groups of univariate measurements. In Figure 1.2, it does not clearly reveal the relationship of height and voice range. True, we see that the heights in the bottom four panels tend to be greater than the heights in the top four panels. But the bottom heights are all men and the top are all women, so we have merely seen the obvious. The visualization tools in Chapter 2 show far more of the structure of the singer data. They include quantile plots, q-q plots, normal q-q plots, box plots, and fitting methods. The venerable histogram, an old favorite, but a weak competitor, will not be encountered again.

Bivariate Data

Figure 1.3 is a scatterplot of data from an experiment on the scattering of sunlight in the atmosphere [7]. The vertical scale is the Babinet point, the scattering angle at which the polarization of sunlight vanishes. The horizontal scale is the atmospheric concentration of solid particles in the air. The goal is to determine the dependence of the Babinet point on concentration, so the Babinet point is a response and the concentration is a factor. The polarization data are bivariate data: paired measurements of two quantitative variables. The visualization of bivariate data is treated in Chapter 3.

The polarization data have two components of variation. One component is a smooth underlying pattern — a decrease in the overall level of the Babinet point as concentration increases. Fitting such bivariate data means determining a smooth curve that describes the underlying pattern. The second component is residual variation about this underlying pattern — the vertical deviations of the points from the smooth curve.

The scatterplot is a useful exploratory method for providing a first look at bivariate data to see how they are distributed throughout the plane, for example, to see clusters of points, outliers, and so forth.

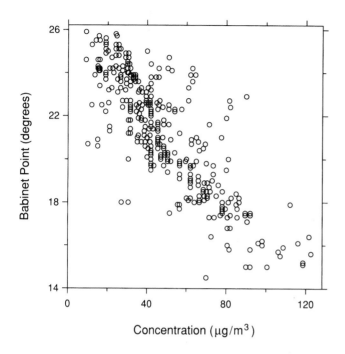

1.3 An exploratory scatterplot graphs the Babinet point against particulate concentration.

But for factor-response data such as the polarization data in Figure 1.3, we should be prepared to move almost immediately to fitting the data and visualizing the fit and residuals. It is part of the folklore of data display that a good method for putting a smooth curve through bivariate data is to stare at an unfitted scatterplot and fair a smooth curve through the data by the mind's eye. In fact, the residual variation often interferes with the visual smoothing. For example, Figure 1.3 suggests that the underlying pattern is linear in the middle with a hint of curvature at the ends, but it is not possible to assess this nonlinearity with precision, or to even determine if it exists. In Chapter 3, a curve is fitted to the polarization data using the fitting method *loess*, and a pattern not readily apparent from the scatterplot emerges. Conversely, when the underlying smooth pattern is a major component of the data, with steep slopes, the pattern interferes with our assessment of the residual variation. In Chapter 3, residual variation is visualized by many methods; for the polarization data, interesting patterns emerge.

Trivariate and Hypervariate Data

   Oxides of nitrogen, NO_x, are one of the major pollutants in
automobile exhaust. An experiment was run to study how the
concentration of NO_x depends on two engine factors: E, the equivalence
ratio, a measure of the richness of the air and fuel mixture, and C, the
compression ratio of the engine [12]. The observations, which consist of
88 measurements of the three quantitative variables, are trivariate data.
Measurements of four or more quantitative variables are hypervariate
data. The visualization of trivariate data is discussed in Chapter 4, and
the visualization of hypervariate data is discussed in Chapter 5.

   Figures 1.4 and 1.5 graph NO_x against the factors. The scatterplot of
NO_x against E reveals a strong nonlinear pattern. The scatterplot of NO_x
against C shows little apparent relationship between the two variables.
Should we conclude that concentration does not depend on C? There is a
precedent for doing this [17]. Still, we will withhold judgment. The data
live in three dimensions, but each scatterplot is a projection onto only
two dimensions. It is possible for 2-D projections not to reveal 3-D
structure. As we go from one point to the next on the scatterplot of NO_x
against C, the value of E changes, so the graph is not providing a proper
view of how NO_x depends on C for E held fixed. It would be imprudent
to conclude at this point that NO_x does not depend on C. For example, a
strong dependence of concentration on E could mask a subtler
dependence on C.

   We need a way of seeing the dependence of NO_x on C without the
interference from E. Visualization tools discussed in Chapters 4 will do
this for us. For example, the coplot is a particularly incisive method for
studying conditional dependence. And, of course, we will fit the data.

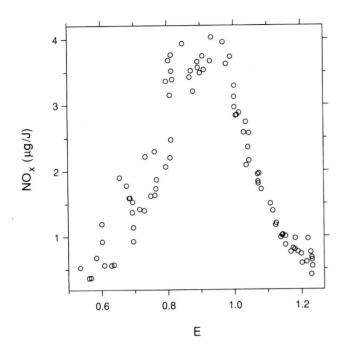

1.4 Oxides of nitrogen are graphed against equivalence ratio.

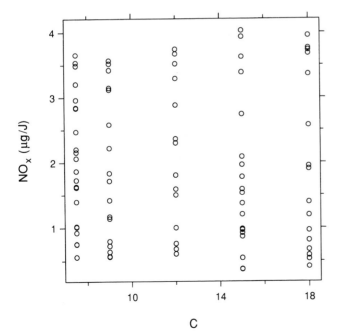

1.5 Oxides of nitrogen are graphed against compression ratio.

Multiway Data

The barley data discussed at the beginning of the chapter are graphed
in Figure 1.6 by a multiway dot plot with a format different from that of
the display of the data in Figure 1.1. The barley measurements are
multiway data: a quantitative variable is measured for each combination
of the levels of two or more categorical variables. The quantitative
variable in this case is yield and the categorical variables are variety, site,
and year. The visualization of multiway data is discussed in Chapter 6.
The chief visualization tool is the multiway dot plot.

1.2   Visualization and Probabilistic Inference

Probabilistic inference is the classical paradigm for data analysis in
science and technology. It rests on a foundation of randomness;
variation in data is ascribed to a random process in which nature
generates data according to a probability distribution. This leads to a
codification of uncertainly by confidence intervals and hypothesis tests.
Pascal, Fermat, and Huygens laid the foundations of probability theory
in the second half of the 17th century, and by the beginning of the 18th
century, the variation in scientific data was being described by
probability models [47]. But the modern foundations of probabilistic
inference as we practice it today were laid in the early part of the 20th
century by R. A. Fisher [38, 39, 40].

Visualization — with its two components, graphing and fitting — is a
different paradigm for learning from data. It stresses a penetrating look
at the structure of data. What is learned from the look is guided by
knowledge of the subject under study. Sometimes visualization can fully
replace the need for probabilistic inference. We visualize the data
effectively and suddenly, there is what Joseph Berkson called *interocular
traumatic impact*: a conclusion that hits us between the eyes. In other
cases, visualization is not enough and probabilistic inference is needed
to help calibrate the uncertainty of a less certain issue. When this is so,
visualization has yet another role to play — checking assumptions. The
validity of methods of probabilistic inference rest on assumptions about
the structure of the population from which the data came. But if
assumptions are false, results are not valid. Despite its flippancy, the
aphorism, "garbage in, garbage out", is an excellent characterization.

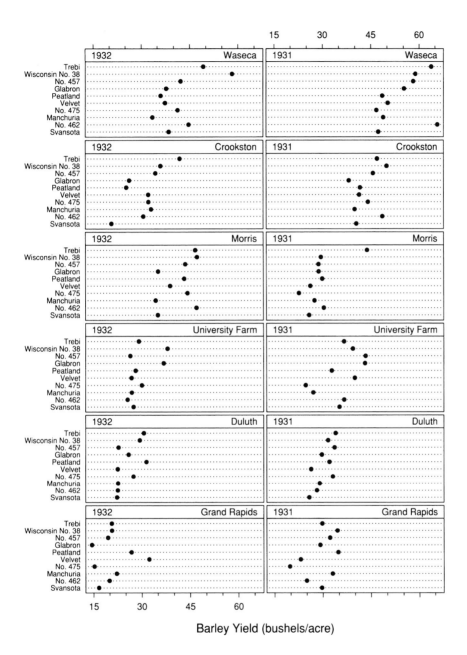

1.6 The barley data are graphed by a multiway dot plot with the data for each site on two panels, one for 1931 and one for 1932.

Without a careful checking of assumptions, validity is replaced by large leaps of faith; one can only hope that the probabilistic assertions of confidence intervals and hypothesis tests are valid. Visualization reduces leaps of faith by providing a framework for studying assumptions.

Carrying out probabilistic inference without checking assumptions deserves an unflattering name. *Rote data analysis* achieves this and describes its character well. Ample examples in the book attest to its dangers.

1.3   Direct Manipulation

Imagine us at the University of Leiden in 1637, trying to understand new data: measurements of the heights and weights of 25 adult males in Leiden. A colleague comes into the office and says, in Dutch, of course:

> I just met a Frenchman named René Descartes and he has an interesting idea for representing mathematical functions of a single variable. Associated with each point in the plane are two numbers: the distances of the point from two perpendicular lines. If the function is f, then the function value $f(x)$ is represented geometrically by showing the point associated with x and $f(x)$. This can be done for many values of x, and the result is a geometric representation of the function that gives you much insight into its behavior. I wonder if we could use this idea to study our height and weight data.

The colleague then reveals Descartes' *La Géométrie* [34].

Cartesian coordinates provide a visual medium within which data can be visually displayed. Most graphical methods use this medium. In 1637 in Leiden, had we been sufficiently creative, we might have exploited Cartesian coordinates and graphed the weights and heights by a scatterplot. This would have made us way ahead of our time. The scientific community only slowly exploited the medium, first on a limited basis in the 1600s and early to middle 1700s, and then with much more energy toward the end of the 1700s [28, 45].

In the 1960s, over three centuries after Descartes' *La Géométrie*, computer scientists created a new visual medium that would be as revolutionary for data display as Cartesian coordinates. *Direct manipulation graphics* appeared on computer screens. The user visually addresses a display using an input device such as a mouse, and causes the display to change in real time. Direct manipulation would become a standard medium not only for data display but also for user interfaces, affecting the basic way that people interface with computer software. But unlike three centuries earlier, scientists were quick off the mark to exploit this new medium for data display. For example, Edward Fowlkes, a statistician, saw the possibilities for graphing data and quickly invented several new methods [2, 43]. As the medium became widely available, the invention of direct manipulation graphical methods grew and intensified [6, 24, 41, 62, 73].

This book presents several direct manipulation methods. This is no small challenge to do on the static pages of a book. But the ideas manage to get through, if not the excitement. The excitement must await the video version of the book.

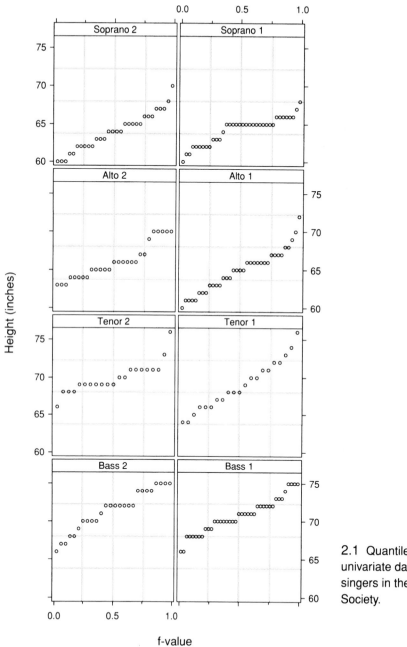

2.1 Quantile plots display univariate data: the heights of singers in the New York Choral Society.

2 Univariate Data

Figure 2.1 graphs data introduced in Chapter 1 — heights of singers in the New York Choral Society [16]. The vertical scale on the panels is height; the horizontal scale, which will be explained shortly, ranges from 0 to 1. The singers are divided into eight voice parts, shown by the panel labels in the figure. The altos and sopranos are women and the tenors and basses are men. The pitch intervals of the voice parts are different. Starting from the lower left panel in Figure 2.1, the pitch interval increases as we progress through the panels from left to right and from bottom to top. For example, the second basses must sing lower pitches than the first basses, who in turn sing lower pitches than the second tenors.

The singer heights are *univariate data*: measurements of a single quantitative variable. The measurements are broken up into groups by the categorical variable, voice part. The goal in analyzing the singer data is to determine whether voice part is related to height. One might expect this because taller people tend to be larger overall, and larger vocal tracts would have lower resonance frequencies, and thus produce lower tones.

2.1 Quantile Plots

The singer heights for each voice part occupy positions along the measurement scale. The collection of positions is the *distribution* of the data. Thus the goal in analyzing the data is to compare the eight height distributions.

Quantiles

Quantiles are essential to visualizing distributions. The f quantile, $q(f)$, of a set of data is a value along the measurement scale of the data with the property that approximately a fraction f of the data are less than or equal to $q(f)$. The property has to be approximate because there might not be a value with exactly a fraction f of the data less than or equal to it. The 0.25 quantile is the *lower quartile*, the 0.5 quantile is the *median*, and the 0.75 quantile is the *upper quartile*.

The graphical methods in this chapter are largely visualizations of quantile information. Quantiles provide a powerful mechanism for comparing distributions because f-values provide a standard for comparison. To compare distributions we can compare quantiles with the same f-values. For example, for the singer heights, the median of the second basses is 72 inches, 4 inches greater than the median of the first tenors. This is a meaningful and informative comparison.

An explicit rule is needed for computing $q(f)$. Consider the first tenor heights. Let $x_{(i)}$, for $i = 1$ to n, be the data ordered from smallest to largest; thus $x_{(1)}$ is the smallest observation and $x_{(n)}$ is the largest. For the first tenors, $n = 21$, $x_{(1)} = 64$ inches, and $x_{(21)} = 76$ inches. Let

$$f_i = \frac{i - 0.5}{n} .$$

These numbers increase in equal steps of $1/n$ beginning with $1/2n$, which is slightly above zero, and ending with $1 - 1/2n$, which is slightly below one. For the first tenors, the values go from $1/42$ to $41/42$ in steps of $1/21$. We will take $x_{(i)}$ to be $q(f_i)$. For the first tenors the values are

f	x	f	x	f	x
0.02	64	0.36	67	0.69	71
0.07	64	0.40	68	0.74	71
0.12	65	0.45	68	0.79	72
0.17	66	0.50	68	0.83	72
0.21	66	0.55	69	0.88	73
0.26	66	0.60	70	0.93	74
0.31	67	0.64	70	0.98	76

The precise form of f_i is not important; we could have used $i/(n+1)$, or even i/n, although this last value would prove inconvenient later for visualization methods that employ the quantiles of a normal distribution.

So far, $q(f)$ has been defined just for f-values that are equal to f_i. The definition is extended to all values of f from 0 to 1 by linear interpolation and extrapolation based on the values of f_i and $q(f_i)$. Figure 2.2 illustrates the method using the first tenor heights. The plotting symbols are the points $(f_i, x_{(i)})$; the interpolation and extrapolation are shown by the line segments.

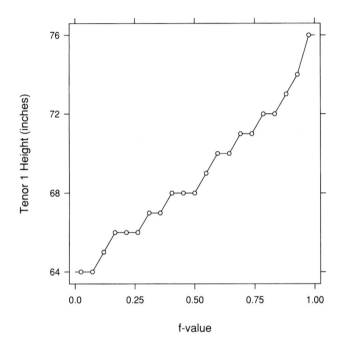

2.2 The symbols and the line segments show the quantile function of the first tenor heights.

Graphing Quantiles

On a *quantile plot*, $x_{(i)}$ is graphed against f_i. In other words, we visualize the f_i quantiles. The panels of Figure 2.1 are quantile plots of the singer heights. The interpolated and extrapolated values of $q(f)$ are not shown because they do not appreciably enhance our visual assessment of the distribution of the data. Rather, the interpolation or extrapolation is used when, for some other purpose, we need a quantile whose f-value does not happen to be one of the values of f_i.

Graphing univariate measurements on a quantile plot is a simple and effective way to have a first look at their distribution. First, the values of all of the data are displayed; we can assess both overall behavior and unusual occurrences. And information about quantiles is conveyed.

Figure 2.1 shows several properties of the singer data: the heights are rounded to the nearest inch; the values for each voice part have a reasonably wide range, about one foot in some cases; there are many first soprano heights equal to 65 inches; and the data have no particularly unusual values, for example, no exceptionally tall or short singers. The height distributions vary substantially with the voice part. At one extreme, the median height is 65 inches for first sopranos, diminutive women piercing the air with notes as high as two octaves above middle C. At the other extreme, the median height is 72 inches for the second basses, tall men vibrating the stage with notes as low as two octaves below middle C. Shortly, other methods for visualizing quantiles will reveal more about the shift in the distributions.

Graphical Order and Visual Reference Grids

Figure 2.1 uses an important convention that will be followed in the remainder of the book; when the panels of a multi-panel display are associated with an ordered variable, such as pitch interval, the variable will increase as we go from left to right and from bottom to top. If the ordered variable were graphed in some way along a horizontal scale, it would increase in going from left to right; if the variable were graphed in some way along a vertical scale, it would increase in going from bottom to top. The *graphical order* of the panels simply follows the established convention.

Figure 2.1 has *visual reference grids*, the vertical and horizontal lines in gray. Their purpose is not to enhance scale reading, or *table look-up*, which is the determination of numerical values from the scales; the tick marks are sufficient for table look-up. Rather, their purpose is to enhance the comparison of patterns, or gestalts, on different panels. By providing a common visual reference, the grids enhance our comparison of the relative locations of features on different panels [21]. For example, in Figure 2.1, the grids make it easy to see that almost all second basses are taller than all of the first sopranos.

2.2 Q-Q Plots

The *quantile-quantile plot*, or *q-q plot*, of Wilk and Gnanadesikan is a powerful visualization method for comparing the distributions of two or more sets of univariate measurements [80]. When distributions are compared, the goal is to understand how the distributions *shift* in going from one data set to the next. For the singers, the goal is to understand how the height distributions shift with voice part.

The most effective way to investigate the shifts of distributions is to compare corresponding quantiles. This was the insightful observation of Wilk and Gnanadesikan, and their invention could not be more simple or elegant — two distributions are compared by graphing quantiles of one distribution against the corresponding quantiles of the other.

Suppose there are just two sets of univariate measurements to be compared. Let $x_{(1)}, \ldots, x_{(n)}$ be the first data set, ordered from smallest to largest. Let $y_{(1)}, \ldots, y_{(m)}$ be the second, also ordered. Suppose $m \leq n$. If $m = n$, then y_i and x_i are both $(i - 0.5)/n$ quantiles of their respective data sets, so on the q-q plot, $y_{(i)}$ is graphed against $x_{(i)}$; that is, the ordered values for one set of data are graphed against the ordered values of the other set. If $m < n$, then y_i is the $(i - 0.5)/m$ quantile of the y data, and we graph y_i against the $(i - 0.5)/m$ quantile of the x data, which typically must be computed by interpolation. With this method, there are always m points on the graph, the number of values in the smaller of the two data sets. Of course, if m is a big number say 10^3, then we can select fewer quantiles for comparison.

Figure 2.3 graphs quantiles of the 26 second basses against quantiles of the 21 first tenors. The size of the smaller data set is 21, so 21 quantiles with f-values equal to $(i - 0.5)/21$ are compared. Because some of the plotting symbols overlap, only 18 distinct points appear on the graph. Ordinarily, such overlap would require a remedy discussed in Chapter 3 — jittering, an addition of uniform random noise to coordinates of the points. But on a q-q plot, the points portray what is actually an increasing continuous curve, one quantile function against another, so breaking up the overlap is not necessary. When $i = 1$, the f-value is 0.024. The point in the lower left corner of the data region is the 0.024 quantile for the basses against the 0.024 quantile for the tenors. When $i = 21$, the f-value is 0.976. The point in the upper right corner of the data region is the 0.976 quantile for the basses against the 0.976 quantile for the tenors.

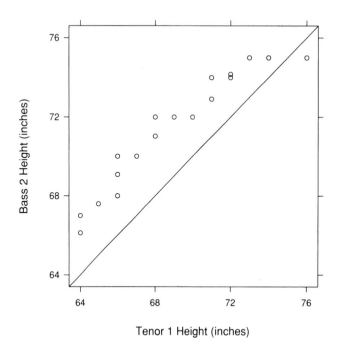

2.3 The first tenor and second bass height distributions are compared by a q-q plot.

Tenor 1 Height (inches)

The line in Figure 2.3 is $b = t$, where b stands for bass and t stands for tenor. Let $(t_i,\ b_i)$ be the coordinates of the points graphed on the panel. Our goal in studying the q-q plot is to determine how the points deviate from the line $b = t$. If the distributions of the tenor and bass heights were the same, the points would vary about this line. But they are not the same. There is a shift between the distributions; the underlying pattern of the points is a line

$$b = t + c.$$

Before interpreting this pattern, we will make one more graph to visualize it in a different way.

Tukey Mean-Difference Plots

A *Tukey mean-difference plot*, or *m-d plot*, can add substantially to our visual assessment of a shift between two distributions. Figure 2.4 is an m-d plot derived from the q-q plot in Figure 2.3. The differences, $b_i - t_i$, are graphed against the means, $(b_i + t_i)/2$. The line $b = t$ on the q-q plot becomes the zero line on the m-d plot, and a shift is assessed by judging deviations from the zero line. This often enhances our perception of effects because we can more readily judge deviations from a horizontal line than from a line with nonzero slope.

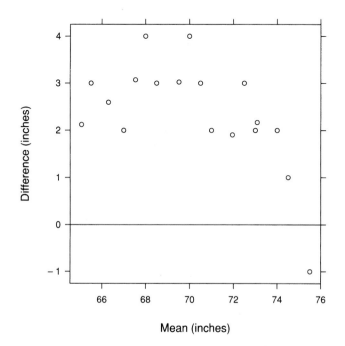

2.4 The first tenor and second bass height distributions are compared by a Tukey m-d plot.

Figures 2.3 and 2.4 show that the tenor and bass distributions differ in an exceedingly simple way: the quantiles of the bass distribution are roughly equal to the quantiles of the tenor distribution plus a constant of about 2.5 inches. There is an *additive shift* of about 2.5 inches. The comparison of the two distributions can be summarized by the simple statement that the distribution of the bass heights is about 2.5 inches greater. This is good news; later examples will show that shifts between distributions can be complex.

Pairwise Q-Q Plots

The goal in analyzing the singer data is to compare the distributions of all voice parts and determine the shifts. Figure 2.5 shows the q-q plots of all possible pairs of voice parts. For example, the second row from the bottom has q-q plots of the first basses against all other voice parts. The second column from the left also compares the distribution of the first basses with all others, but now the first bass quantiles are on the horizontal axis instead of the vertical axis. Thus we can scan either the second row or column to compare the first basses with all other voice parts.

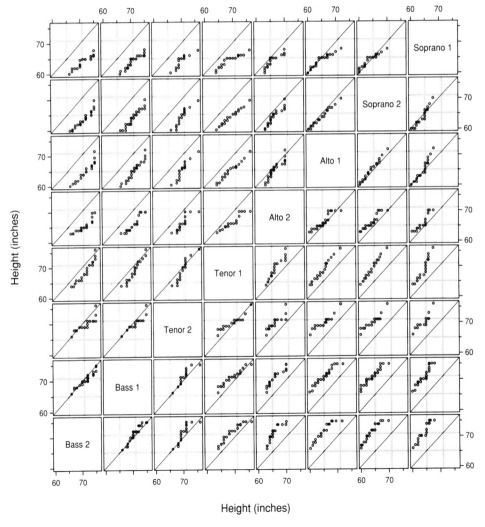

2.5 The height distributions are compared by q-q plots for all pairs of singer voice parts.

There is a great deal of information in Figure 2.5. Overall, there is a suggestion that shifts between pairs of distributions are additive. But we need a way to distill the information because there are so many pairs to compare. Coming methods help with the distillation.

2.3   Box Plots

One method for distilling the information on q-q plots is Tukey's *box plot* [76]. Instead of comparing many quantiles, as on the q-q plot, a limited number of quantities are used to summarize each distribution, and these summaries are compared.

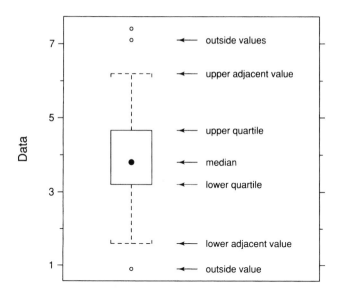

2.6 The diagram defines the box plot display method.

The method of summary is illustrated in Figure 2.6. The filled circle encodes the median, a measure of the center, or *location*, of the distribution. The upper and lower ends of the box are the upper and lower quartiles. The distance between these two values, which is the *interquartile range*, is a measure of the *spread* of the distribution. The middle 50% or so of the data lie between the lower and upper quartiles. If the interquartile range is small, the middle data are tightly packed around the median. If the interquartile range is large, the middle data spread out far from the median. The relative distances of the upper and lower quartiles from the median give information about the *shape* of the distribution of the data. If one distance is much bigger than the other, the distribution is *skewed*.

The dashed appendages of the box plot encode the *adjacent values*. Let r be the interquartile range. The upper adjacent value is the largest observation that is less than or equal to the upper quartile plus $1.5r$. The lower adjacent value is the smallest observation that is greater than or equal to the lower quartile minus $1.5r$. Figure 2.7, a quantile plot, demonstrates their computation. The adjacent values also provide summaries of spread and shape, but do so further in the extremes, or *tails*, of the distribution.

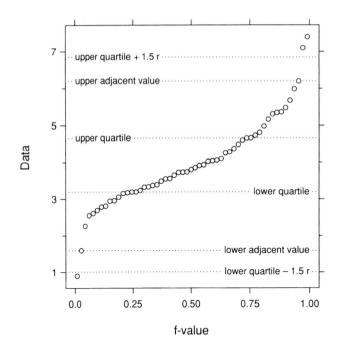

2.7 The diagram illustrates the computation of the adjacent values, which are used in the box plot display method.

Outside values, observations beyond the adjacent values, are graphed individually. Sometimes, the upper adjacent value is the maximum of the data, so there are no outside values in the upper tail; a similar statement holds for the lower tail. Outside values portray behavior in the extreme tails of the distribution, providing further information about spread and shape. If there happen to be outliers — unusually large or small observations — they appear as outside values, so the box plot method of summarizing a distribution does not sweep outliers under the rug.

Figure 2.8 shows box plots of the singer heights. The visualization effectively conveys the relationship of voice part and height. Part of the reason is the perceptual effectiveness of the display method. Each specific aspect of the distributions that is encoded — medians, upper quartiles, lower quartiles, and so forth — can be readily visually decoded [21, 77]. For example, it is easy to see the medians as a whole, and visually assess the values. Also, the format is horizontal to enhance the readability of the labels. Figure 2.8 shows that for the men singers, the tenors and basses, height tends to decrease as the pitch interval increases; the same is true of the women singers, the sopranos and altos. One exception to this pattern is the first sopranos, whose height distribution is quite similar to that of the second sopranos. This might be due to a bias in the measurements; the collector of the data noticed a tendency for the shortest sopranos to round their heights strongly upward.

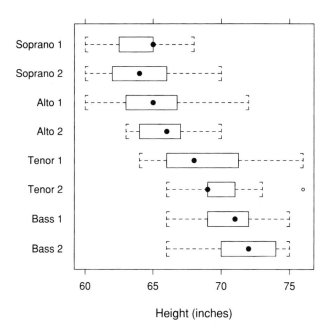

2.8 The eight singer distributions are compared by box plots.

2.4   Normal Q-Q Plots

The box plots in Figure 2.8 show certain effects that accord with our prior knowledge of height and pitch interval, and that we would expect to be reproduced if we were to study another set of singer heights. One such reproducible effect is the general decrease in the height distributions with increasing pitch interval. But the box plots also show spurious effects: unreproducible variation, and variation that is an artifact of rounding to the nearest inch. This spurious variation does not speak to the relationship of height and voice part. For example, for the first sopranos, the median is equal to the upper quartile; for the second tenors, the median is equal to the lower quartile; and the two tallest singers are a first tenor and a second tenor. There is nothing to be learned about height and voice part from these properties of the data. In this section and the next, we move from the graphical methods of the previous sections, which give full vent to the variation in the data, both informative and spurious, to methods whose purpose is to impose structure on the data in an attempt to help us decide what variation appears meaningful and what variation it is better to ignore.

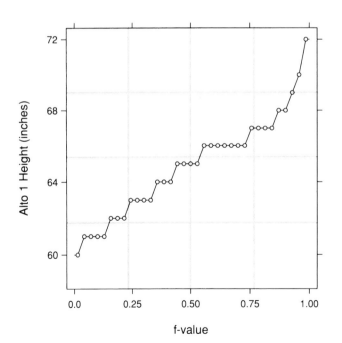

2.9 The plotting symbols and the line segments display the quantile function of the first altos.

Data Quantiles and Normal Quantiles

Figure 2.9 graphs the quantile function, $q(f)$, of the first alto heights. This is the quantile function of a data distribution, a set of real-life univariate measurements. Figure 2.10 graphs quantiles of a mathematical distribution, the normal distribution, a staple of probabilistic inference. It has no reality in the sense that no set of data could ever have such a normal distribution or even be construed as genuinely being a sample from a normal population of potential measurements. It implies, among other things, that measurements range from $-\infty$ to ∞ and have infinite accuracy. Yet it is still helpful to check if the normal quantile function, however imaginary, serves as a reasonable approximation to the real thing, the data distribution.

The normal distribution is a family of distributions. Each normal distribution in the family is specified by two numerical values: the mean, μ, and the standard deviation, σ. The mean is a measure of the location of the distribution, and the standard deviation is a measure of the spread of the distribution about its mean. Given μ and σ, we can

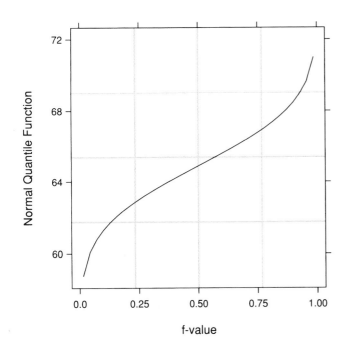

2.10 The curve displays the quantiles of a normal distribution for f-values from 1/70 to 69/70, which are the f-values of the minimum and maximum heights of the first altos.

compute the quantile function, $q_{\mu,\sigma}(f)$, of the specified distribution; in Figure 2.10, the specified mean is the sample mean of the first alto heights,

$$\bar{x} = \frac{1}{35} \sum_{i=1}^{35} x_i = 64.9 \text{ inches} ,$$

and the specified standard deviation is the sample standard deviation of these heights,

$$s = \sqrt{\frac{1}{34} \sum_{i=1}^{35} (x_i - \bar{x})^2} = 2.8 \text{ inches} .$$

Most people think about the normal distribution in terms of random variables and probabilities. Suppose nature generates a value, x, of a random variable with a normal distribution. Let f be a probability between 0 and 1. Then the probability that x is less than or equal to $q_{\mu,\sigma}(f)$ is f. That is, a fraction f of the mass of the normal distribution is less than or equal to $q_{\mu,\sigma}(f)$. Notice that the definition of the normal quantile is analogous to the definition of the quantile, $q(f)$, of a set of data; approximately a fraction f of the mass of the data is less than or equal to $q(f)$.

Graphing Data Quantiles and Normal Quantiles

A *normal quantile-quantile plot*, or *normal q-q plot*, is a graphical method for studying how well the distribution of a set of univariate measurements is approximated by the normal. As before, let $x_{(i)}$ be the data, ordered from smallest to largest, and let $f_i = (i - 0.5)/n$. Suppose the distribution of the data is well approximated by some normal distribution with mean μ and standard deviation σ. $x_{(i)}$ is the f_i

quantile of the data, and $q_{\mu,\sigma}(f_i)$ is the corresponding normal f_i quantile of the approximating distribution. If $x_{(i)}$ is graphed against $q_{\mu,\sigma}(f_i)$, the overall pattern is a line with intercept 0 and slope 1. An important property of normal quantiles is that

$$q_{\mu,\sigma}(f) = \mu + \sigma q_{0,1}(f) ,$$

where $q_{0,1}(f)$ is the quantile function of the unit normal distribution, which has $\mu = 0$ and $\sigma = 1$. In other words, to go from unit normal quantiles to general normal quantiles, we simply multiply by σ and add μ. Thus, if the distribution of the $x_{(i)}$ is well approximated by a normal distribution, then on a graph of $x_{(i)}$ against $q_{0,1}(f_i)$, the overall pattern is a line with intercept μ and slope σ.

A graph of $x_{(i)}$ against $q_{0,1}(f_i)$ is a normal q-q plot. To judge the normal approximation, we judge the underlying pattern of the points on the graph. If the pattern is linear, or nearly so, the data distribution is well approximated by the normal. If not, the deviations from linearity convey important information about how the data distribution deviates from the normal.

Figure 2.11 shows normal q-q plots of the singer data. On each panel, a line is superposed to help us judge the straightness of the pattern. The line passes through the upper and lower quartiles, $(q_{0,1}(0.25), q(0.25))$ and $(q_{0,1}(0.75), q(0.75))$. In each case, the overall pattern appears nearly straight; that is, the eight distributions are reasonably well approximated by normal distributions. The deviations from the overall pattern are inflated by rounding to the nearest inch, which produces strings of points positioned at integer values along the vertical scale. Such discreteness is a departure from normality, because the normal distribution is a continuous one in which any value is possible. But the rounding in this case is not so severe that the approximation is seriously jeopardized.

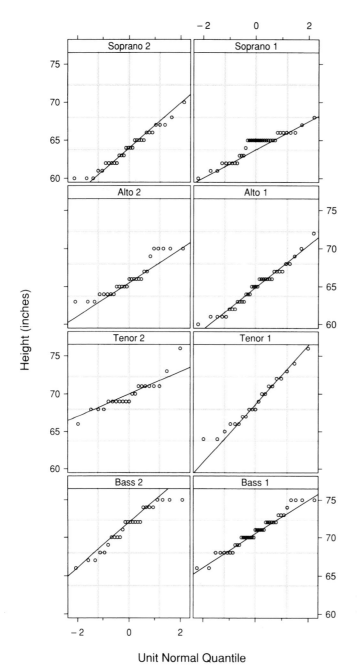

Height (inches)

Unit Normal Quantile

2.11 Normal q-q plots compare the eight height distributions with the normal distribution.

The Normal Approximation

Many good things happen when data distributions are well approximated by the normal. First, the question of whether the shifts among the distributions are additive becomes the question of whether the distributions have the same standard deviation; if so, the shifts are additive. The slope of the pattern of points on a normal q-q plot is an indicator of the standard deviation of the approximating normal, so judging whether standard deviations are equal from normal q-q plots involves judging whether the slopes are equal. For the singer data, the slopes in Figure 2.11 do vary, but not by a large amount. Most importantly, the variation in the slopes is not related to the means of the distributions. If there were a meaningful change in the standard deviations of the singer distributions, we would expect it to take the form of an increase in the voice-part standard deviations as the voice-part means increase. This is not the case.

A second good happening is that methods of fitting and methods of probabilistic inference, to be taken up shortly, are typically simple and on well understood ground. For example, statistical theory tells us that the sample mean, $\bar{x}$, provides a good estimate of the location of the distribution, and the sample standard deviation, s, provides a good estimate of the spread of the distribution.

A third good thing is that the description of the data distribution is more parsimonious. A data distribution needs n values to completely determine it, the n observations x_i. If the distribution is well approximated by the normal, these n values can be replaced by two values, $\bar{x}$ and s. The quantiles of the data are then described by the quantiles of the normal distribution with a mean equal to $\bar{x}$ and a standard deviation equal to s. For example, with these values, we know that the upper quartile of the data is about $\bar{x} + 0.67s$.

2.5   Fits and Residuals

Fitting data means finding mathematical descriptions of structure in the data. An additive shift is a structural property of univariate data in which distributions differ only in location and not in spread or shape. For example, the visualization of the singer data has so far suggested that the voice-part distributions differ only in location. An additive shift is fitted by *estimating* location — computing a location measure for each distribution.

Fitting Additive Shifts by Location Estimates

Two candidates for location estimation are the median and the mean. For the singer data, since the normal q-q plots showed that the distributions are well approximated by the normal, we will follow the imperatives of statistical theory and use means. The voice-part means are graphed by a dot plot in Figure 2.12. The mean height decreases with increasing pitch interval, except for the means of the first and second sopranos, which are very nearly equal. We saw this property earlier in the box plots of Figure 2.8, which used medians rather than means as the location measure. At that stage of our analysis, which was preliminary and exploratory, we used medians because they are not distorted by a few outliers, a property not shared by the mean; we will return to this issue of distortion in Section 2.8.

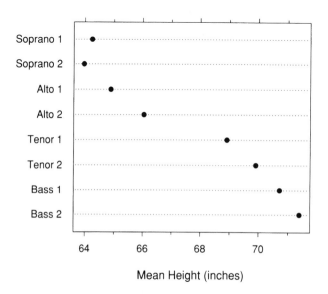

2.12 A dot plot displays the sample means of the height distributions.

Fitted Values and Residuals

For the pth voice part of the singer data, let h_{pi} be the ith measurement of height and let $\bar{h}_p$ be the mean height. In fitting the eight voice-part means to describe the additive shifts, each singer height has had its voice-part mean fitted to it. The *fitted value* for h_{pi} is

$$\widehat{h}_{pi} = \bar{h}_p.$$

The *residuals* are the deviations of the heights from the fitted values,

$$\widehat{\varepsilon}_{pi} = h_{pi} - \widehat{h}_{pi}.$$

Thus the heights have been decomposed into two parts,

$$h_{pi} = \widehat{h}_{pi} + \widehat{\varepsilon}_{pi}.$$

The fitted values account for the variation in the heights attributable to the voice-part variable through the fitting process. The residuals are the remaining variation in the data after the variation due to the shifting means has been removed. This removal is shown in Figure 2.13, which graphs the eight residual distributions. Since the subtraction of means has removed the effect of location, the box plots are centered near zero.

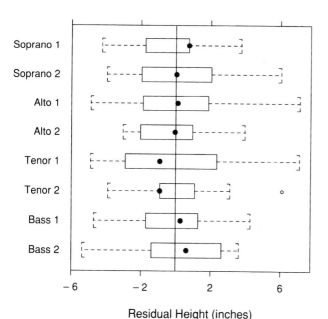

2.13 Box plots compare the distributions of the height residuals for the fit to the data by voice-part means.

Residual Height (inches)

Suppose, as our visualization so far suggests, that the underlying patterns of the eight singer distributions differ by additive shifts. Then the distributions of the eight sets of residuals should be nearly the same because subtracting means eliminates the shifts. Our next task is to compare the distributions of the residuals to see if they appear to be nearly the same; this provides a confirmation of our additive-shift observation.

The residual distributions could be compared by all pairwise q-q plots, but there are 28 pairs, and we would be back to the problem of the pairwise q-q plots of the data in Figure 2.5 — assessing a substantial amount of variation. Figure 2.14 uses another method that results in just eight q-q plots. On each panel, the quantiles of the residuals for one voice part are graphed on the vertical scale against the quantiles of the residuals for all voice parts on the horizontal scale. The line on each panel has slope one and intercept zero. Since the underlying patterns of the points on the eight panels follow these lines, the residual distributions are about the same. This adds credence to a conclusion of additive shifts.

Homogeneity and Pooling

The process of identifying a structure in data and then fitting the structure to produce residuals that have the same distribution lies at the heart of statistical analysis [3, 30, 35, 76]. Such *homogeneous* residuals can be *pooled*, which increases the power of the description of the variation in the data. For the singer data, we have judged the eight residual distributions to be homogeneous, so we can pool them, using the variation in the entire collection of residuals to describe the variation in the residuals for each voice part. This fitting and pooling leads, as we will now show, to a more informative characterization of the variation of the height distribution for each of the voice parts.

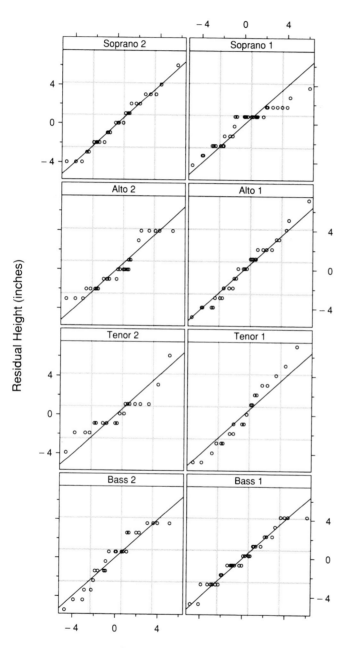

2.14 Each panel is a q-q plot that compares the distribution of the residuals for one voice part with the distribution of the pooled residuals.

Each voice-part distribution can be described by its mean together with the pooled residual variation. Figure 2.15 is a quantile plot of all of the residuals. The 0.025 quantile of the residuals is −4.6 inches and the 0.975 quantile is 4.8 inches. Thus 95% of the residuals lie between about ±4.7 inches. Consider the first sopranos. The mean is 64.3 inches. The resulting description of the 95% first soprano variation is 64.3±4.7 inches, which is 59.6 inches to 69.0 inches. Similarly, the second bass variation is 71.4±4.7 inches, which is 66.7 inches to 76.1 inches. We have been able to use the richer information source of all of the residuals to describe the variation in the second basses and the variation in the first sopranos, rather than relying on just the first soprano heights to describe their variation, and just the second bass heights to describe their variation. Of course, the pooling power has come from imposing structure on the data — an additive-shift structure — and the resulting description is valid only if the structure is valid, but the visualization of the data has made the imposition entirely reasonable.

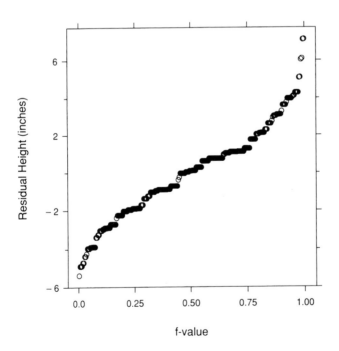

2.15 The pooled residuals are displayed by a quantile plot.

Fitting the Normal Distribution

Once the homogeneity of a set of residuals has been established, we can attempt a fit of the normal distribution to them. Figure 2.16 is a normal quantile graph of the singer residuals. There is a hint of curvature in the underlying pattern, but the effect is relatively minor, so the residual distribution is reasonably well approximated by the normal. Thus we can use a fitted normal to characterize the variability in the residuals.

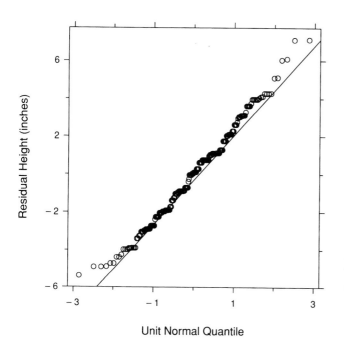

2.16 A normal q-q plot compares the distribution of the pooled residuals with a normal distribution.

Unit Normal Quantile

The sample mean of the residuals is 0 inches because the mean of the residuals for each voice part is 0 inches. The sample standard deviation of the residuals is

$$\sqrt{\frac{1}{n-8}\sum_{p=1}^{8}\sum_{i}\widehat{\varepsilon}_{pi}^{2}} = 2.45 \text{ inches} .$$

Thus the fitted normal has a mean of 0 inches and has a standard deviation of 2.45 inches. The 95% variation about the mean of a normal distribution is ±1.96 times the standard deviation; for the singer residuals, this is ±4.8 inches, a value that is very close to the ±4.7 inches that arose from the residual quantiles. Thus, using this normal fit, the description of the 95% variability in the first soprano heights is 59.5 inches to 69.1 inches and the 95% variability in the second bass heights is 66.6 inches to 76.2 inches. The description via the normal approximation is attractive because it is more parsimonious than the description based on the residual quantiles.

The Spreads of Fitted Values and Residuals

It is informative to study how influential the voice-part variable is in explaining the variation in the height measurements. The fitted values and the residuals are two sets of values each of which has a distribution. If the spread of the fitted-value distribution is large compared with the spread of the residual distribution, then the voice-part variable is influential. If it is small, the voice-part variable is not as influential. Figure 2.17 graphs the two distributions by quantile plots; since it is the spreads of the distributions that are of interest, the fitted values minus their overall mean are graphed instead of the fitted values themselves. This *residual-fit spread plot*, or *r-f spread plot*, shows that the spreads of the residuals and the fitted values are comparable. Thus the voice-part variable accounts for a significant portion of the variation in the height data, but there is a comparable amount of variation remaining.

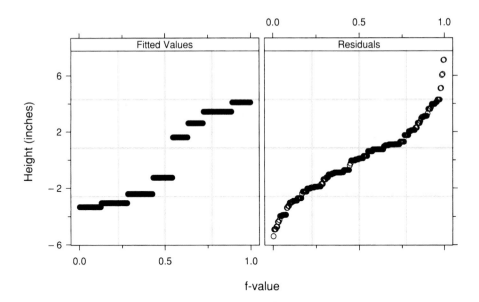

2.17 An r-f spread plot compares the spreads of the residuals and the fitted values minus their mean for the fit to the singer data.

Fitting and Graphing

This approach to studying the singer distributions — fitting sample means to the data, subtracting them to get residuals, and then graphing the fit and residuals — illustrates the visualization paradigm of fitting and graphing. For the singer heights, it has led us to a more powerful description of the data. The sample means fitted to the data summarize the locations of the distributions. The graphs of the residuals make it clear that the distributions of the residuals are homogeneous and well approximated by the normal distribution. The pooling of the residuals to characterize the variation for each voice part and the approximation of the pooled residual distribution by the normal increase the information in the description of the variation of the data. The final result is a convincing, quantified picture of the relationship between height and pitch interval.

2.6 Log Transformation

In 1960 Bela Julesz sprang an ingenious invention on the scientific world of visual perception — the random dot stereogram [56, 57]. An example, designed by Julesz, is shown in Figure 2.18. Each of the two images has the appearance of a collection of random dots. But when the images are looked at in stereo — which means that one image falls on the left retina and the other image falls on the right — a 3-D object is seen. In this case, the object is a diamond-shaped region floating above or below the plane of the page.

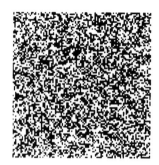 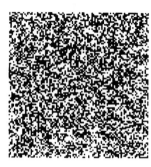

2.18 A diamond-shaped region is shown in 3-D by a random dot stereogram.

One way to fuse the two images in Figure 2.18 — that is, to see the 3-D effect — is to use a stereo viewer, which channels the left image to the left retina and the right image to the right retina. This makes the diamond float above the page. Another method requires no equipment — fixing on a point between the two images and defocusing the eyes by looking through the images, bringing them together in the middle. It is helpful to vary the distance of the image from the eyes to find an optimal position for fusion. When fusion is accomplished, the visual system actually sees three images, with the center one in 3-D, and, again, the diamond floats above the page. It is hard to make this method work the first time, but after a first success, it is typically easy to do again. A third method is crossing the eyes; since this sends the left image to the right retina and the right image to the left retina, the diamond floats below the page. For those without a stereo viewer, mastering the technique of viewing with the unaided eye will have a benefit. A visualization method in Chapter 4 uses stereo to display trivariate data.

The idea of the random dot stereogram is simple and elegant. Embedded in the right view is a region, in this case a diamond, that is exactly repeated in the left view, but is shifted slightly to the right. Quite incredibly, this *binocular disparity* is enough to enable fusion. Julesz's invention demonstrated that the visual system can process local detail to construct an object in 3-D, and needs no other information about the form of the object.

Typically, a viewer concentrating on a random dot stereogram achieves fusion after a few seconds or more. The fusion is not achieved by conscious thought, for example, by the processes that allow us to reason about the world. But fusing the stereogram once makes it easier to do again, so something stored in the brain's memory can decrease fusion time. An experiment was run to study the effect of prior knowledge of an object's form on fusion time [44]. The experimenters measured the time of first fusion for a particular random dot stereogram. There were two groups of subjects. The NV subjects received either no information or verbal information. The VV subjects received a combination of verbal and visual information, either suggestive drawings of the object or a model of it. Thus the VV subjects actually saw something that depicted the object, but the NV subjects did not. The goal in analyzing the fusion times is to determine if there is a shift in the distribution of the VV times toward lower values compared with the NV times. The experimenters used a classical method of probabilistic inference to analyze the data, and concluded that there is no shift. We will use visualization methods to re-examine this result.

Skewness

Figure 2.19 shows quantile plots of the fusion times. The data are *skewed toward large values*. Small values are tightly packed together, and the large values stretch out and cover a much wider range of the measurement scale. The extreme case is the largest NV time, 47.2 seconds, which is more than twice the value of the next largest observation. The skewing gradually increases as we go from small to large values; the result is a strongly convex pattern.

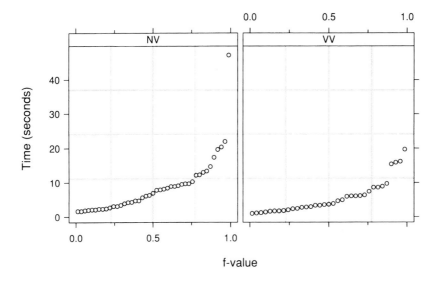

2.19 Quantile plots display the two distributions of the fusion-time data.

As before, let $q(f)$ be the f quantile of the data. Let $d(f)$ be the distance of $q(f)$ from the median,

$$d(f) = |q(0.5) - q(f)|.$$

A distribution is symmetric if $d(f)$ is symmetric about 0.5 as a function of f; that is, $d(f) = d(1 - f)$. The values shown on the quantile plot in Figure 2.20 are symmetric. A distribution is skewed toward large values if $d(f)$ is bigger than $d(1 - f)$ for f in the interval 0.5 to 1, and the disparity increases as f goes from 0.5 to 1, that is, from the center of the distribution to the tails. The values shown on the quantile plot of Figure 2.21 are skewed toward large values.

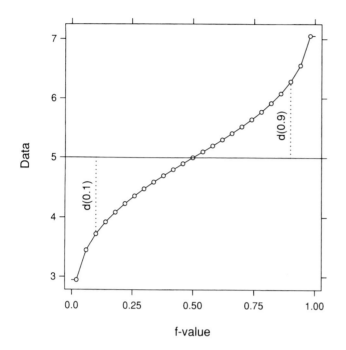

2.20 The graph shows the quantile function of data with a symmetric distribution.

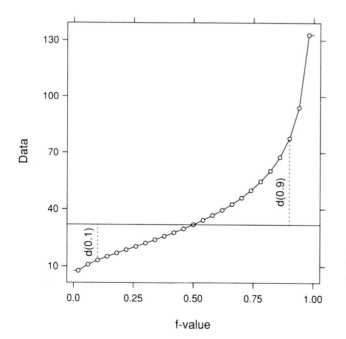

2.21 The graph shows the quantile function of data that are skewed toward large values.

Figure 2.22 shows normal q-q plots of the fusion times. The skewness toward large values creates the same convex pattern as on the quantile plot. This deviation from normality occurs because the normal distribution is symmetric. This behavior contrasts with that of the distributions of the singer heights, which are nearly symmetric and are well approximated by the normal distribution.

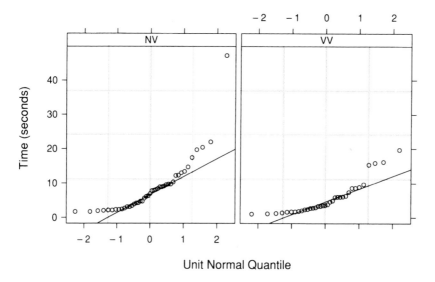

2.22 Normal q-q plots compare the distributions of the fusion-time data with the normal distribution.

Data that are skewed toward large values occur commonly. Any set of positive measurements is a candidate. Nature just works like that. In fact, if data consisting of positive numbers range over several powers of ten, it is almost a guarantee that they will be skewed. Skewness creates many problems. There are visualization problems. A large fraction of the data are squashed into small regions of graphs, and visual assessment of the data degrades. There are characterization problems. Skewed distributions tend to be more complicated than symmetric ones; for example, there is no unique notion of location and the median and mean measure different aspects of the distribution. There are problems in carrying out probabilistic methods. The distribution of skewed data is not well approximated by the normal, so the many probabilistic methods based on an assumption of a normal distribution cannot be applied. Fortunately, remedies coming in later sections can cure skewness.

Monotone Spread

In Figure 2.23, box plots of the fusion-time distributions show that the median of the NV times is greater than the median of the VV times, and the spread of the NV times is greater than the spread of the VV times. In other words, the spreads increase with the locations. The same phenomenon can also be seen on the normal q-q plots in Figure 2.22. The slope of the line on each panel is the interquartile range of the data divided by the interquartile range of the unit normal distribution. This measure of spread is just a rescaling of the interquartile range of the data. In Figure 2.22, the slope for the NV times is greater than the slope for the VV times.

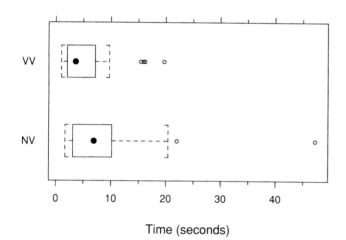

2.23 The distributions of the fusion times are compared by box plots.

Time (seconds)

When the distributions of two or more groups of univariate data are skewed, it is common to have the spread increase monotonically with location. This behavior is *monotone spread*. Strictly speaking, monotone spread includes the case where the spread decreases monotonically with location, but such a decrease is much less common for raw data. Monotone spread, as with skewness, adds to the difficulty of data analysis. For example, it means that we cannot fit just location estimates to produce homogeneous residuals; we must fit spread estimates as well. Furthermore, the distributions cannot be compared by a number of standard methods of probabilistic inference that are based on an assumption of equal spreads; the standard t-test is one example. Fortunately, remedies for skewness can cure monotone spread as well.

Transformation by Logs

For positive univariate measurements, it is often more natural to consider multiplicative effects rather than additive ones. The fusion times are one example. Consider times of 4 seconds and 6 seconds for two individuals. The interesting information is that the second individual took 1.5 times as long. The two individuals differ by a lot more in their fusion performance than two individuals with times of 20 seconds and 22 seconds. Even though the absolute difference, 2 seconds, is the same in both cases, the poorer performer in the first case took 50% longer, whereas the poorer performer in the second set took only 10% longer. Taking logs amounts to changing the units of the data — from seconds to log seconds for the fusion times — in such a way that equal differences now mean equal multiplicative factors. This simplifies the interpretation of the measurement scale because, to put it simplistically, addition is easier than multiplication.

The logarithm is one of many transformations that we can apply to univariate measurements. The square root is another. Transformation is a critical tool for visualization or for any other mode of data analysis because it can substantially simplify the structure of a set of data. For example, transformation can remove skewness toward large values, and it can remove monotone increasing spread. And often, it is the logarithm that achieves this removal.

Figure 2.24 shows normal q-q plots of the logs of the fusion times. The data are now much closer to symmetry, although there is a small amount of remaining skewness; the points in the lower tail of each distribution lie somewhat above the line. In other words, the data quantiles in the lower tail are a bit too big, or too close to the median. The effect is small, but there is a plausible explanation. There is a minimum amount of time that a subject needs to consciously realize that the visual system has fused the stereogram, and then to signal that fusion has occurred. Effectively, this makes the origin somewhat bigger than 0 seconds. We could try to bring the lower tail into line by subtracting a small constant such as 0.5 seconds from all of the data, but this gets fussier than we need to be.

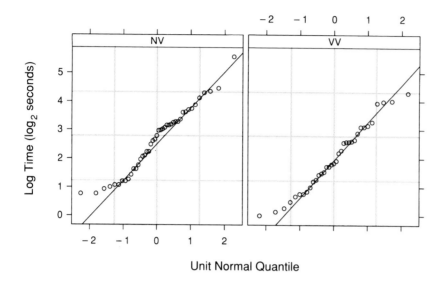

2.24 Normal q-q plots compare the distributions of the log fusion times with the normal distribution.

In graphing the log fusion times, log base 2 has been used. Thus, a change of one unit on the transformed scale means a change on the original scale by a factor of two. When data range through just a few powers of 10, $\log_2$ is easier to interpret than $\log_{10}$ because fractional powers of 10 are harder to fathom than integer powers of 2 [20].

Except for the outlier, the fusion times range from 1 second to 22 seconds. On the $\log_2$ scale, this range becomes 0 $\log_2$ seconds to 4.5 $\log_2$ seconds. On the $\log_{10}$ scale, the range becomes 0 $\log_{10}$ seconds to 1.3 $\log_{10}$ seconds, and we must expend effort fathoming fractional powers of 10 to comprehend the multiplicative effects.

S-L Plots

   Monotone spread, when it occurs, can typically be spotted on box
plots. For example, Figure 2.23 revealed the monotone spread of the
fusion times. But the box plot is a general-purpose visualization tool for
exploring many aspects of distributions, not just spread. The
spread-location plot, or *s-l plot*, provides a more sensitive look at
monotone spread because it is a specialized tool whose sole purpose is
to detect changes in spread. The s-l plot translates looking at spread to
looking at location. First, medians are fitted to the distributions of the
data, x_i. Measures of location for the absolute values of the residuals,
$|\widehat{\varepsilon}_i|$, are measures of spread for the x_i. For example, the *median absolute
deviations*, or *mads*, of the distributions of the x_i are the medians of the
distributions of the $|\widehat{\varepsilon}_i|$ [51, 65].

   Figure 2.25 is an s-l plot of the fusion times. The circles graph the
square roots of the $|\widehat{\varepsilon}_i|$ for the two distributions against the fitted values,
which take on two values, the medians of the two distributions. To
prevent undue overlap of the plotting symbols, the locations of the
symbols are jittered by adding uniform random noise to the fitted
values. Jittering will discussed further in Chapter 3.

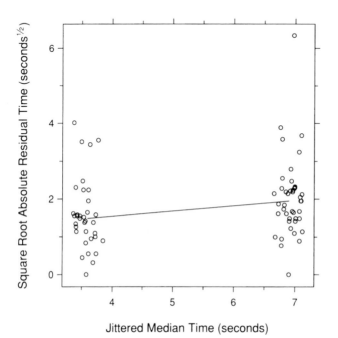

2.25 The s-l plot for the fusion
times checks for nonuniform spread.

The square root transformation is used because absolute residuals are almost always severely skewed toward large values, and the square root often removes the asymmetry. Also, the square roots of the two mads are graphed against the two medians by connecting the plotting locations by a line segment.

The s-l plot for the fusion times adds to our understanding of the monotone spread of the distributions. It shows a convincing upward shift in the location of the $\sqrt{|\widehat{\varepsilon}_i|}$ for the NV times.

Figure 2.26 is an s-l plot for the log fusion times. The log transformation, in addition to removing most of the skewness, makes the spreads nearly equal. It is not unusual for a single transformation to do both. Nature is frequently kind enough to allow this.

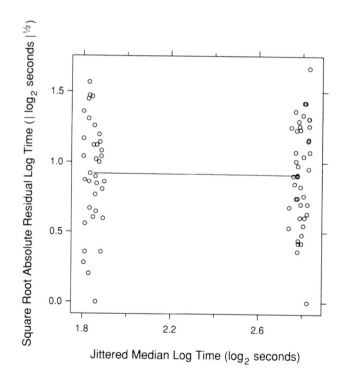

2.26 The s-l plot for the log fusion times checks for nonuniform spread.

Multiplicative and Additive Shifts

As we saw for the fusion times, logs can simplify structure by changing severe skewness to near symmetry and by changing monotone spread to nearly equal spread. It can also simplify structure by changing multiplicative shifts among distributions to additive shifts.

Figure 2.27 is a q-q plot of the fusion times on the original scale, before taking logs. There is a shift in the two distributions, but unlike the singer heights, it is not additive. The underlying pattern is a line through the origin with a slope of about 2/3. The shift is multiplicative, and quantiles with large f-values differ by more than those with small ones. This multiplicative shift is more complicated than an additive one because it results in a difference not just in the locations of the distributions but in the spreads as well. This produces the monotone spread.

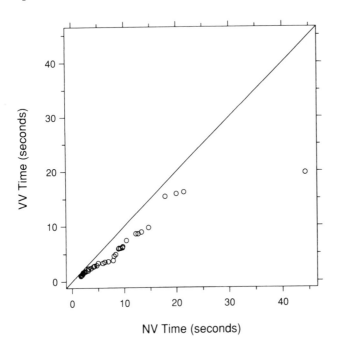

2.27 The q-q plot compares the distributions of the fusion times.

Figure 2.28 is a q-q plot of the log fusion times, and Figure 2.29 is a corresponding m-d plot. Now, on the log scale, the effect is additive. On the average, the log VV times are about 0.6 $\log_2$ seconds less than the log NV times. Back on the original scale, this is just the multiplicative effect with a multiplicative constant of $2^{-0.6} = 0.660 \approx 2/3$.

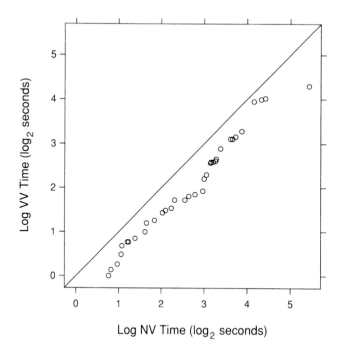

2.28 The q-q plot compares the distributions of the log fusion times.

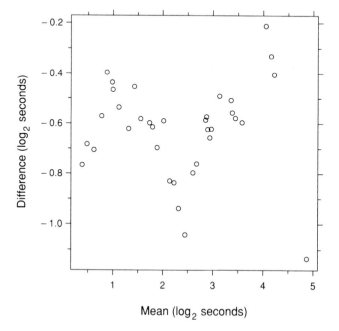

2.29 The m-d plot provides more information about the shift of the log fusion times.

Fitting and Residuals

Since logs result in an additive shift of the fusion times, the fitting on the log scale only needs to account for a shift in location. Since the distributions are not far from the normal, means can be used to estimate locations. The mean for the log NV times is 2.6 $\log_2$ seconds, and the mean for the log VV times is 2.0 $\log_2$ seconds. Figure 2.30 shows q-q plots of the residuals; the quantiles of each residual distribution are graphed against the quantiles of the pooled residuals. The patterns lie close to the lines, which have intercept 0 and slope 1, so the two residual distributions are nearly the same. The residuals are homogeneous and can be pooled to characterize the variation in the data.

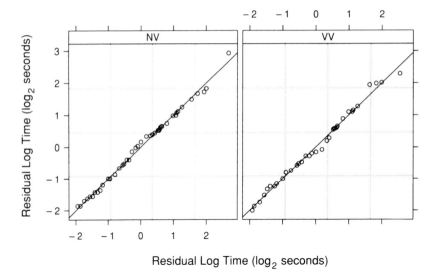

2.30 Each panel is a q-q plot that compares the distribution of the residuals for one group of log times with the distribution of the pooled residuals.

Figure 2.31, a normal q-q plot of the pooled residuals, shows the lifting of the lower tail observed earlier. The departure from normality begins at a value of -1 on the horizontal axis. This is the 0.16 quantile of the unit normal distribution. Thus the upper 84% of the distribution of the pooled residuals is well approximated by the normal. Figure 2.32, an r-f spread plot, shows that the spread of the residuals is considerably greater than the spread of the fitted values. Thus the effect of the increased VV information is small compared with other factors that affect fusion time.

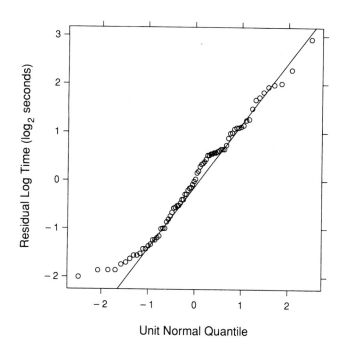

2.31 A normal q-q plot compares the normal distribution with the distribution of the pooled residuals for the fit to log fusion time.

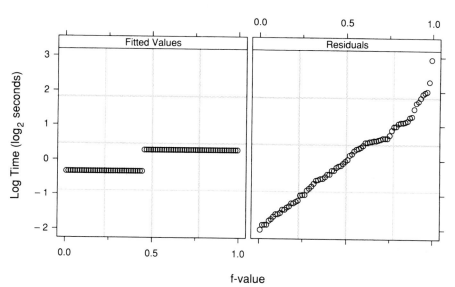

2.32 An r-f spread plot compares the spreads of the residuals and the fitted values minus their mean for the fit to log fusion time.

In the original analysis of the fusion-time data, the experimenters concluded that there was no support for the hypothesis that prior information about the object reduces fusion time. Yet our analysis here does seem to suggest an effect: the VV distribution is shifted toward lower values by a factor of 2/3. This apparent conflict between the original analysis and the analysis here is discussed in the final section of this chapter where it is argued that our visualization of the data has yielded valid insight that was missed by the experimenters.

2.7   Power Transformation

We need more than just the logarithm in our arsenal of transformation methods. Logs cannot be used for data with zeros unless the data are adjusted. And a transformation other than the logarithm is often the one that leads to a simple data structure; in many cases the logarithm can fail to cure skewness and monotone spread, but another transformation does so.

Power transformations are a class of transformations that includes the logarithm. Let x be the variable under study. The power transformation with parameter τ is defined to be x^τ if $\tau \neq 0$ and $\log(x)$ if $\tau = 0$. For $\tau = 1$, the transformation is just x, so this leaves the data alone. For $\tau = 1/2$, the transformation is the square root, $\sqrt{x}$. For $\tau = -1$, it is the inverse of the data, $1/x$. It might seem artificial to define the power transformation for $\tau = 0$ to be the logarithm, but in fact it belongs there because x^τ for τ close to zero behaves much like the logarithm; for example, the derivative of $\log x$ is x^{-1}, and the derivative of $x^{0.001}$ is proportional to $x^{-.999}$. The parameter τ can be any number if the data are positive, but τ must be greater than 0 if the data have zeros. Of course, if the data have negative values, no power transformation is possible without some adjustment of the data.

Figure 2.33 shows normal q-q plots of the VV fusion times transformed by seven power transformations with values of τ equal to $-1, -1/2, -1/4, 0, 1/4, 1/2$, and 1. The panels are in graphical order: the value of τ increases as we go from left to right and from bottom to top through the panels. The figure illustrates a phenomenon that occurs for many data sets that are skewed toward large values. As τ decreases from 1, the skewness is reduced until the data become nearly symmetric, and then as τ is further reduced, the data become more and more skewed again. When τ goes from 1 to $1/2$, the transformation pushes the upper tail closer to the center and pulls the lower tail further from the center. This continues as τ decreases, although when τ goes negative, the transformation reverses the upper and lower tails, so the continued force of the transformation pulls out the upper tail and pushes in the lower.

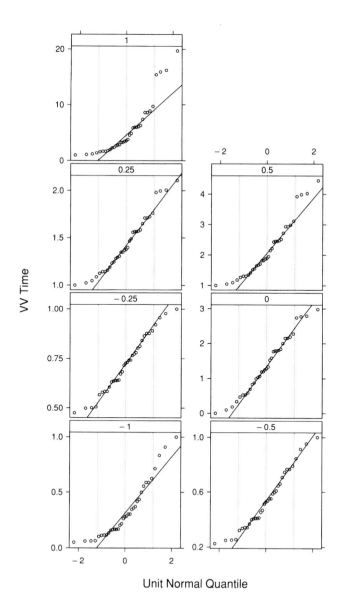

2.33 Seven power transformations of the VV times are displayed by normal q-q plots.

Unit Normal Quantile

Figure 2.33 illustrates the method for discovering the power transformation that brings a distribution the closest to symmetry — trial and error. We simply choose a selection of values of τ, graph the transformed data for each transformation, and assess the symmetry. The seven values of τ in Figure 2.33 are a good starting set because they provide a representative collection of power transformations. For the VV times, the logarithm and the inverse fourth root do the best job. They also do the best job for the NV times. But, of course, a tie goes to the logarithm because of the multiplicative interpretation.

Food Webs

The food web for the animal species in an ecosystem is a description of who eats whom. A chain is a path through the web. It begins with a species that is eaten by no other, moves to a species that the first species eats, moves next to a species that the second species eats, and so forth until the chain ends at a species that preys on no other. If there are 7 species in the chain then there are 6 links between species, and the length of the chain is 6. The mean chain length of a web is the mean of the lengths of all chains in the web.

A two-dimensional ecosystem lies in a flat environment such as a lake bottom or a grassland; movement of species in a third dimension is limited. In a three-dimensional ecosystem, there is considerable movement in three dimensions. One example is a forest canopy; another is a water column in an ocean or lake. A mixed ecosystem is made up of a two-dimensional environment and a three-dimensional environment with enough links between the two to regard it as a single ecosystem. An interesting study reports the mean chain lengths for 113 webs [11]. Quantile plots display the data in Figure 2.34. Here, we will study how the distributions of mean chain lengths vary for the three classes — two-dimensional, mixed, and three-dimensional. In doing this, we regard the dimensionality of the mixed webs as lying between that of the two-dimensional webs and the three-dimensional webs.

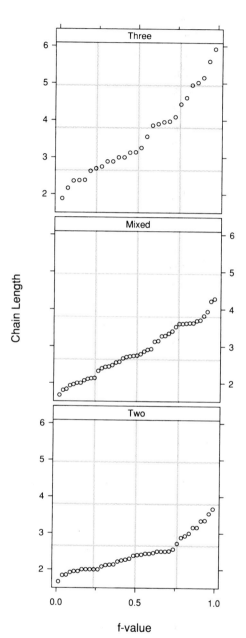

2.34 Quantile plots display the chain length measurements for three ecosystem dimensions.

Skewness and Monotone Spread

Figure 2.35 is an s-l plot of the three distributions of chain length. There is monotone spread. Normal q-q plots in Figure 2.36 reveal mild skewness toward large values. Also, the middle panel shows a peculiarity in the upper tail of the webs of mixed dimension. At a length of about 3.5, there is a knee in the distribution caused by five webs with very nearly identical values.

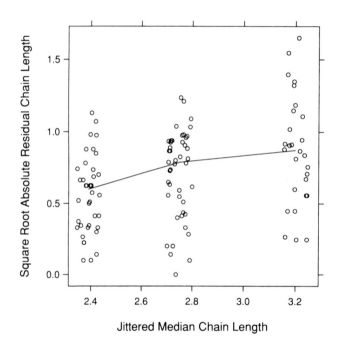

2.35 The s-l plot for the chain lengths checks for nonuniform spread.

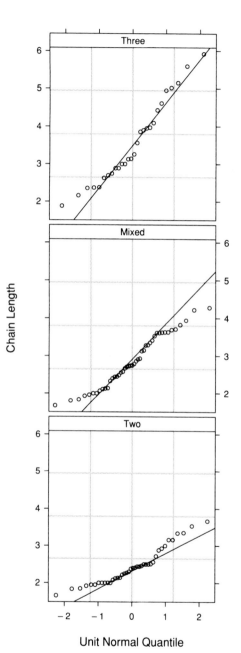

2.36 Normal q-q plots compare the chain length distributions with the normal distribution.

The skewness and monotone spread of the food web data are not cured by the logarithm, although the transformation does reduce their severity. Figure 2.37 is an s-l plot for the logs. The monotone spread remains, although the magnitude has been substantially reduced. Figure 2.38 shows normal q-q plots. Skewness remains, particularly for dimension two. We need a smaller value of τ.

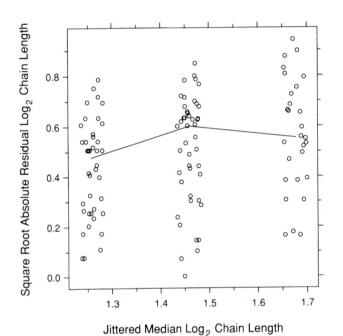

2.37 The s-l plot for the log chain lengths checks for nonuniform spread.

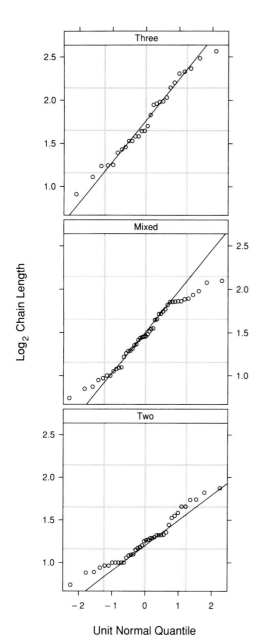

2.38 Normal q-q plots compare the log chain length distributions with the normal distribution.

The inverse transformation, which is $\tau = -1$, does the best job although the improvement over the logarithm is small. Figure 2.39 is the s-l plot for the inverse lengths; monotone spread no longer occurs. Figure 2.40 shows normal q-q plots of the inverses. The peculiar behavior for the mixed dimension now occurs in the lower tail because the inverse transformation has changed the order of the measurements. The other two panels, however, show a small amount of convexity in the lower tail of the distribution, so some of the peculiar behavior for the mixed dimension appears to be part of a general pattern.

The inverse transformation provides a natural measurement scale for the food web data. The measurement scale for chain length is links per chain. The measurement scale for inverse chain length is chains per link, or the *link fraction*. There is no reason to prefer links per chain to chains per link.

Fitting and Residuals

The normal q-q plots of the distributions in Figure 2.40 suggest that the shifts in the link-fraction distributions are additive on the inverse scale. Thus we will fit the data by estimating location, using means

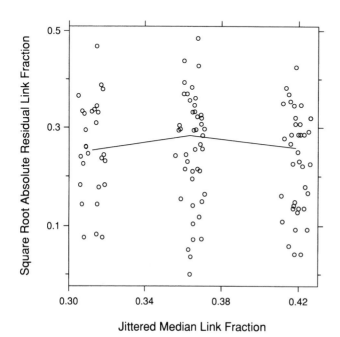

2.39 The s-l plot for the inverse chain lengths, or link fractions, checks for nonuniform spread.

because the distributions are not badly nonnormal. The mean link fractions are 0.43, 0.37, and 0.31 for two, mixed, and three. Note that these values are very close to 7/16, 6/16, and 5/16. Noting this form is likely just pure numerology, a taking of pleasure from detecting a simple pattern, but without theoretical significance.

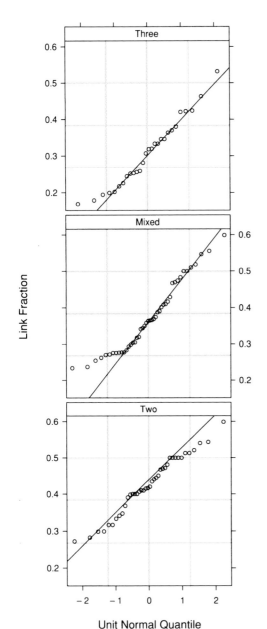

2.40 Normal q-q plots compare the normal distribution with the distributions of link fractions.

Figure 2.41 is a q-q plot of the residuals; the quantiles of each residual distribution are graphed against the quantiles of all residuals. The distributions are reasonably similar, so we can pool them.

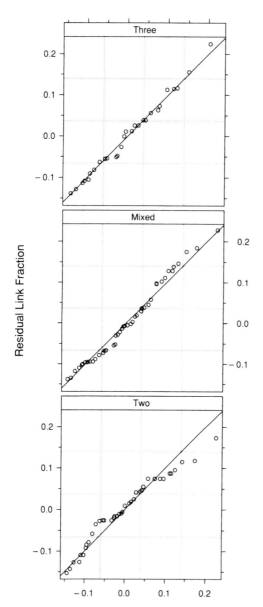

2.41 Each panel is a q-q plot that compares the distribution of the residuals for one group of link fractions with the distribution of the pooled residuals.

of 11 values: 125, 250, 500, and so forth by factors of 2 up to 128000. There were 25 runs for each of the 11 different numbers of weights, which makes $25 \times 11 = 275$ runs in all. For each run of the experiment, the performance of the algorithm was measured by the total amount of empty space in the bins that were used. We will study log empty space to enhance our understanding of multiplicative effects.

Shifts in Location, Spread, and Shape

Figure 2.43 displays the bin packing data by box plots. The shifts in the 11 distributions are complex. The locations tend to increase with n, the number of weights. For example, the medians increase with n except for the two smallest values of n. The box plots also show that the spreads of the distributions tend to decrease as n increases. Both the interquartile ranges and the ranges of the adjacent values tend to decrease with n.

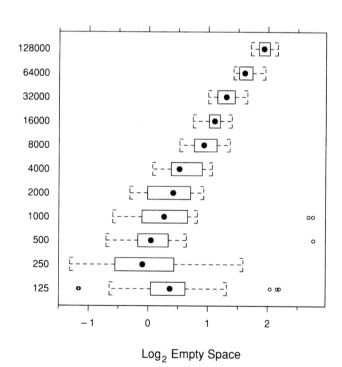

2.43 Box plots compare the distributions of the bin packing data.

Figure 2.44, normal q-q plots of the bin packing data, show that not all of the bin packing distributions are well approximated by the normal. For n equal to 2000 to 128000, the patterns are reasonably straight, but for lesser values of n, there are marked deviations from linear patterns. In other words, not only do the distributions differ in location and spread, they differ in shape as well. To study this shape in more detail, we will fit the data, compute residuals, and study the residual distributions. But since both location and spread change, we need to estimate both in fitting the data.

Figure 2.44 reveals enough information about shape to have a major impact on how we carry out the fitting of location and spread. For $n = 125$, the line follows the middle of the data; if the entire distribution were well approximated by the normal, the points in the tails would lie near this line. Instead, the points in the upper tail are above the line, and the points in the lower tail are below the line. In other words, with respect to a normal distribution as determined by the middle of the data, the values in the tails are too spread out. Distributions with this property occur frequently enough that there is a term to describe their shape — *leptokurtic*. The root "lepto" means slender. For data that are leptokurtic, the relative density of the data in the middle of the distribution compared with the density in the tails is less (thinner) than for a normal distribution. In cases where leptokurtosis affects only the extreme tails, the result can be just a few outliers. For n equal to 500 and 1000, three observations are considerably larger than the others. These outliers are likely just a remnant of a leptokurtosis that moves further and further into the tails of the distribution as n increases through 1000.

The opposite of leptokurtosis is *platykurtosis*. With respect to a normal distribution as determined by the middle of the data, the values in the tails of the data are a bit too close to the middle, that is, not sufficiently spread out. The root "platy" means broad. For data that are platykurtic, the relative density of the data in the middle of the distribution compared with the density in the tails is greater (broader) than for a normal distribution. Shortly, we will also see platykurtosis in the bin packing data.

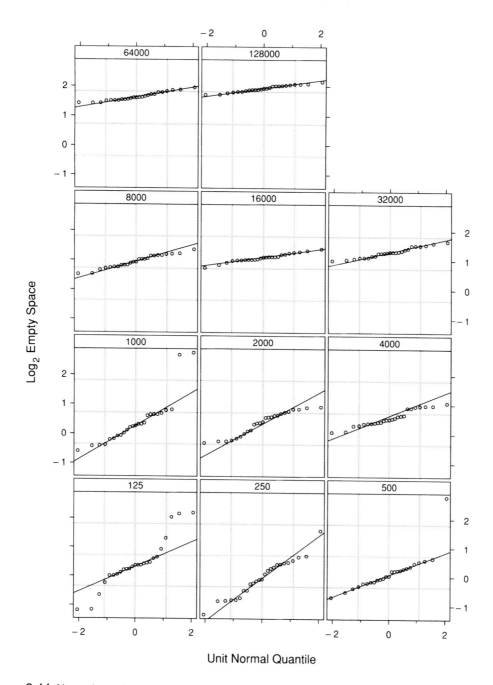

2.44 Normal q-q plots compare the distributions of the bin packing data with the normal distribution.

Robust Estimation

For the singer heights, the log fusion times, and the link fractions, the distributions of the different groups of measurements are reasonably well approximated by the normal. For this reason, in fitting the data, we used sample means to estimate the locations of the distributions. Had it been necessary to account for changing spread, we would have used sample standard deviations to fit spread. Statistical theory tells us that sample means and standard deviations are the right thing to use when the distributions are close to the normal. And when a distribution is mildly platykurtic, sample means and standard deviations are typically satisfactory.

But in the presence of leptokurtosis, means and standard deviations can perform disastrously. Even just a few outliers can yield a silly answer. Suppose we have 20 observations ranging from 10 to 20 with a mean of 16.3. Suppose we add one new observation, an outlier equal to 99. The mean of the new data now becomes

$$(20 \times 16.3 + 99)/21 = 20.2 \ .$$

This is not a sensible description of the location of the data because it exceeds all of the observations except one. The sample standard deviation is also sensitive to a small number of outliers.

The median is typically *robust*: resistant to a few outliers or to more extreme leptokurtosis [51, 65]. Suppose that for the 20 observations above, the two middle observations — that is, the 10th and 11th largest observations — are 14 and 15. Then the median is 14.5. When the outlier is added, the median changes to 15, a sensible answer. Similarly, the mad, introduced earlier for use on s-l plots, is a robust estimate of spread [51, 65]. Thus we will use medians to fit the locations of the bin packing distributions, and mads to fit the spreads.

Let b_{in} be the ith log empty space measurement for the bin packing run with n weights. Let ℓ_n be the medians, and let s_n be the mads. The fitted values are

$$\widehat{b}_{in} = \ell_n \, ,$$

the residuals are

$$\widehat{\varepsilon}_{in} = b_{in} - \widehat{b}_{in} \, ,$$

and the *spread-standardized residuals* are

$$\frac{\widehat{\varepsilon}_i}{s_n} \, .$$

In Figure 2.45, the distributions of the 11 sets of spread-standardized residuals are graphed by normal q-q plots. As before, the leptokurtosis is clearly revealed, but now we also see that once n is above 1000, the distributions turn mildly platykurtic. But a few outliers for distributions with $n \leq 1000$ squash the spread-standardized residuals for $n > 1000$ into a small region of the vertical scale, which interferes with our assessment of the platykurtosis. To enhance the assessment, we will eliminate the four distributions with $n \leq 1000$, and analyze the remaining seven residual distributions. Figure 2.46 shows q-q plots of each residual distribution against the pooled distribution of the seven sets. The departures for the three smaller values of n appear somewhat bigger than for the remaining, so there are differences among the distributions, but the effect is slight.

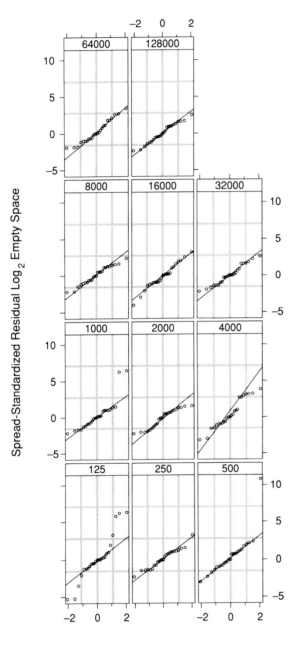

2.45 Normal q-q plots display spread-standardized residuals from the robust fit to the bin packing data.

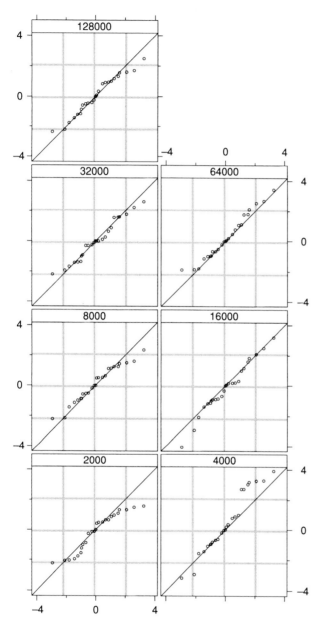

2.46 The q-q plots compare distributions of spread-standardized residuals for seven values of n with the pooled values of the seven distributions.

Spread-Standardized Residual $\log_2$ Empty Space

While Figure 2.46 has suggested some differences among the seven distributions with $n > 1000$, the magnitudes of the differences appear small, so we will pool the residuals anyway to further study the platykurtosis of the distributions. Figure 2.47, a normal q-q plot of the pooled values, shows that the shortening of the tails with respect to the normal begins near the quartiles of the data.

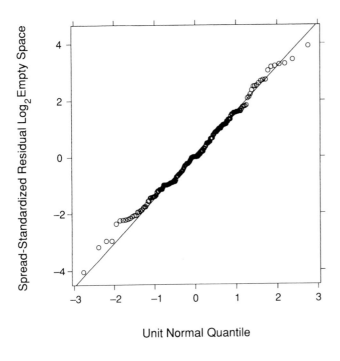

2.47 The normal q-q plot compares the normal distribution with the distribution of the pooled spread-standardized residuals for seven values of n.

Figure 2.48 graphs ℓ_n against $\log n$. Theoretical results suggest that when n gets large, ℓ_n is linear in $\log n$ with a slope of $1/3$ [8]. The line in Figure 2.48 has a slope of $1/3$ and passes through the rightmost point. The points for the largest values of $\log n$ do indeed appear to be increasing with this slope, but for the smaller values of $\log n$, the pattern of the points is convex and the slopes are less. In other words, before the asymptotics take over, the rate of growth in log empty space is less than $1/3$, and the rate increases as n increases.

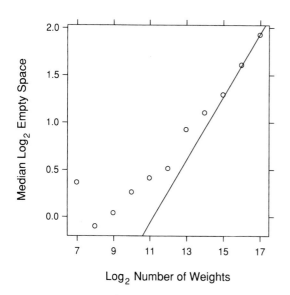

2.48 Median log empty space is graphed against log number of weights.

To study the behavior of s_n as a function of n, Figure 2.49 graphs log s_n against log n. The underlying pattern is linear, and a line with a slope of $-1/3$ would fit the pattern. This triggers an uncomfortable thought.

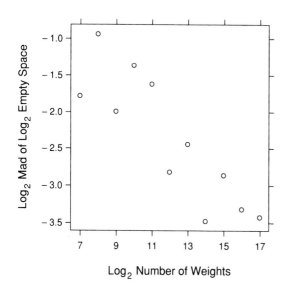

2.49 The logs of the mads for log empty space are graphed against log number of weights.

Since the log medians grow with a slope of $1/3$ as a function of $\log n$, and the log mads grow with a slope of $-1/3$ as a function of $\log n$, the log mads as a function of the log medians should have a slope of -1. This is checked in Figure 2.50; each s_n is divided by the minimum of the s_n, the log is taken, and the values are graphed against ℓ_n. This is simply an alternative form of the s-l plot; instead of graphing square root absolute residuals and square root mads against the medians, the log relative mads are graphed against the medians. The pattern is indeed linear with a slope of -1. In other words, there is monotone spread — a decrease in the spread with location. The discomfort is this. If the spreads of distributions do not depend on the locations, then taking logs can create monotone spread with exactly the pattern observed in Figure 2.50. We took the logs of the measurements of empty space at the outset to enhance the interpretation of multiplicative effects, but it is now likely that the transformation has induced the monotone spread.

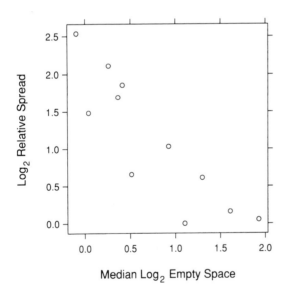

2.50 Log relative mads for log empty space are graphed against median log empty space.

This is checked in Figure 2.51; the alternate s-l visualization method employed in Figure 2.50 is also used, but for empty space without transformation. Quite clearly, there is no monotone spread.

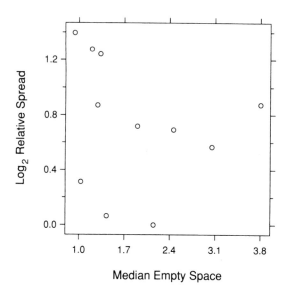

2.51 Log relative mads for empty space are graphed against median empty space.

Backing Up

By taking logs at the outset to enhance the interpretation of multiplicative effects, we have induced some of the variation in the spreads of the distributions of empty space. With the benefit of visualization hindsight, it appears that we would be better off fitting empty space rather than log empty space. Then, we can always take logs of fits to study multiplicative properties. Thus, we should go back to the beginning and analyze the data again without transformation. We will not do so in this account since the data have been treated enough. Such backing up is common. It speaks to the power of visualization to show us mistaken actions that we have no way of judging until we visualize the results.

2.9   *Direct Manipulation: Outlier Deletion*

Outliers not only force us to use robust fitting, they ruin the
resolution of graphical displays. A single large outlier that expands the
range of the data by a factor of, say 2, squashes all of the remaining data
into 50% of the scale on a graph. The normal q-q plot of the
spread-standardized residuals in Figure 2.45 was the victim of such
squashing. The range of all spread-standardized residuals is -5.28 to
10.82. But 97% of them lie between ± 4, so 3% of the spread-standardized
residuals take up about 50% of the vertical scale. The result is a reduction
in our ability to assess the nonnormality of the distributions aside from
the outlier behavior. For example, the platykurtosis for n greater than
1000 is barely noticeable on the display. The remedy was to continue the
visualization for the distributions with $n > 1000$. This removed the
outliers. Another sensible procedure would have been to make
Figure 2.45 again, but deleting the points whose vertical scale values lie
beyond ± 4. The result of this outlier deletion is shown in Figure 2.52.

Direct manipulation provides an effective way to delete outliers.
Since we identify outliers through the visualization process, it is natural
to visually designate points for deletion by touching them with an input
device. By their nature, outliers are typically few in number, so the
process can be carried out quickly. By contrast, in computing
environments that allow only static graphics, outlier deletion must be
carried out by a less natural process. Scales must be read to determine
cutoffs such as the ± 4 used for Figure 2.52, then commands must be
issued to determine those observations that do not survive the cutoff,
then more commands must be issued to delete them from the data given
to the graphical routine, and finally the graph must be redrawn.

Outlier deletion by direct manipulation is so attractive that in 1969
Edward Fowlkes made it one of the first tools in the arsenal of direct
manipulation methods discussed in Chapter 1. And outlier deletion was
among the first operations of brushing, a direct manipulation tool that
will be described in Chapter 3.

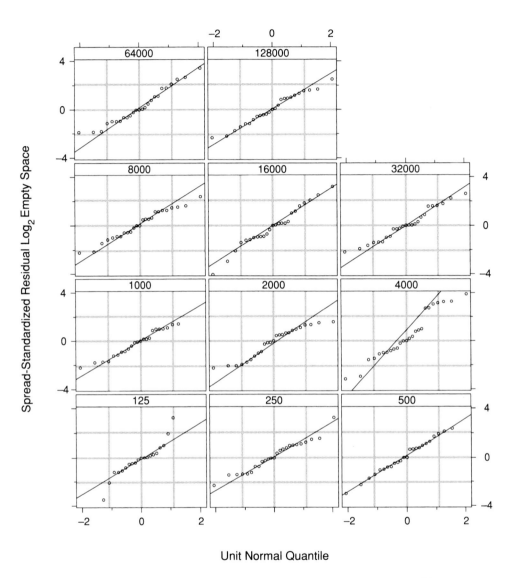

Unit Normal Quantile

2.52 The outliers in the spread-standardized residuals have been removed. Direct manipulation provides a convenient environment for such point deletion.

2.10   Visualization and Probabilistic Inference

Visualization can serve as a stand-alone framework for making inferences from data. Or, it can be used to support probabilistic inferences such as hypothesis tests and confidence intervals. The fusion times provide a good example of this interplay between visualization and probabilistic inference.

The Julesz Hypothesis

Fusing a complicated random dot stereogram requires movements of the eyes to the correct viewing angle to align the two images. These movements happen very quickly in viewing a real scene; they bring focus to the scene as we shift our attention among objects at different distances. A more complex series of movements is needed to fuse a complicated random dot stereogram for the first time. But viewers can typically drastically reduce the time needed to fuse it by repeated viewing. Practice makes perfect because the eyes learn how to carry out the movements.

From informal observation, Bela Julesz noted that prior information about the visual form of an object shown in a random dot stereogram seemed to reduce the fusion time of a first look [57]. It certainly makes sense that if repeated viewing can reduce the fusion time, then seeing a 3-D model of the object would also give the viewer some information useful to the eye movements. This Julesz observation led to the experiment on fusion time, a rough pilot experiment to see if strong effects exist.

Reproducibility

Our visualization of the fusion times showed an effect; the distribution shifts toward longer times for reduced prior information. But the r-f plot showed the effect is small compared with the overall variation in fusion time. This makes it less convincing. Perhaps the better performance of increased information is spurious. Another experiment run in the same way might yield data in which decreased prior information produced shorter times. Once we begin thinking like this, it is time for probabilistic inference, not that we expect a definitive answer, but just simply to extract further information to help us judge the reproducibility of the results.

Statistical Modeling

But we must make the big intellectual leap required in probabilistic inference. We imagine that the subjects in the experiment are a random sample of individuals who can use a stereogram to see in depth. (A small fraction of individuals get no depth perception from stereo viewing.) Thus the log times for each group, NV and VV, are a random sample of the population of times for all of our specified individuals. Let μ_v be the population mean of the log VV times and let μ_n be the population mean of the log NV times.

Validating Assumptions

The normal q-q plots in our analysis showed that the two distributions of log times are reasonably well approximated by normal distributions. The lower tails are slightly elevated, but the departures are small. Thus it is reasonable to suppose that our two populations of log fusion times are well approximated by the normal distribution. The q-q plots and the fitting for viewing showed that it is reasonable to suppose the two population distributions have an additive shift. In particular, this means the standard deviations of the two populations are the same. With this checking of assumptions through visualization, we have earned the right to use the standard t-method to form a confidence interval for the difference in the two population means. Also, the visualization has revealed that it would be improper to use this method on the original data, which are severely nonnormal and do not differ by an additive shift.

Confidence Intervals

The sample mean of the 35 log VV times is $\bar{x}_v = 2.00 \log_2$ seconds. The sample mean of the 43 log NV times is $\bar{x}_n = 2.63 \log_2$ seconds. The estimate of the sample standard deviation from the residuals, $\hat{\varepsilon}_i$, is

$$ s = \sqrt{\frac{1}{76} \sum_{i=1}^{78} \hat{\varepsilon}_i{}^2} = 1.18 \; \log_2 \text{ seconds} . $$

A 95% confidence interval for the difference in population means, $\mu_n - \mu_v$, is

$$ (\bar{x}_n - \bar{x}_v) \pm 1.99 \, s \sqrt{\frac{1}{43} + \frac{1}{35}} , $$

where 1.99 is the 0.975 quantile of a t-distribution with 76 degrees of freedom. The lower and upper values of the 95% interval are 0.09 and 1.15. Furthermore, the interval (0, 1.24) is a 97.7% interval. In other words, there is reasonable evidence that the results of the experiment are reproducible because a value of 0, which means no effect, does not enter a confidence interval until the confidence level is 97.7%.

Rote Data Analysis

The fusion-time experimenters based their conclusions on rote data analysis: probabilistic inference unguided by the insight that visualization brings. They put their data into an hypothesis test, reducing the information in the 78 measurements to one numerical value, the significance level of the test. The level was not small enough, so they concluded that the experiment did not support the hypothesis that prior information reduces fusion time. Without a full visualization, they did not discover taking logs, the additive shift, and the near normality of the distributions. Such rote analysis guarantees frequent failure. We cannot learn efficiently about nature by routinely taking the rich information in data and reducing it to a single number. Information will be lost. By contrast, visualization retains the information in the data.

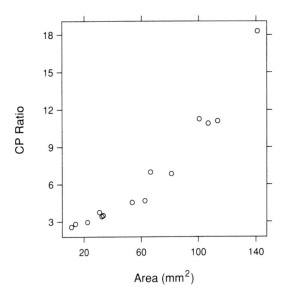

3.1 A scatterplot displays bivariate data: measurements of retinal area and CP ratio for 14 cat fetuses.

3 Bivariate Data

Figure 3.1 is a scatterplot of two variables from a study in animal physiology [60]. For species with highly developed visual systems, such as cats and man, the distribution of ganglion cells across the surface of the retina is not uniform. For example, cats at birth have a much greater density of cells in the central portion of the retina than on the periphery. But in the early stages of fetal development, the distribution of ganglion cells is uniform. The nonuniformity develops in later stages. Figure 3.1 is a scatterplot of data for 14 cat fetuses ranging in age from 35 to 62 days of gestation. The vertical scale is the ratio of the central ganglion cell density to the peripheral density. The horizontal scale is the retinal area; this variable is nearly monotonically increasing with age, so age tends to increase from left to right along the scale. The scatterplot shows that the ratio increases as the retinal area increases.

The ratios and areas in Figure 3.1 are *bivariate data*: paired measurements of two quantitative variables. The goal in this case is to study how the ratios depend on the areas. Ratio is the *response* and area is the *factor*. In other examples of this chapter, neither variable is a factor or response, and the goal is to study the distribution of the observations in the plane and to determine how the variables are related.

3.1   Smooth Curves and Banking

The scatterplot is an excellent first exploratory graph to study the dependence of a response on a factor. An important second exploratory graph adds a smooth curve to the scatterplot to help us better perceive the pattern of the dependence.

Loess Curves

Figure 3.2 adds a *loess* curve to the ganglion data; loess is a fitting tool that will be described in the next section [19, 22, 23]. The fitted curve has a convex pattern, which means that the rate of change of CP ratio with area increases as area increases. In this example, the existence of the curvature is apparent from the unadorned scatterplot in Figure 3.1, but the graphing of the curve provides a more incisive description. In examples coming later, even the broad nature of the curvature is not revealed until a curve is added.

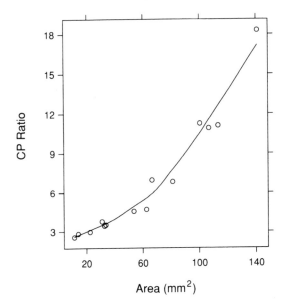

3.2 A loess curve has been added to the scatterplot of the ganglion data. The aspect ratio of the graph has been chosen to bank the curve to 45°.

Visual Perception: Banking

The *data rectangle* of a graph just encloses the data on the graph. In Figure 3.2, the upper right corner of the data rectangle is at the data point in the upper right corner, and the lower left corner of the rectangle is at the data point in the lower left corner. The *aspect ratio* of a graph is the height of the data rectangle divided by the width. In Figure 3.2, the aspect ratio is 1.08.

The fitted curve in Figure 3.2 is made up of a collection of connected line segments. First, the fit was evaluated at 100 equally spaced values of the factor, which results in 100 points in the plane; then the curve was drawn by connecting the 100 points by line segments.

Our perception of a curve is based on judgment of the relative orientations of the line segments that make up the curve. Suppose we measure orientation in degrees. A line segment with slope 1 has an orientation of 45°, and a line segment with slope −1 has an orientation of −45°. Typically, the judgments of a curve are optimized when the absolute values of the orientations are centered on 45°, that is, when the location of the distribution of absolute orientations is 45° [21, 25]. Chapter 4 contains an analysis of the data from the perceptual experiment that led to the discovery of this 45° principle.

It is the aspect ratio that controls the orientations of line segments on a graph. This is illustrated in Figure 3.3, which draws the same curve with three aspect ratios: 0.5 in the upper left panel, 0.05 in the lower panel, and 5 in the upper right panel. The absolute orientations are centered on 45° in the upper left, on 5.7° in the lower, and on 84° in the upper right. The upper left panel provides the best perception of the properties of the curve; the left half of the curve is convex and the right half is linear. Choosing the aspect ratio of a graph to enhance the perception of the orientations of line segments is *banking*, a display method whose name suggests the banking of a road to affect its slope. Choosing the aspect ratio to center the absolute orientations on 45° is *banking to 45°*. In Figure 3.2, the aspect ratio has been chosen by banking the segments of the loess curve to 45°. At the end of this section, a method will be given for finding the aspect ratio that banks a collection of segments to 45°.

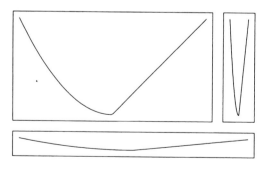

3.3 The same curve is graphed with three different aspect ratios: 0.5 in the upper left panel, 5 in the upper right panel, and 0.05 in the bottom panel. The aspect ratio of 0.5 banks the curve to 45°.

Banking is a vital aspect of visualizing curves, and will be widely invoked in this and later chapters. It is not always practical to bank to 45° because the aspect ratio that produces it can be too small or too large for the resolution of the physical display device. In some cases, as we will see later in this chapter, a display can be redesigned to enable the optimal value. In other cases we will simply take the aspect ratio to be as close to the optimal value as possible.

For the Record: A Method for Banking to 45°

Let v be the length in physical units of a vertical side of the data rectangle of a graph. In Figure 3.2, the scatterplot of the ganglion data with the loess curve, the value of v is 5.5 cm. Let $\ddot{v}$ be the length of the vertical side in data units. In Figure 3.2, the value of $\ddot{v}$ is 15.7 units of CP ratio, or 15.7 cpr. Similarly, let h be the length in physical units of a horizontal side of the data rectangle, and let $\ddot{h}$ be the length in data units.

Consider the length in data units of any interval on the measurement scale of a variable. For example, suppose for the CP ratio scale that the length is 5 cpr. Then $v/\ddot{v}$ is the conversion factor that takes the length in the units of the data and changes it to a length in physical units on the graph. For example, for Figure 3.2, 5 cpr becomes

$$5 \text{ cpr } \frac{5.5 \text{ cm}}{15.7 \text{ cpr}} = 1.8 \text{ cm}.$$

Similarly, $h/\ddot{h}$ is the conversion factor for the horizontal scale.

The aspect ratio of the data on the graph is

$$a(h, v) = v/h.$$

Suppose the units of the data are fixed so that $\ddot{v}$ and $\ddot{h}$ are fixed values. The values of v and h are under our control in graphing the data. The aspect ratio is determined by our choice of v and h, which is why in the notation we show the dependence of a on v and h.

Consider a collection of n line segments inside the data region. Let $\ddot{v}_i$ be the change in data units of the ith line segment along the vertical scale, and let $v_i(v)$ be the change in physical units when the vertical length of the data rectangle is v. Define $\ddot{h}_i$ and $h_i(h)$ similarly. Let

$$\bar{v}_i = \ddot{v}_i/\ddot{v}$$

and

$$\bar{h}_i = \ddot{h}_i/\ddot{h} \ .$$

The orientation of the ith segment is

$$\theta_i(h, v) = \arctan\left(\frac{v_i(v)}{h_i(v)}\right) = \arctan\left(a(h, v)\bar{v}_i/\bar{h}_i\right) \ .$$

The physical length of the ith segment is

$$\ell_i(h, v) = \sqrt{h_i^2(h) + v_i^2(v)} = h\sqrt{\bar{h}_i^2 + a^2(h, v)\bar{v}_i^2} \ .$$

One method for banking the n segments to $45°$ is to choose $a(h, v)$ so that the mean of the absolute orientations weighted by the line segment lengths is $45°$. Thus

$$\frac{\sum_{i=1}^n \theta_i(h, v)\ell_i(h, v)}{\sum_{i=1}^n \ell_i(h, v)} = \frac{\sum_{i=1}^n \arctan\left(a(h, v)\bar{v}_i/\bar{h}_i\right)\sqrt{\bar{h}_i^2 + a^2(h, v)\bar{v}_i^2}}{\sum_{i=1}^n \sqrt{\bar{h}_i^2 + a^2(h, v)\bar{v}_i^2}}$$

is equal to $45°$. Notice that the right side of this formula depends on v and h only through $a(h, v)$. As is intuitively clear, if we multiply v and h by the same factor, the orientations of the segments do not change. Only their ratio matters. Thus it is the aspect ratio that controls banking.

There is no closed-form solution for the aspect ratio that makes the above weighted mean absolute orientation equal to $45°$. The value of a needs to be found by iterative approximation. But the approximation can be fast because the weighted mean is a monotone function of a.

3.2   Fitting: Parametric and Loess

Figure 3.2 has shown clearly that the underlying pattern in the ganglion data is convex. Astonishingly, the three experimenters who gathered and analyzed the data, fitted a line. Figure 3.4 shows the fit. As expected, there is *lack of fit*. Figure 3.5 shows the fit of a quadratic. The fitted function now describes the underlying pattern in the data. The lack of fit has been eliminated.

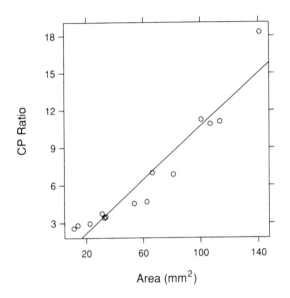

3.4 The least-squares line has been added to the scatterplot of the ganglion data.

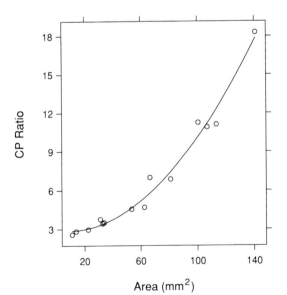

3.5 The least-squares fit of a quadratic polynomial has been added to the scatterplot of the ganglion data. The curve is banked to 45°.

Parametric Families of Functions

Fitting a line to data is an example of *parametric fitting*. Lines, or linear polynomials,

$$y = a + bx \, ,$$

are a parametric family of functions that depend on two parameters, a and b. Fitting the linear family to data means selecting, or estimating, a and b so that the resulting line best describes the underlying dependence of y on x. Quadratic polynomials,

$$y = a + bx + cx^2 \, ,$$

are a parametric family with three parameters: a, b, and c.

The classical method for fitting parametric families is *least-squares*. The parameters are estimated by finding the member of the family that minimizes the sum of the squares of the vertical deviations of the data from the fitted function. For example, for linear polynomials, the least-squares estimates of a and b are the values that minimize

$$\sum_{i=1}^{n} (y_i - a - bx_i)^2 \, ,$$

where the x_i are the measurements of the factor, and the y_i are the measurements of the response. Least-squares was used for the linear and quadratic fits to the ganglion data. The linear fit is

$$y = 0.0140 + 0.107x \, ,$$

and the quadratic fit is

$$y = 2.87 - 0.0120x + 0.000839x^2 \, .$$

Least-squares is a good method to use provided the data have certain properties; checking to see if the data have these properties will be taken up in the next section.

Flexible Fitting

Parametric fitting is very useful but not nearly enough. When the underlying pattern in a set of data is simple — for example, the quadratic pattern in the ganglion data — we can expect to find a parametric family that will provide a good fit. But nature is frequently not so obliging. The patterns in many bivariate data sets are too complex to be described by a simple parametric family. For visualization, we need a method of fitting that will handle these complex cases. Loess fitting does just this. Figure 3.6 shows an example. The loess curve on the graph follows a pattern that defies fitting by a simple parametric function.

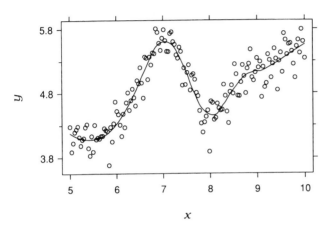

3.6 The data are fitted by loess. The curve is banked to $45°$.

The name *loess* — pronounced (*lō´ is*) and from the German *löss* — is short for *local regression*. The name also has semantic substance. In Chapter 4, loess is used to fit surfaces to data in three dimensions, and geologists and hikers know well that a loess is a surface of sorts — a deposit of silt, or fine clay, typically found in valleys. Loess is just one of many curve-fitting methods that are often referred to as nonparametric regression [49]. But loess has some highly desirable statistical properties [36, 48], is easy to compute [23], and, as we will see, is easy to use.

A Graphical Look at How Loess Works

Two parameters need to be chosen to fit a loess curve. The first parameter, α, is a smoothing parameter; it can be any positive number but typical values are $1/4$ to 1. As α increases, the curve becomes smoother. The second parameter, λ, is the degree of certain polynomials that are fitted by the method; λ can be 1 or 2. Guidance on the choices of α and λ will be given later.

Figure 3.7 shows how the loess fit, $\hat{g}(x)$, is computed at $x = 8$ for data that are graphed by the circles in the upper left panel. The values of the loess parameters are $\lambda = 1$ and $\alpha = 0.5$. The number of observations, $n = 20$, is multiplied by α, which gives the value 10. A vertical strip, depicted by the dashed vertical lines in the upper left panel of Figure 3.7, is defined by centering the strip on x and putting one boundary at the 10th closest x_i to x.

The observations $(x_i,\ y_i)$ are assigned *neighborhood weights*, $w_i(x)$, using the weight function shown in the upper right panel. The function has a maximum at 8, decreases as we move away from this value in either direction, and becomes zero at the boundaries of the strip. The observations whose x_i lie closest to x receive the largest weight, and observations further away receive less.

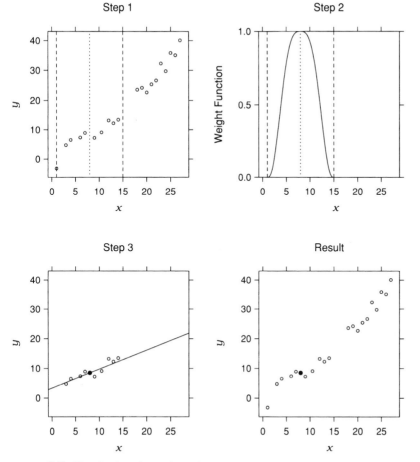

3.7 The display shows how the loess fit is computed at $x = 8$.

A line is fitted to the data using weighted least-squares with weight $w_i(x)$ at (x_i, y_i). The fit is shown in the lower left panel. The $w_i(x)$ determine the influence that each $(x_i,\ y_i)$ has on the fitting of the line. The influence decreases as x_i increases in distance from x, and finally becomes zero. The loess fit, $\hat{g}(x)$, is the value of the line at x, depicted by the filled circle.

Thus the computations illustrated in Figure 3.7 result in one value of the loess fit, $\hat{g}(8)$. This value is shown by the filled circle in the lower right panel.

The same operations can be carried out for any other value of x. Figure 3.8 shows them at $x = 27$, which happens to be the value of the largest x_i. The right boundary of the strip does not appear in the top panels because it is beyond the right extreme of the horizontal scale line.

Since $\lambda = 1$, a linear polynomial has been fitted in Figures 3.7 and 3.8. This is *locally linear fitting*. If $\lambda = 2$, a quadratic polynomial is used, which is *locally quadratic fitting*.

A loess fit is displayed by evaluating it at a grid of equally spaced values from the minimum value of the x_i to the maximum, and then connecting these evaluated curve points by line segments. The number of evaluations is typically in the range 50 to 200.

The Two Loess Parameters

In any specific application of loess, the choice of the two parameters α and λ must be based on a combination of judgment and of trial and error. There is no substitute for the latter. As the chapter progresses, many examples will illustrate how residual plots allow us to judge a particular choice. But the following description of the influence of changing the parameters, together with experience in using loess, can help to provide educated first guesses.

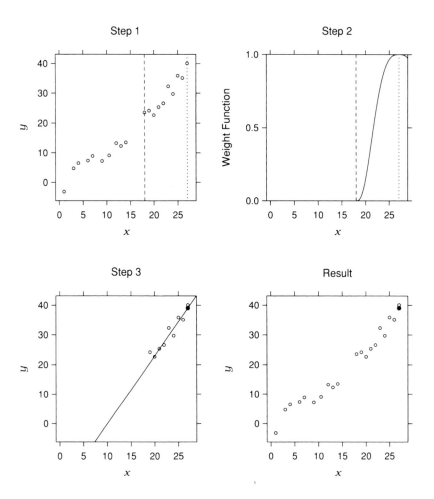

3.8 The display shows how the loess fit is computed at $x = 27$.

As α increases, a loess fit becomes smoother. This is illustrated in Figure 3.9. In all panels, $\lambda = 2$, so the fitting is locally quadratic. In the top panel, $\alpha = 0.6$. The fitted function is very smooth, but there is *lack of fit*; both the peak and the valley are missed because α is too large. In the middle panel, α has been reduced to 0.3. Now the curve is less smooth, but it follows the pattern of the data. In the bottom panel, α has been reduced still further to 0.1. The underlying pattern is tracked, but there is *surplus of fit*; the local wiggles do not appear to be supported by the data. The goal in choosing α is to produce a fit that is as smooth as possible without unduly distorting the underlying pattern in the data. In this example, $\alpha = 0.3$ is a good choice that follows the pattern without undue wiggles.

If the underlying pattern of the data has gentle curvature with no local maxima and minima, then locally linear fitting is usually sufficient. But if there are local maxima or minima, then locally quadratic fitting typically does a better job of following the pattern of the data and maintaining local smoothness. This is illustrated in Figure 3.10. The top panel shows the fit from the middle panel of Figure 3.9, which has $\lambda = 2$ and $\alpha = 0.3$. The substantial curvature, in particular the peak and valley, are adequately tracked by the curve. In the middle panel of Figure 3.10, λ has been changed to 1, with α remaining at 0.3. The fit does poorly. Because of the curvature in the data, locally linear fitting is not able to accommodate the peak and valley; the curve lies below the peak and above the valley. In the bottom panel, $\lambda = 1$, and α has been reduced to 0.1 in an attempt to follow the pattern. The curve tracks the data, but it has surplus of fit because α is small. But if we increase α by more than just a very small amount, still using locally linear fitting, the curve becomes smoother but no longer tracks the data. Locally linear fitting is not capable of providing an adequate fit in this example.

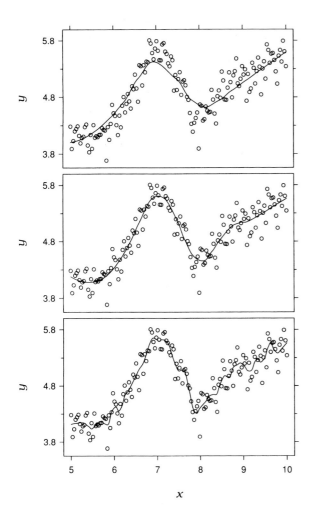

3.9 The three loess curves have three different values of the smoothing parameter, α. From the bottom panel to the top the values are 0.1, 0.3, and 0.6. The value of λ is 2.

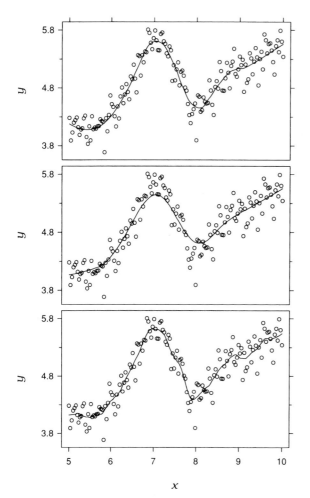

3.10 Three loess fits are shown. From the bottom panel to the top the two parameters, α and λ, are the following: 0.1 and 1; 0.3 and 1; 0.3 and 2.

For the Record: The Mathematical Details of Loess

The following describes in detail the loess fit, $\widehat{g}(x)$, at x. Suppose first that $\alpha \leq 1$. Let q be αn truncated to an integer. We will assume that α is large enough so that q is at least 1, although in most applications, q will be much larger than 1.

Let $\Delta_i(x) = |x_i - x|$ be the distance from x to the x_i, and let $\Delta_{(i)}(x)$ be these distances ordered from smallest to largest. Let $T(u)$ be the *tricube weight function*:

$$T(u) = \begin{cases} (1 - |u|^3)^3 & \text{for } |u| < 1 \\ 0 & \text{otherwise} . \end{cases}$$

Then the neighborhood weight given to the observation (x_i, y_i) for the fit at x is

$$w_i(x) = T\left(\frac{\Delta_i(x)}{\Delta_{(q)}(x)}\right) .$$

For x_i such that $\Delta_i(x) < \Delta_{(q)}(x)$, the weights are positive and decrease as $\Delta_i(x)$ increases. For $\Delta_i(x) \geq \Delta_{(q)}(x)$, the weights are zero. If $\alpha > 1$, the $w_i(x)$ are defined in the same manner, but $\Delta_{(q)}(x)$ is replaced by $\Delta_{(n)}(x)\alpha$.

If $\lambda = 1$, a line is fitted to the data using weighted least-squares with weight $w_i(x)$ at (x_i, y_i); values of a and b are found that minimize

$$\sum_{i=1}^{n} w_i(x)(y_i - a - bx_i)^2 .$$

Let $\widehat{a}$ and $\widehat{b}$ be the minimizing values, then the fit at x is

$$\widehat{g}(x) = \widehat{a} + \widehat{b}x .$$

If $\lambda = 2$, a quadratic is fitted to the data using weighted least-squares; values of a, b, and c are found that minimize

$$\sum_{i=1}^{n} w_i(x)(y_i - a - bx_i - cx_i^2)^2 .$$

Let $\widehat{a}$, $\widehat{b}$, and $\widehat{c}$ be the minimizing values, then the fit at x is

$$\widehat{g}(x) = \widehat{a} + \widehat{b}x + \widehat{c}x^2 .$$

3.3 Visualizing Residuals

In Chapter 2, one method for fitting univariate data was to estimate the locations of the distributions. An example is the singer heights; let h_{pi} be the ith height for the pth voice part. Locations were estimated by the voice-part means, $\bar{h}_p$. Each height has a fitted value,

$$\widehat{h}_{pi} = \bar{h}_p \,,$$

and a residual,

$$\widehat{\varepsilon}_{pi} = h_{pi} - \widehat{h}_{pi} \,.$$

The fitted values account for the variation in the heights attributable to the voice-part variable through the fitting process. The residuals are the remaining variation in the data.

The fitting in this chapter has so far followed a parallel course: estimating location. Whether we use parametric fitting or loess, the result is a function, $y = \widehat{g}(x)$, that describes the location of the measurements of the response, y, when the value of the factor is x. This is illustrated by the loess fit, $\widehat{g}(x)$, in Figure 3.11. The vertical strip contains observations whose x values are nearly the same. The loess fit in the strip, which is nearly constant, describes the location of the

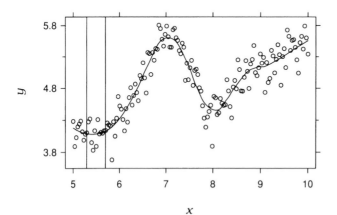

3.11 The display illustrates the purpose of curve fitting — describing the location of the distribution of the response given the factor.

distribution of the y values of observations in the strip. Furthermore, for each observation, (x_i, y_i), there is a fitted value

$$\widehat{y}_i = \widehat{g}(x_i) \, ,$$

and a residual

$$\widehat{\varepsilon}_i = y_i - \widehat{y}_i \, .$$

The $\widehat{y}_i$ are the variation in the response, y, attributable to the factor, x, through the fitting process. The $\widehat{\varepsilon}_i$ are the remaining variation. Thus the y_i are decomposed into fitted values and residuals,

$$y_i = \widehat{y}_i + \widehat{\varepsilon}_i \, .$$

And as with univariate data, an important part of visualizing bivariate data is the graphing of residuals from fits.

Residual Dependence Plots

If a fitted function suffers from lack of fit, the aspect of the underlying pattern not accounted for by the fit comes out in the residuals. A line did not fit the ganglion data. Figure 3.12 graphs the residuals against area together with a loess curve. This *residual dependence plot* shows a remaining dependence of the residuals on area. The location of the distribution of the residuals still varies with area.

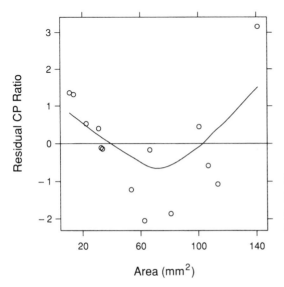

3.12 On this residual dependence plot, the residuals from the linear fit to CP ratio are graphed against area. The parameters of the loess curve on the plot are $\alpha = 1$ and $\lambda = 1$.

If a fit is adequate, the location of the residual distribution at each x should be zero. A quadratic appeared to adequately fit the ganglion data. Figure 3.13 is a residual dependence plot. The location of the residual distribution no longer depends on area.

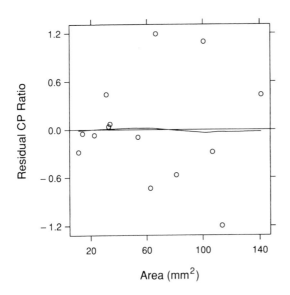

3.13 On this residual dependence plot, the residuals from the quadratic fit to CP ratio are graphed against area. The parameters of the loess curve on the plot are $\alpha = 1$ and $\lambda = 1$.

A residual dependence plot is an excellent diagnostic for detecting lack of fit when it exists. Of course, for the linear fit to the ganglion data, lack of fit is so blatant that it is obvious just from Figure 3.4, the scatterplot of the data with the fit superposed. But in other cases, lack of fit can be more subtle, and we must rely on the residual dependence plot to make a reliable judgment.

S-L Plots

The quadratic fit to the ganglion data has resulted in residuals whose location does not depend on area. Still, the residuals might not be homogeneous. Aspects of the residual distribution other than location might depend on area. As with univariate data, one type of nonhomogeneity is monotone spread: the spread of the residuals increases or decreases as the fitted values increase. And as with univariate data, we can check for monotone spread by an s-l plot.

Figure 3.14 is an s-l plot for the quadratic fit to the ganglion data. The square roots of the absolute residuals, $\sqrt{|\hat{\varepsilon}_i|}$, are graphed against the fitted values, $\hat{y}_i$, and a loess curve is added. There is monotone spread. Thus the residuals are not homogeneous, which makes the characterization of the dependence of the response on the factor more complicated. When the residuals are homogeneous, the residual variation at any x can be described by the distribution of all of the residuals. In other words, the power of pooling, discussed in Chapter 2, can be brought to bear. But if the residual variation changes, we must take the change into account in characterizing the variation.

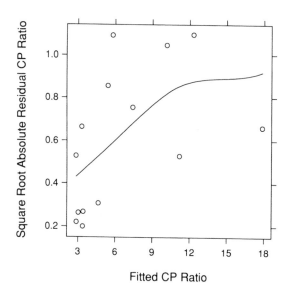

3.14 On this s-l plot, the square root absolute residuals from the quadratic fit to CP ratio are graphed against the fitted values to check for monotone spread. The parameters of the loess curve are $\alpha = 2$ and $\lambda = 1$.

As with univariate data, transformation — in this case, of the response — can cure monotone spread. Figure 3.15 graphs log CP ratio against area with a loess curve superposed. Something fortuitous has occurred; the overall pattern now appears nearly linear, which is simpler than the curved pattern before transformation. Figure 3.16 shows a line

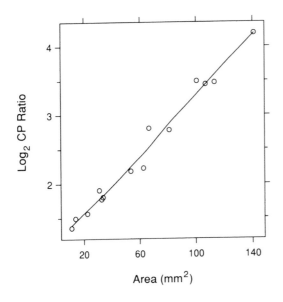

3.15 Log CP ratio is graphed against area. The curve is a loess fit with $\alpha = 2/3$ and $\lambda = 1$.

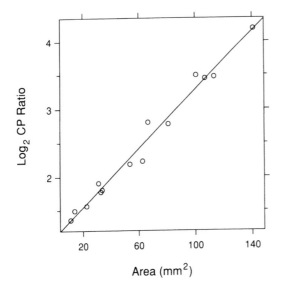

3.16 Log CP ratio is graphed against area. The line is the least-squares fit.

fitted by least-squares, and Figure 3.17 is a residual dependence plot.
There is no dependence of the location of the residuals on area.
Figure 3.18 is an s-l plot. There is no longer any dependence of spread
on location; the log transformation has removed the monotone spread
and, along the way, the nonlinearity of the underlying pattern.

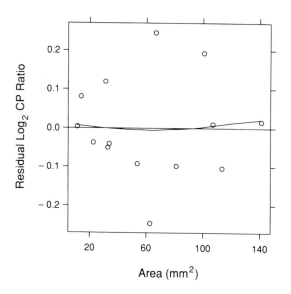

3.17 On this residual dependence plot, the residuals from the linear fit to log CP ratio are graphed against area. The parameters of the loess curve on the plot are $\alpha = 1$ and $\lambda = 1$.

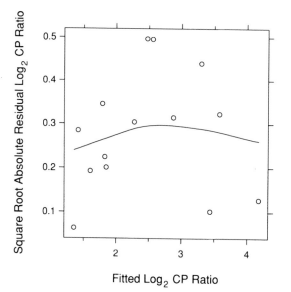

3.18 An s-l plot for the linear fit to log CP ratio checks for monotone spread. The parameters of the loess curve are $\alpha = 2$ and $\lambda = 1$.

R-F Spread Plots

As with univariate data, an r-f spread plot consists of quantile plots that compare the spreads of the residuals and the fitted values minus their mean. This shows how much variation in the data is explained by the fit and how much remains in the residuals. Figure 3.19 is an r-f spread plot for the fit to log CP ratio. The spread of the residual distribution is considerably smaller than that of the fitted values; the fit explains most of the variation in the data.

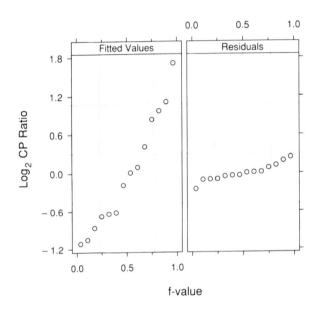

3.19 An r-f spread plot compares the spreads of the residuals and the fitted values minus their mean for the linear fit to log CP ratio.

Fitting the Normal Distribution

Figure 3.20, a normal quantile plot of the residuals, shows that the residual distribution is well approximated by the normal. This justifies our use of least-squares to fit the data. The theory of statistics tells us that least-squares is appropriate for bivariate fitting when the distribution of the random variation of the response about the underlying pattern is well approximated by the normal, just as it tells us that means are appropriate for univariate fitting when the variation of univariate data is well approximated by the normal. When outliers or other forms of leptokurtosis are present in the residuals, robust methods of fitting are needed, just as they are for univariate data. This is taken up in Section 3.4.

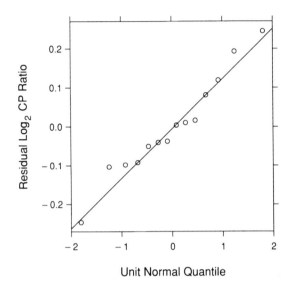

3.20 A normal q-q plot compares the normal distribution with the distribution of the residuals for the linear fit to log CP ratio.

The Dependence of Ratio on Area

The final result of the visualization of the ganglion data is a simple description of how CP ratio depends on area. The simplicity arises because log CP ratio is linear in area, the residuals are homogeneous, and the normal distribution provides a good approximation to the residual distribution. Let y be the $\log_2$ ratio and let x be area. The least-squares fit is

$$y = 1.11 + 0.022x \ .$$

If area changes by $1/0.022$ mm^2 = 45 mm^2, the $\log_2$ CP ratio changes by 1, which means the CP ratio doubles. The areas of the ganglion data set vary by 130 mm^2, so $\log_2$ CP ratio changes by about 2.8 overall, and the CP ratio changes by a factor of $2^{2.8} = 7.0$. The sample standard deviation of the residuals is 0.13. Thus, using the normal approximation to the residuals, about 95% of the residual distribution lies between $\pm 1.96 \times 0.13 = \pm 0.25$, which on the CP ratio scale are factors of 0.84 and 1.19.

Log Transformation

The tortuous path to the logarithm in the analysis of the ganglion data might have been avoided at the outset. The scatterplot of the data with the loess fit in Figure 3.2, which showed a convex pattern, might have inspired us to take logs to attempt a straightening of the pattern, rather than moving to a quadratic fit. But even more fundamentally, we might have taken the logs of the ratios before visualizing the data. A ratio, which has a numerator and denominator, is a strong candidate for a log transformation. When the numerator is bigger, the ratio can go from 1 all the way to infinity, but when the denominator is bigger, the ratio is squeezed into the interval 0 to 1. The logarithm symmetrizes the scale of measurement; when the numerator is bigger, the log ratio is positive, and when the denominator is bigger, the log ratio is negative. The symmetry often produces simpler structure.

3.4   Robust Fitting

Ages of many ancient objects, such as archeological artifacts and fossils, are determined by carbon dating. Organic material absorbs ^{14}C, which then decays at a known rate through time. Carbon dating, which consists of measuring the remaining ^{14}C, is not a fully accurate timepiece because the amount of ^{14}C in the environment available for absorption by organic material has fluctuated through time. Tree-ring dating was at first used to calibrate carbon dating, but this method of calibration works only back to about 9 kyr BP (kiloyears before present).

A second dating method, first reported in 1990, provides calibration back to at least 30 kyr BP by measuring the decay of uranium to thorium [5]. The group that invented the method took core samples in coral off the coast of Barbados and dated the material back to nearly 30 kyr BP using both the carbon and thorium methods. The thorium results were used to study the accuracy of the carbon method. Of course, this is valid only if the thorium method is itself accurate, but the consensus appears to be that it is [64].

Figure 3.21 shows the results of dating 19 coral samples by both methods; thorium age minus carbon age is graphed against carbon age. The display shows that carbon dating using the old method of calibration underestimates the true age. The scatterplot suggests a linear pattern, but there are two outliers, deviant observations that do not conform to the pattern of the remaining observations. Both lie well below the linear pattern suggested by the other observations.

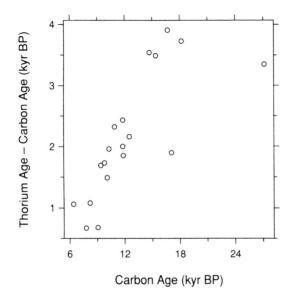

3.21 The differences of carbon age and thorium age for 19 coral samples are graphed against the carbon ages.

Figure 3.22 shows the least-squares fit of a line to the dating data. The fit does not follow the underlying linear pattern; the slope is too small because the line has been pulled down by the outliers. Figure 3.23 is a residual dependence plot; there is a pronounced remaining dependence on carbon age.

In Chapter 2, the distortion of the mean by outliers was discussed. Like the mean, least-squares estimates are not robust. If fact, the mean of univariate data is a least-squares estimate; it is the value of a that minimizes

$$\sum_{i=1}^{n} (y_i - a)^2 .$$

Least-squares is appropriate for bivariate fitting when the distribution of the random variation of the response about the underlying pattern is well approximated by the normal. And its performance is satisfactory if the distribution is moderately platykurtic. But in the presence of leptokurtosis, even in the form of just a few outliers, least-squares can be a disaster. And because loess is based on least-squares fitting of many polynomials locally, it too is not robust.

Bisquare

In Chapter 2, when a distribution appeared leptokurtic, we moved to the median, a robust estimate of location that is not adversely affected by leptokurtosis. For bivariate data, we will use the robust estimation method *bisquare* [51, 65]. Bisquare is added to the least-squares method for fitting a parametric family and is added to loess to turn these nonrobust methods into robust ones.

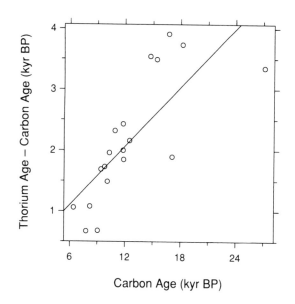

3.22 The least-squares fit of a line has been added to the scatterplot of the dating data.

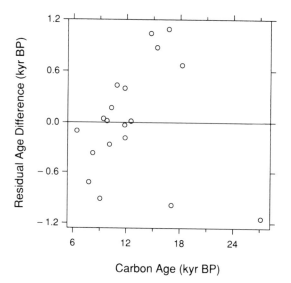

3.23 The residuals from the least-squares fit to the dating data are graphed against carbon age.

Figure 3.24 illustrates bisquare fitting of a line with the dating data. The first step is to fit by least-squares; this is shown in the upper right panel. The two outliers are graphed by the "+" plotting symbols. The second step is to assign a robustness weight, r_i, to each observation (x_i, y_i), based on the size of the residual for that observation. The weights are assigned by the value of a weight function called *bisquare*, from which the fitting procedure gets its name. The residuals and the weight function are graphed in the middle left panel of Figure 3.24. Residuals close to 0 have a weight close to 1. As the absolute values of the residuals increase, the weights decrease; for example, the largest and smallest residuals have weights of about 0.6. In the next step, the parameters are re-estimated using weighted least-squares with the weights r_i. In our example, we are fitting the parametric family

$$y = a + bx \, .$$

Thus, the weighted least-squares estimates are the values of a and b that minimize

$$\sum_{i=1}^{n} r_i(y_i - a - bx_i)^2 \, .$$

The new fit is shown in the middle right panel of Figure 3.24. Next, new weights are computed, and a line is fitted using weighted least-squares with the new weights. This iterative procedure is continued until the fit converges. The bottom left panel of Figure 3.24 shows the weights for the final fit, and the bottom right panel shows the fit; the outliers receive zero weight in this final fit.

In a similar way, loess can be altered by the bisquare method to make it robust. The details of how bisquare iterations are added to least-squares parametric fitting and how the iterations are added to loess curve fitting are given at the end of this section.

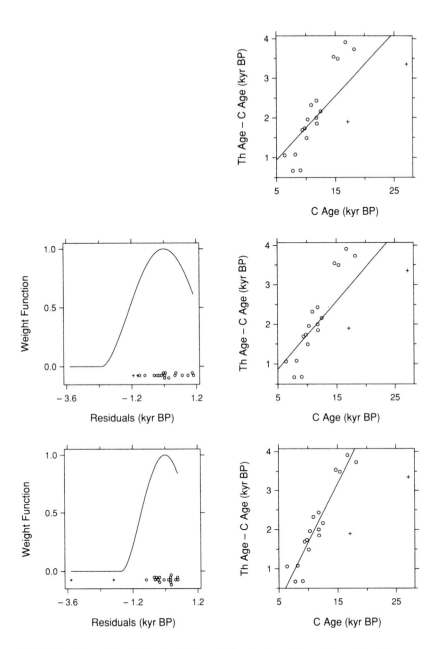

3.24 The figure illustrates the fitting of a line to the dating data by the bisquare method of robust estimation.

A Robust Analysis of the Dating Data

The bisquare line is graphed again in Figure 3.25. A residual dependence plot is shown in Figure 3.26. There is no remaining dependence in the residuals; the fit describes the overall pattern of the majority of the data. Figure 3.27 is a normal quantile plot of the residuals. Except for the outliers, the points have a linear pattern.

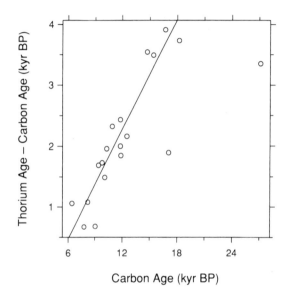

3.25 The bisquare fit of a line has been added to the scatterplot of the dating data.

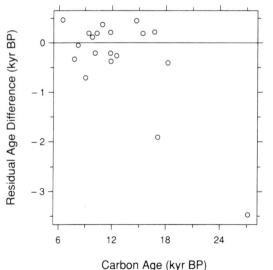

3.26 The residuals from the bisquare fit are graphed against carbon age.

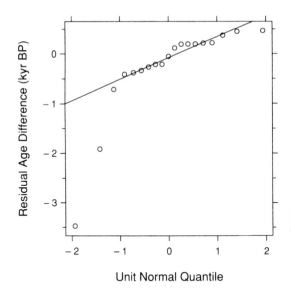

3.27 A normal q-q plot displays the residuals from the bisquare fit to the dating data.

The equation of the fitted bisquare line is

$$y = -1.3 + 0.30x \ .$$

The response y is zero when x is 4.3 kyr BP. Thus the fitted line suggests that a departure between carbon and thorium ages begins near 4.3 kyr BP. After that time point, the underestimation of age by carbon dating grows at a rate of 0.3 kyr for each kyr of carbon age. Thus for a carbon age of 15 kyr BP, the underestimation is about

$$0.3(15 - 4.3) \text{ kyr BP} = 3.2 \text{ kyr BP} \ .$$

The underestimation of age by traditional carbon dating is substantial. Carbon dating specialists had been aware that the method was biased, but the magnitude of the bias came as a surprise [64].

The Scope of Bisquare

Bisquare has been introduced in this chapter for use with bivariate data. It will also be used in coming chapters because it extends in a straightforward way to trivariate, hypervariate, and multiway data. For univariate data, the median was used in Chapter 1 for robust estimation because it is simple, widely known, and almost always performs well when robustness to outliers is needed. But we can also use bisquare for univariate data; the initial estimate is the mean, and subsequent estimates in the iterations are weighted means with bisquare weights computed from the residuals [51, 65]. Thus bisquare is attractive because a single method can be used for all the data types in the book to produce robust estimates.

For the Record: The Details of Bisquare

For fitting a parametric family, the only detail of bisquare that remains is the formula for the robustness weights, r_i. Let s be the median absolute deviation for the least-squares fit or any subsequent weighted fit. Thus

$$s = \text{median}\,|\widehat{\varepsilon}_i|,$$

where the $\widehat{\varepsilon}_i$ are the residuals from the fit. Let $B(u)$ be the bisquare weight function,

$$B(u) = \begin{cases} (1 - u^2)^2 & \text{for } |u| < 1 \\ 0 & \text{otherwise} . \end{cases}$$

The robustness weight for the observation (x_i, y_i) is

$$r_i = B\left(\frac{\widehat{\varepsilon}_i}{6s}\right).$$

As discussed in Chapter 2, s is a measure of the spread of the residuals. If a residual is small compared with $6s$, the robustness weight will be close to 1; if a residual is greater than $6s$, the weight is 0. Large residuals tend to be associated with outliers, so unusual observations are given reduced weight. The constant 6 has been chosen so that if the random variation of the response about the underlying pattern has a distribution that is well approximated by the normal, then bisquare does nearly as well as least-squares.

For loess, an initial fit is carried out with no robustness weights. The fit is evaluated at the x_i to get the fitted values, $\widehat{y}_i$, and the residuals,

$$\widehat{\varepsilon}_i = y_i - \widehat{y}_i .$$

Bisquare weights, r_i, are computed from the residuals using the bisquare weight function exactly as described for fitting a parametric function. Thus each observation (x_i, y_i) has a robustness weight, r_i, whose value depends on the magnitude of $\widehat{\varepsilon}_i$. Weighted local fitting is again carried out, but now the weight for (x_i, y_i) for the fit at x is $r_i w_i(x)$. Thus, (x_i, y_i) is given reduced weight if x_i is far from x or if $\widehat{\varepsilon}_i$ is large in absolute value. The second fit is used to define new residuals which are used to define new robustness weights, and the local fitting is carried out again. This process is repeated until the loess curve converges.

3.5   *Transformation of a Factor and Jittering*

Figure 3.28 is a scatterplot of 355 observations from an experiment at the University of Seville on the scattering of sunlight in the atmosphere [7]. The response is the *Babinet point*, the scattering angle at which the polarization of sunlight vanishes. The factor is the concentration of particulates, which are solid particles in the air. These data were briefly discussed in Chapter 1.

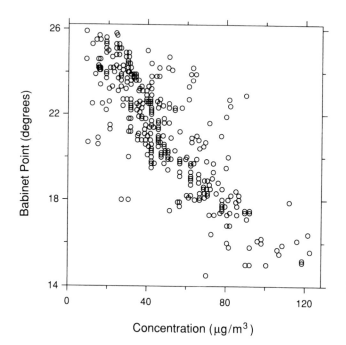

3.28 The scatterplot displays the polarization data.

Transformation

Transformation was first introduced in Chapter 2 as a tool for simplifying the structure of data. Power transformation cured skewness toward large values and monotone spread. For bivariate data, transformation of the response can also cure these ills. The ganglion data are one example.

For bivariate data, power transformation of the factor can also simplify structure. This is especially true of a factor whose measurements are observational and not specified by an experimenter. The particulate concentrations are one example; they are at the mercy of atmospheric conditions and the amount of air pollution.

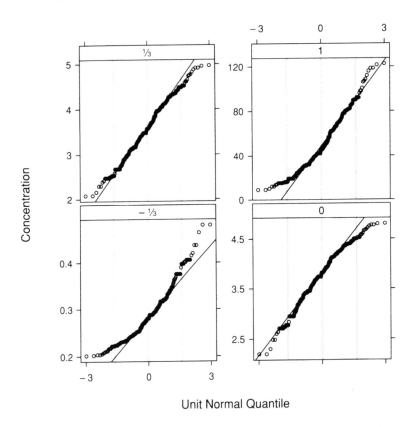

3.29 Normal q-q plots display four power transformations of the particulate concentrations.

Figure 3.28 suggests that the particulate concentrations, as a univariate data set, are somewhat skewed toward large values. One result is a few observations in the lower right corner that straggle somewhat from the remaining. If a power transformation can remove the skewness, it might simplify the dependence of the Babinet point on concentration. Figure 3.29 shows normal q-q plots for four power transformations of the concentrations. The cube roots appear to symmetrize the distribution of the data. Figure 3.30 graphs the Babinet point against cube root concentration. The effect is not dramatic, but we have pulled the lower right stragglers into line.

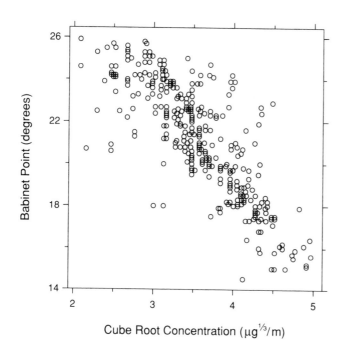

3.30 The measurements of the Babinet point are graphed against the cube root concentrations.

Visual Perception: Jittering

There is still a problem to be cured on the scatterplot in Figure 3.30; observations are obscured because the data on each scale are rounded, which results in a multiplicity of points at many of the plotting locations. One solution to the overlap problem, a particularly simple one, is jittering [20]. A small amount of uniform random noise is added to the data before graphing. It can be added to the measurements of just one of the variables or to the measurements of both.

Jittering is used in Figure 3.31 to display the polarization data. Noise has been added to the measurements of both variables; for each variable the noise was generated from a uniform distribution on an interval that is centered on zero and that is small compared with the range of the measurements. Now, most of the plotting symbols can be visually detected.

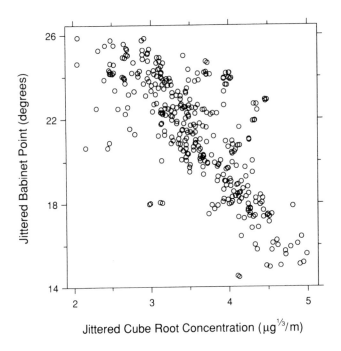

3.31 The measurements of the Babinet point are graphed again against the cube root concentrations, but this time the locations of the plotting symbols have been jittered.

3.6   The Iterative Process of Fitting

Fitting mathematical structures to data must be relentlessly iterative. The analysis of the ganglion data provides one illustration. The first fit, a line fitted to CP ratio, was quite obviously inadequate. On the second pass, a loess fit showed a pattern that appeared simple enough to be fitted by a quadratic function. On the third pass, a quadratic polynomial was fitted; there was no lack of fit, but an s-l plot detected monotone spread. On the fourth pass, logs were taken and the loess fit showed a linear pattern. On the fifth pass, log CP ratio was fitted by a line. The fit passed the visualization tests for lack of fit, and the residuals proved to be homogeneous with a distribution well approximated by the normal.

The single task of fitting a loess curve typically needs to be iterative as well. It is often possible to make an initial correct guess of λ and of whether bisquare is needed or not, but the choice of α usually requires a few trial values, with the final choice based on the visualization of fits and residuals. The polarization data provide one example.

Interestingly, without a smooth curve superposed, Figure 3.31 appears to have an underlying pattern that is linear; loess fits will show that this is not the case. However, the scatterplot does indicate that λ should be one, for even if we do not fully trust our unaided eyes, we can trust them enough to conclude that whatever curvature might be present is not likely to have peaks and valleys in need of locally quadratic fitting. Figure 3.31 also suggests that we should use bisquare iterations to make the loess fitting robust. There are a number of observations that deviate substantially in the vertical direction from the underlying pattern. For example, at a cube root concentration of $c = 3\sqrt[3]{\mu g}/m$, and a Babinet point of $b = 18°$, there is a small cluster of deviant observations. Finally, we will use $\alpha = 3/4$ as a trial value.

Figure 3.32 graphs a robust loess fit with $\alpha = 3/4$ and $\lambda = 1$. The pattern suggested by the curve is two straight lines with a break point near $3\sqrt[3]{\mu g}/m$. Figure 3.33 is a residual dependence plot. There appears to be a remaining dependence of the residuals on the factor. There is lack of fit because α is too large. Figure 3.34 graphs a robust loess fit with α reduced to $1/6$, and Figure 3.35 is a residual dependence plot. There is no remaining residual dependence, but the fitted curve in Figure 3.34 has undue wiggles that do not appear to be supported by the data. There is surplus of fit because α is now too small. In choosing α, we want a curve that is as smooth as possible without introducing lack of fit. Figure 3.36 graphs a robust loess fit with α increased to $1/3$, and Figure 3.37 is a residual dependence plot. No residual dependence appears to be present, yet the fitted curve is smooth — the unnecessary wiggles are gone. These loess parameters appear to be a good choice. Figure 3.38 is a normal quantile plot of the residuals from the final fit. The residual distribution is strongly leptokurtic; the robust loess fitting is needed in this example. Figure 3.39 is an r-f spread plot. The amounts of variation in the two distributions are roughly commensurate. Most residuals lie between $\pm 3°$, but a small fraction deviate by much more, some getting as large as $\pm 6°$. The range of the fitted values is about $9°$.

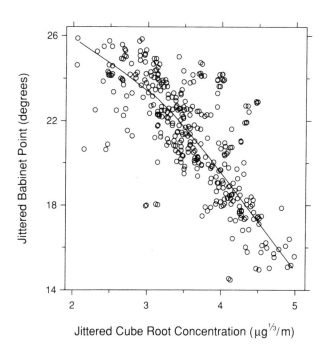

3.32 The curve is a robust loess fit to the polarization data with $\alpha = 3/4$ and $\lambda = 1$. The aspect ratio has been chosen to bank the curve to $45°$.

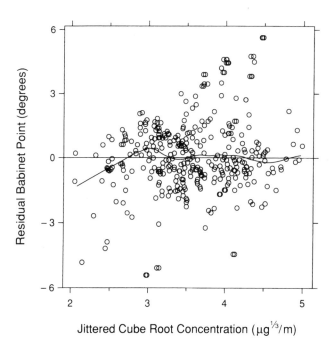

3.33 The residuals from the robust loess fit are graphed against cube root concentration. The parameters of the robust loess curve on the plot are $\alpha = 1/3$ and $\lambda = 1$.

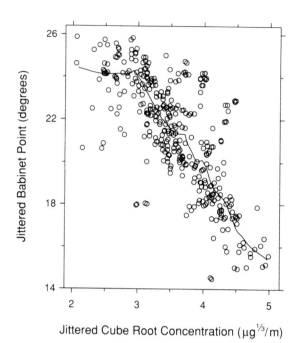

3.34 The curve is a robust loess fit to the polarization data with $\alpha = 1/6$ and $\lambda = 1$. The curve is banked to $45°$.

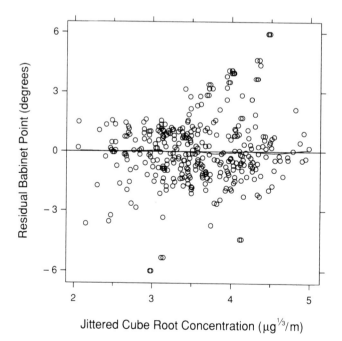

3.35 The residuals from the second robust loess fit are graphed against cube root concentration. The parameters of the robust loess curve on the plot are $\alpha = 1/3$ and $\lambda = 1$.

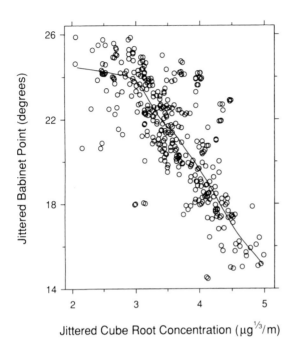

3.36 The curve is a robust loess fit to the polarization data with $\alpha = 1/3$ and $\lambda = 1$. The curve is banked to $45°$.

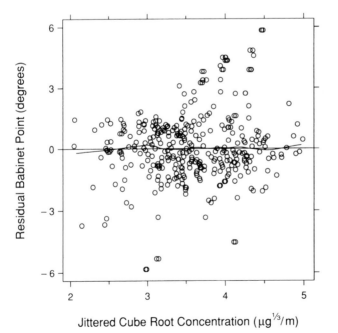

3.37 The residuals from the third robust loess fit are graphed against cube root concentration. The parameters of the robust loess curve on the plot are $\alpha = 1/3$ and $\lambda = 1$.

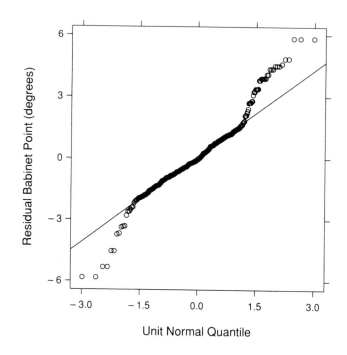

3.38 A normal q-q plot displays the distribution of the residuals from the final robust loess fit to the polarization data.

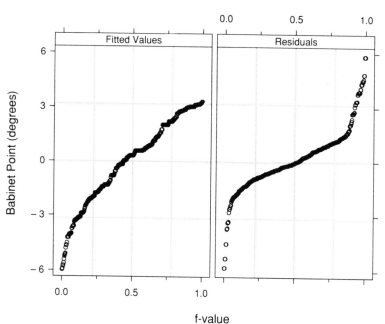

f-value

3.39 An r-f spread plot compares the spreads of the residuals and the fitted values minus their mean for the final robust loess fit to the polarization data.

3.7   Slicing

The full purpose in analyzing factor-response data is to visualize the change in the distribution of the measurements of the response as the factor changes. This is illustrated in Figure 3.40 by the polarization data. The vertical slice contains observations whose values of c, the cube root particulate concentration, lie in a small interval. For these observations, the values of b, the Babinet point, are a set of univariate data with a distribution. We can pick many such slices and compare the resulting distributions to see how the distribution of b changes as c changes. The robust loess curve fitted to these data in Section 3.5 shows the change in the location of b with c, but there are other aspects of the distribution to consider.

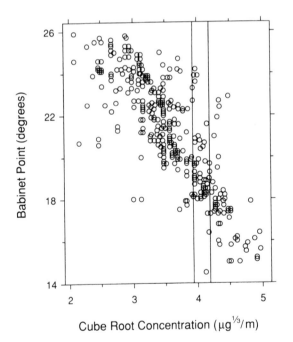

3.40 The display illustrates slicing, a method for studying the conditional distribution of the response given the factor.

Stated in this way, the goal of the analysis of the polarization data becomes that for univariate data, studied in Chapter 2. For example, distributions of singer heights for different voice parts were compared to study how height depends on voice part. For the polarization data, we will compare distributions of values of b for different slices to study how b depends on c.

Visualizing Residual Distributions

In Chapter 2, distributions were visualized by a number of tools such as box plots and q-q plots. We could apply these directly to distributions of b formed from slices on c. But there is a problem that is illustrated by Figure 3.41, which displays the polarization data and the final robust loess fit of Section 3.6. Within the slice, the location of the distribution of b given c is not constant. Thus, the values of b within the slice are not homogeneous. Were we to compare with another slice where the location is constant but the spread is the same, say around $c = 2.5\sqrt[3]{\mu g}/\mathrm{m}$, the distribution for the first slice might look as if it had greater spread simply because the location is changing. The change in location interferes with a study of other aspects of the distribution of b given c.

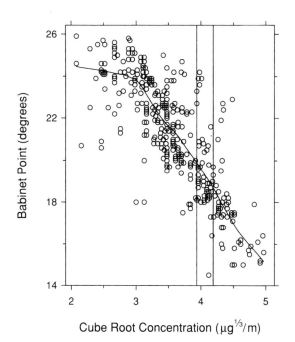

3.41 The robust loess curve describes how the location of the distribution of the response changes with the factor.

One remedy to the problem of a changing location would be to condition on very small intervals so that the change within each slice is small. But the result would be many groups of measurements and only a few measurements within each group. There is a better solution: carrying out the analysis with residuals from the robust loess fit. This is illustrated with Figure 3.42. With the fit removed, the location is now constant, not just within the slice but overall since we have determined from the residual dependence plot in Figure 3.37 that there is no remaining dependence of the location of b on c. In removing the change in the location, the hope is that the remaining aspects of the distribution change less precipitously so that we can use wider slices.

Just from Figure 3.42 itself there is a suggestion that aspects of the distribution of b given c other than location might be changing. For example, in the interval of values of c from about 3.5 $\sqrt[3]{\mu g}/\text{m}$ to 4.5 $\sqrt[3]{\mu g}/\text{m}$, the upper tail of the residual distribution appears stretched out. Slicing will provide more information about this effect.

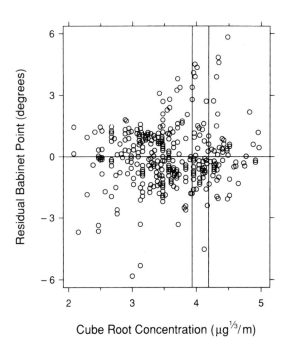

3.42 The display illustrates slicing the residuals to study how aspects of the distribution of the response other than location change with the factor.

Slicing Intervals

Figure 3.43, a *given plot*, shows intervals of c that we will use for slicing. The intervals are output from the *equal-count algorithm*. The input is the number of intervals and the target fraction of values shared by successive intervals. For Figure 3.43, the number of intervals is 15 and the target fraction is 1/2. The algorithm takes the input and selects intervals to make the numbers of values in the intervals as nearly constant as possible, and to make the fraction of values shared by each pair of successive intervals as nearly equal to the target fraction as possible. The lower boundary of the lowest interval is the minimum value of the measurements of c, and the upper boundary of the highest interval is the maximum value of the measurements. The algorithm, which is described at the end of this section, does its best, but achieving equality is typically not possible. For example, for the intervals in Figure 3.43, the number of values of c ranges from 45 to 61. This variation occurs in large part because there are many ties among the measurements of c; this can be seen in Figure 3.42.

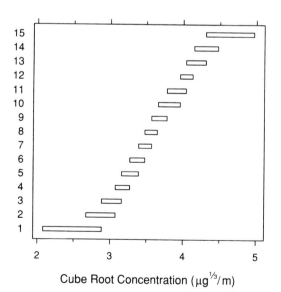

3.43 The given plot shows 15 intervals selected by the equal-count method. The target fraction of overlap is 1/2.

Sliced Distribution Plots

Figure 3.44 shows box plots of the 15 sets of residuals formed by the slicing intervals of the given plot in Figure 3.43. As we go from bottom to top through the box plots, the corresponding intervals go from bottom to top on the given plot. The box plots reveal a change in the distribution of the residuals. As the intervals of c increase, there is a migration from a stretching out of the lower tail to a stretching out of the upper tail. Thus there is substantial nonhomogeneity in the distribution of the residuals. The ideal case, as in Chapter 2, is a location fit that produces homogeneous residuals; then we can pool them to produce a more powerful description of variation about the fit. For example, for the singer heights in Chapter 2, once the means of the voice parts are subtracted, the residual distribution no longer depends on voice part; the eight residual distributions are homogeneous and can be pooled. For the analysis of the ganglion data in previous sections of this chapter, the residuals for the quadratic fit to CP ratio produced nonhomogeneous residuals; their spread increased with the location. But a log transformation resulted in a fit with homogeneous residuals. For the

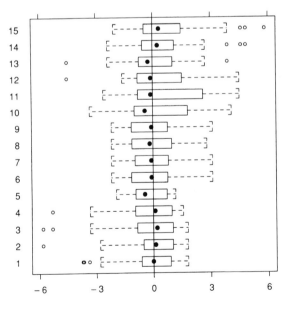

Residual Babinet Point (degrees)

3.44 Fifteen conditional distributions of residual Babinet point are compared by box plots.

polarization data, the residuals are not homogeneous, but in this case, there is no simple remedy such as transformation to make them so. Thus we cannot pool all of the residuals to characterize the behavior of the distribution at each value of c. The distribution at c must be characterized by residuals corresponding to cube root concentrations close to c, for example, by the box plots in Figure 3.44. Sometimes the results of a data analysis are unavoidably complicated.

Choosing the Slicing Intervals

The two parameters of the equal-count algorithm used in slicing typically need to be chosen by trial and error. There is no one correct solution; different choices can show different properties. Still, there are considerations that affect the choice.

Suppose the number of observations is n, the number of intervals is k, and the target fraction of overlap is f. As shown in a coming section that is for the record, the target value for the number of observations in each interval is

$$r = \frac{n}{k(1 - f) + f} .$$

The value of r, which is not necessarily an integer, increases as k decreases or as f increases.

The numbers of values in the intervals must be controlled to be neither too small nor too large. If they are too small, there is no basis for comparison. If they are too large, there is a risk that within an interval there is a significant change in the distribution that is masked by too much pooling.

Unless there is an enormous amount of data, it is preferable to have the intervals overlap. The slicing intervals then move gradually along the scale of the factor, which provides greater sensitivity in detecting nonhomogeneity than would be provided by intervals that do not overlap and thus change less gradually. This same principle is used in loess fitting. For the fit at a single value of x, a vertical slice contains the observations that receive positive weight in the fitting; since the loess fit is evaluated typically at a grid of x values with far smaller spacing than the widths of the slices, the fit is determined by a sequence of slices that slide along the factor scale. In loess fitting, the widths of the slices are controlled by the choice of the smoothing parameter, α. In slicing to compare residual distributions, the widths of the slices are controlled by the choices of the parameters k and f.

For the Record: The Equal-Count Algorithm

Let x_i be the values of the factor, ordered from smallest to largest, so x_1 is the smallest and x_n is the largest. The equal-count algorithm finds intervals whose endpoints are values of x_i. Let ℓ_j be the lower endpoint of the jth interval, and let u_j be the upper.

Consider, first, a special case with three properties: (1) there are no ties among the x_i; (2) there are intervals for which the actual fractions of values shared by successive intervals are all equal to f; (3) the numbers of values in these intervals are equal to a constant, r. The total number of values in all of the intervals collectively is the number of conditioning intervals, k, times the number of values, r, in each interval. But also, since two successive intervals share fr values, and since there are $(k-1)$ separate sets of such shared values, the total number of values is $n + (k-1)fr$. Thus

$$rk = n + (k-1)fr$$

and

$$r = \frac{n}{k(1-f)+f}.$$

Now we can compute the interval endpoints. For the first interval,

$$\ell_1 = x_1$$

and

$$u_1 = x_r.$$

For the second interval,

$$\ell_2 = x_{1+(1-f)r}$$

and

$$u_2 = x_{r+(1-f)r} \cdot$$

The formulas for the endpoints of the jth interval are

$$\ell_j = x_{1+(j-1)(1-f)r}$$

and

$$u_j = x_{r+(j-1)(1-f)r} \cdot$$

In the general case, we cannot necessarily make the actual fractions exactly equal to f, or make the numbers of points in the intervals constant, because the indices that define ℓ_j and u_j in the above formulas are not necessarily integers. In the general case, we simply compute the values $1 + (j-1)(1-f)r$ and $r + (j-1)(1-f)r$, and round them to the nearest integer to get indices. In all cases, $\ell_1 = x_1$ and $u_n = x_n$, so the first interval has a left endpoint of x_1 and the last interval has a right endpoint of x_n.

3.8   Discrete Values of a Factor

In 1924, a journal article reported 823 observations from a genetics experiment on flies' eyes [50] . Stocks of the ubiquitous species Drosophila melanogaster Meig were hatched in nine incubators whose temperatures varied from 15°C to 31°C in equal steps of 2°C. The number of facets of the eyes of each hatched fly were reported in units that essentially make the measurement scale logarithmic. The goal of the experiment was to see how facet number depends on temperature.

In Figure 3.45, the facet numbers are graphed against the temperatures; most plotting symbols are visually lost because of the repeat measuring at each temperature and the rounding of the facet numbers. In Figure 3.46, the data are graphed with temperature and facet number jittered to alleviate the overlap.

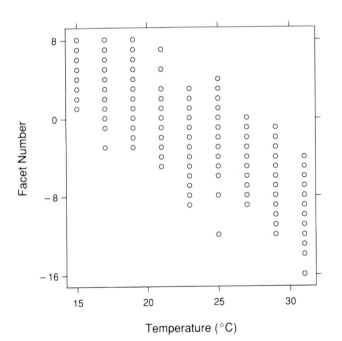

3.45 Facet number is graphed against temperature.

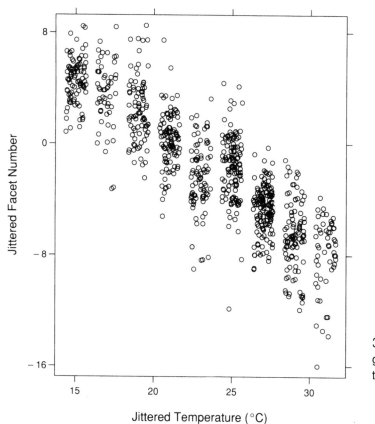

3.46 Facet number is graphed against temperature.

In the fly experiment, the measurements of the factor are discrete; there are many measurements of the response for each unique value of the factor. The data at the outset are ready for slicing. The facet numbers at each temperature serve as a single slice. Since there is no variation of the factor within each slice, there is no problem of a changing location within a slice, and we can begin the data analysis with slicing rather than waiting until we have residuals from a location fit.

Figure 3.47 graphs the nine distributions of facet number by box plots. The overall impression is that the shifts in the distributions are additive, varying exclusively in location, and that the distributions are symmetric. Furthermore, the shifts are large compared with the spreads of the distributions, which means that temperature is an important factor in determining facet number.

Figure 3.48 shows normal q-q plots, not of the facet numbers themselves, but of the residuals from the means because this provides a better look at the normal approximation. If we graph the facet numbers, the large change in location forces the data on each panel into a narrow interval along the vertical scale, which interferes with our ability to assess the shape of the underlying pattern of the points. The nine residual distributions appear well approximated by the normal. The biggest deviation, that for the largest temperature, is mild skewness.

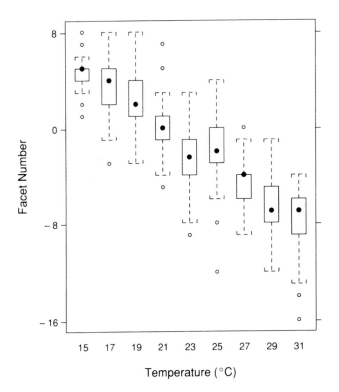

3.47 The conditional distributions of facet number given temperature are compared by box plots.

For 15°C, the underlying pattern is linear but the quartile line does not follow the pattern because facet number at 15°C takes on only eight distinct values and about half of the data are equal to the two central values. The slopes of the underlying patterns for the nine temperatures are quite similar. The normality together with the similar slopes appears to confirm the impression from the box plots that the distributions differ by additive shifts.

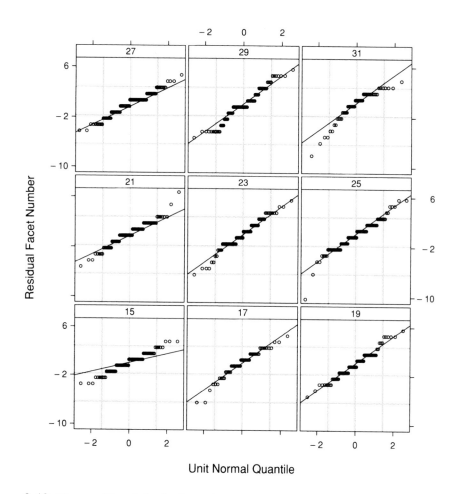

3.48 The conditional distributions of facet number given temperature are compared with the normal distribution by normal q-q plots of the residuals from the means.

Our goal now is to determine how the locations of the distributions of facet number vary with temperature. The box plots in Figure 3.47 suggest that the overall effect is linear. But there is anomalous behavior at 23°C and 25°C; the distribution at 25°C is shifted upward compared to the distribution at 23°C, which runs counter to the trend. The overall trend and the anomaly are probed further by the visualizations in Figures 3.49 and 3.50. The first figure displays both the least-squares fit of a line to the data and the means of the nine distributions. The second figure displays the residuals of the nine means from the least-squares line. Clearly the means at 23°C and 25°C vary by large amounts from the overall pattern.

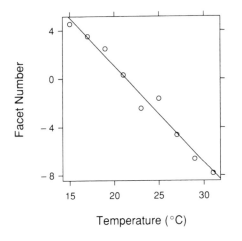

3.49 The plotting symbols graph the means of the nine conditional distributions of facet number given temperature. The line is the least-squares fit to the 823 measurements of facet number and temperature.

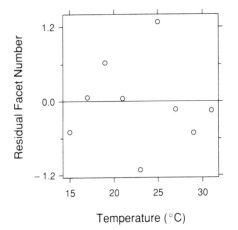

3.50 The deviations of the conditional means from the least-squares line are graphed against temperature.

The scientific question is this. Should we conclude that there is a reproducible anomaly in the dependence of facet number on temperature? Or, is the effect linear, and some aspect of the experiment has caused a result that would not appear in a more carefully controlled experiment? Two pieces of information are important for making the decision. First, a linear decrease of facet number measured on a log scale is expected based on zoological reasoning and other data. The experimenters state:

> Seyster ('19) and Krafka ('20) showed that the number of facets decreases with the increase in temperature in bar and ultra-bar races of Drosophila. The rate of decrease is proportional to the number of facets within any given stock, so that we are dealing with an instance of 'the compound interest law'.

Second, the values of the factor are nominal values and not necessarily what was achieved. The average temperature of an incubator fluctuates with time, and the temperature at a point in time is not constant throughout the incubator. Here is what the experimenters write about the control of temperature in the experiment:

> Errors in the study may arise from fluctuating temperatures. The fluctuations are not the same in all cases; 15°, 17°, 25°, and 27° showed a variation of ±0.5°. 23° varied as much as 3°. The record of 29° showed a variation from 28.0° to 29.5°. Temperature readings taken of the food by a thermometer graded in tenths of degrees, showed a total variation of 1.4° in the 31° aquarium, and of 1.3° in the 21° aquarium. The 19° aquarium was more unsatisfactory and varied sometimes as much as 5°. In every case, however, an attempt was made to have the proper temperature during the facet reaction period, though this may not have been accomplished because the period may not be the same for the heterozygotes as for the homozygotes for which it has been determined. Nominal temperatures in accompanying tables and figures are to be considered with these remarks in mind.

Note, in particular, the large uncertainty in the temperature at 23°C. The visualization of the data, the zoological reasoning, and the information about the experimental protocol suggest the conclusion that there is no meaningful temperature anomaly and that the dependence of facet number on temperature is linear.

Using probablistic methods to enhance our inductive inference on this matter would require incorporating the uncertainty of the temperature measurements into the analysis, which would be complicated. And attempting to carry out probabilistic methods without accounting for the uncertainty would be uninformative or worse yet, misleading. Surprisingly, R. A. Fisher, the founder of modern statistical theory, made such an attempt. This will be discussed in the final section of the chapter.

3.9   Transforming Factor and Response

In 1801, William Playfair published his *Statistical Breviary* [67], which contains many displays of economic and demographic data. One display, beautifully reproduced by Tufte [74], graphs the populations of 22 cities by the areas of circles. The graph also contains a table of the populations, so we can compare the data and the areas of the circles.

Figure 3.51 graphs the data by circles whose areas are proportional to those of Playfair. Using area to encode quantitative information is a poor graphical method. Effects that can be readily perceived in other visualizations are often lost in an encoding by area [20]. For example, Figure 3.52 is a dot plot of the populations that conveys the distribution of the data more effectively than the areas of Figure 3.51.

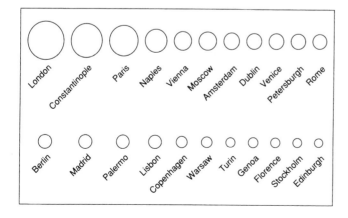

3.51 Circle areas encode the populations of cities at the end of the 1700s.

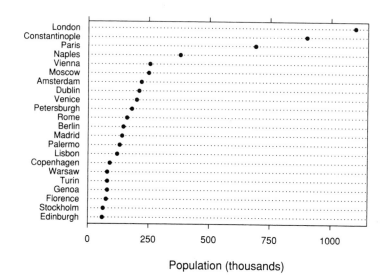

3.52 A dot plot displays the population data.

Population (thousands)

Still, for historical purposes, it is interesting to study Playfair's areas to see how accurately the circles have been drawn. Such study is inspired by the observation that the circle area for Turin is slightly less than that for Genoa, even though the population values recorded on Playfair's graph for these cities are equal. Thus the goal is to study how the areas depend on the populations, so area is a response and population is a factor.

Instead of studying population and area directly, we will work on a square root scale. In place of area, we will use diameter. In place of population, we will use square root population. There are two reasons. First, drawn circles are typically rendered by specifying a linear measure such as a radius or a diameter. Thus we might expect that for the diameters, measurement error would be roughly constant. Second, the distributions of the populations and the areas are substantially skewed toward large values, and taking square roots removes much of the asymmetry. Thus we are transforming both the factor and the response to simplify the analysis.

Let d_i be the diameters of the circles in Tufte's reproduction, and let s_i be the square root populations. In Figure 3.53, d_i is graphed against s_i. If the encoding by circle area were exact, the circle areas would be proportional to the populations, and the transformed data would lie along a line of the form

$$d_i = bs_i \,.$$

This is a linear parametric family with a single parameter b, and an intercept of zero.

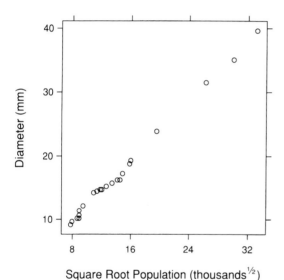

3.53 Circle diameter is graphed against square root population.

Figure 3.54 graphs the data and the least-squares fit of the linear parametric family with zero intercept; the display shows how close the data come to an exact encoding. There is a consistent departure from linearity — an undulation back and forth for those observations with diameters of about 10 mm to 20 mm. However, the magnitude of this undulation is very small compared with the overall variation in the data, so the graph gives us little information about its properties.

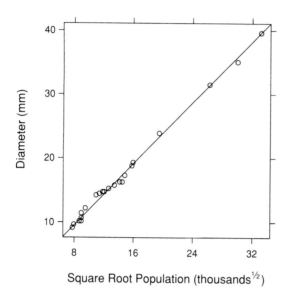

3.54 A line has been fitted to the Playfair data by least-squares.

Square Root Population (thousands$^{1/2}$)

Figure 3.55 is a residual dependence plot. By removing the gross linear effect, the plot magnifies the deviations from a perfect encoding. Now we can perceive the properties of the deviations far more incisively. Their total variation is about ± 1 mm. Furthermore, there is clearly a dependence of the residuals on square root population. This suggests that the deviations are not simply the usual measurement error that would result from laying down a length with a measuring device. Such measurement error should produce a random pattern with no dependence. The true cause of the deviations is likely to remain a mystery without more information about the production of the original graph.

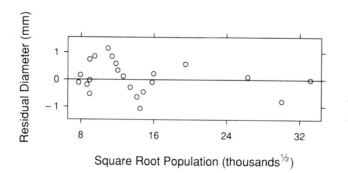

3.55 The residuals from the linear fit to the Playfair data are graphed against square root population.

Square Root Population (thousands$^{1/2}$)

3.10   Bivariate Distributions

For the examples encountered so far in this chapter, the bivariate data consist of a response variable and a factor variable. In other words, the goal of each analysis has been to determine how one variable depends on the other. For many bivariate data sets, however, the goal is simply to determine the *bivariate distribution* of the data in the two-dimensional space of the measurements, rather than determining how the variation in one variable explains the variation in the other. Figure 3.56 shows an example. The bivariate data are 111 measurements of wind speed and temperature on 111 days from May to September of 1973 in the New York City metropolitan region [13]. The temperature measurement is the daily maximum. The wind speed measurement is the average of values at 0700 and 1000. The goal is not to determine how the variation in one explains the variation in the other, but rather to see how wind speed and temperature vary together.

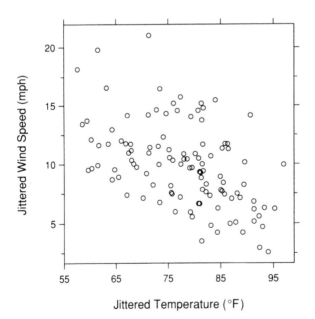

3.56 A scatterplot displays the wind speed and temperature data.

One aspect of a bivariate distribution is the two univariate distributions of the two separate sets of measurements. Figures 3.57 and 3.58 are normal q-q plots of the temperatures and wind speeds. The temperatures are slightly platykurtic. The wind speeds are slightly

skewed toward large values; one result of the univariate skewness for
the bivariate distribution of the data is several stragglers at the top of the
scatterplot of Figure 3.56.

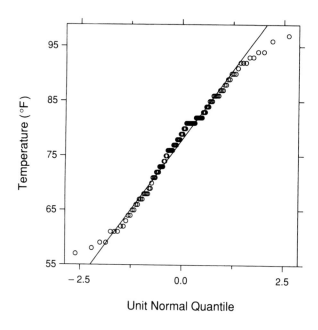

3.57 The univariate distribution of the
temperatures is compared with the
normal distribution by a normal q-q plot.

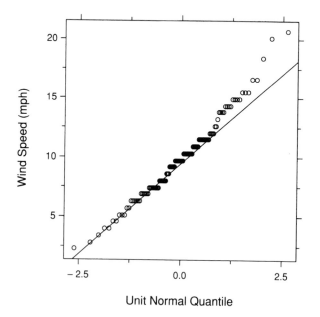

3.58 The univariate distribution of the
wind speeds is compared with the
normal distribution by a normal q-q plot.

Because temperature and wind speed are not designated as factor and response, it is no more informative to see a loess fit to wind speed as a function of temperature than it is to see a loess fit to temperature as a function of wind speed. For this reason, Figure 3.59 graphs both loess fits. The curve with the lesser overall slope is the fit to wind speed, and the curve with the greater overall slope is the fit to temperature.

In Figure 3.59 the fit to wind speed is nearly linear, but the fit to temperature has more curvature. The visualization shows that wind speed and temperature vary together; a decrease in wind speed tends to be associated with an increase in temperature.

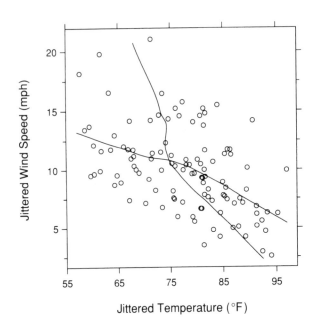

3.59 Two loess curves have been added to the scatterplot of wind speed and temperature. The loess parameters are $\alpha = 3/4$ and $\lambda = 1$.

Bivariate Data with the Same Units

It is common to encounter bivariate distributions where both variables have the same units. Most often, this arises because experimental units, or samples, are measured twice, for example, in two different locations or at two times or by two different measurement techniques. Figure 3.60 shows an example. The data are daily maximum ozone concentrations at ground level on 132 days from May 1, 1974 to September 30, 1974 at two sites in the U.S.A. — Yonkers, New York and

Stamford, Connecticut — which are approximately 30 km from one another [16]. The sample for each measurement is the air mass on a particular day, and the bivariate data arise from two measurements at the two sites.

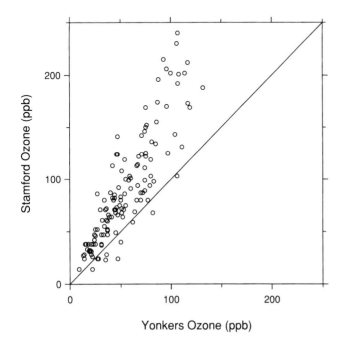

3.60 The scatterplot displays measurements of ground-level ozone concentration at two sites.

Tukey Mean-Difference Plots

Whenever the two axes of a graph of two variables have the same units, a Tukey mean-difference plot, or m-d plot, is a candidate for visualization. For example, m-d plots served as an adjunct display for q-q plots in Chapter 2. Figure 3.61 is an m-d plot of the points of Figure 3.60; the difference in the concentrations at the two sites on each day is graphed against the mean for the two sites. A loess curve has been added to aid our judgment of how the differences change with the mean level.

Figures 3.60 and 3.61 show that ozone concentrations at the two sites are correlated. This is to be expected since both are subject to the same weather systems, and the variation in the systems accounts in large part for the variation in the concentrations through time. It is also clear that

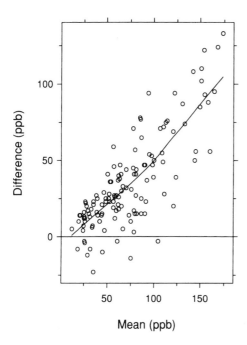

3.61 The Tukey mean-difference plot graphs ozone differences against ozone means. The parameters of the loess curve are $\alpha = 1$ and $\lambda = 1$. The curve is banked to $45°$.

concentrations at Stamford are higher than those at Yonkers; on all but 10 days, Stamford values exceed Yonkers values. Stamford tends to have higher concentrations because it lies downwind of the New York City metropolitan region; the chemical reactions that produce ozone are able to more effectively create the air pollutant once the air mass moves away from the heaviest concentrations of primary pollutants. The amount by which Stamford exceeds Yonkers tends to increase as the levels at the two sites increase. The loess curve in Figure 3.61 shows that the differences increase from about 0 ppb on the cleanest days to about 100 ppb on the dirtiest days.

The m-d plot shows the concentration differences have a complex behavior. But it may be that concentration ratios have a simpler behavior. We can check this by taking logs and making the scatterplot and m-d plot again. This is done in Figures 3.62 and 3.63. The loess curve still increases showing there is an increase in the percentage difference between Stamford and Yonkers as the overall level of ozone increases. But the effect on the log scale is less dramatic. At low concentrations, Stamford exceeds Yonkers by 0.5 $\log_2$ ppb, which is a factor of $2^{0.5} = 1.4$. At high concentrations, the difference is 0.9 $\log_2$ ppb, which is a factor of $2^{0.9} = 1.9$.

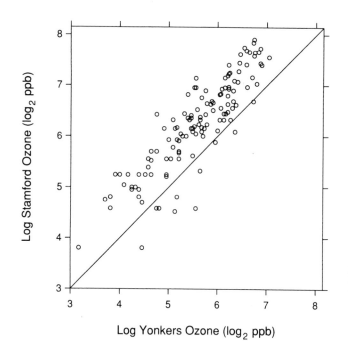

3.62 The scatterplot displays the logs of the ozone measurements.

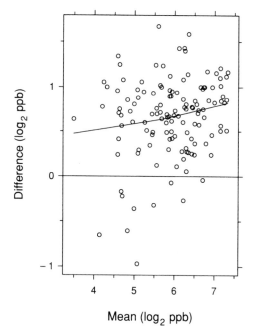

3.63 The m-d plot graphs log ozone differences against log ozone means. The parameters of the loess curve on the plot are $\alpha = 1$ and $\lambda = 1$. The curve is banked by an aspect ratio of 1.5. Banking to $45°$ results in an aspect ratio that is too large.

3.11   Time Series

Figure 3.64 displays yearly incidences of melanoma, the deadly form of skin cancer [53]. The units are age-adjusted cases per 10^6 population. The data are from the state of Connecticut in the U.S.A. A principal cause of melanoma is exposure to solar radiation. For white populations, incidence tends to increase as latitude decreases because of increased exposure to radiation, and incidence is higher at skin sites with more exposure to the sun, such as the face.

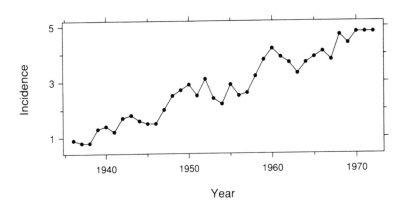

3.64   A time series — yearly age-adjusted melanoma cases per 10^6 population in Connecticut, U.S.A. — is graphed with $45°$ banking of the local segments, the line segments connecting successive observations.

The melanoma data are a time series: measurements of a quantitative variable through time. Melanoma incidence is the response and time is the factor; the goal is to see how incidence varies through time. While the data type is still bivariate data, the special character of the time variable changes the strategy and methods of analysis.

Time Components

Figure 3.64 shows a steady upward trend in the data. Superposed on this trend are oscillations that appear to rise and fall with periods of about 10 years. Figure 3.65 graphs a loess curve fitted to the data to describe the upward trend; the rise is very nearly linear. Figure 3.66 graphs the residuals from the loess fit against time. The oscillations are contained in the residuals since they are not fitted by the trend curve.

Figure 3.67 graphs a loess curve that was fitted to the residuals to describe the oscillations. There are approximately three complete oscillations; since the data cover 36 years, the average period is about 12 years.

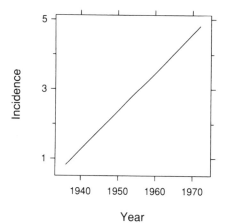

3.65 The display graphs a loess trend fit to melanoma incidence. The local segments are banked to 45°.

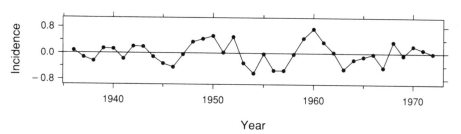

3.66 The display graphs the residuals from the loess trend fit to melanoma incidence. The local segments are banked to 45°.

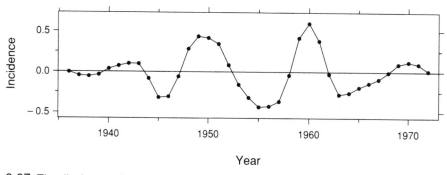

3.67 The display graphs an oscillatory component fitted by loess to the residuals from the trend fit. The local segments are banked to 45°.

This initial visualization of the melanoma data illustrates the principal consequence of having time as a factor. Instead of fitting a single curve to describe dependence — as we did for the previous bivariate data sets in the chapter — we often fit multiple curves to the data to describe multiple *time components*. For the melanoma data, one component is the trend component and another is the oscillatory component. Separate descriptions of different time components of a time series are necessary because different components often have different causes.

Loess Fitting for Time Series

Loess will be our principal tool for fitting time components, which are often complicated functions that defy description by simple parametric functions. We will suppose that the time series under analysis has been measured at equally spaced points in time; this is the case for many series in practice.

Consider the method for computing the loess fit, $\hat{g}(x)$, at a time point x. The first step is to multiply the number of observations, n, times the smoothing parameter, α, and then truncate the result to an integer, q. Then we find the q observation times closest to x and carry out the local fitting using data at these times. For time series applications, we will always take α to be of the form ℓ/n, where ℓ is an integer; thus $q = \ell$, and we will quote ℓ rather than α because it is typically more natural to think in terms of ℓ for a time series. For the trend fit to the melanoma data, $\ell = 30$ and $\lambda = 1$. For the fit to the residuals from the trend fit, $\ell = 9$ and $\lambda = 2$. Locally linear fitting is used for the trend fit because the trend has little or no curvature. Locally quadratic fitting is used for the oscillatory fit because the oscillations have peaks and valleys. The values of ℓ arose from experimenting with several values.

For a times series, we will typically evaluate a loess fit at the times at which the series is measured. This was done to display the loess fits in Figures 3.65 and 3.67.

Repeated Loess Fitting

The above fitting of two curves to the melanoma data is just the first step, or pass, of *repeated loess fitting*, a method for fitting two or more time components. For the first pass, the component with the largest value of ℓ is fitted by loess. For the melanoma data, this is the trend component graphed in Figure 3.65. Then the component is subtracted from the data to form residuals. The component with the second largest ℓ is fitted to the residuals. For the melanoma data, this is the oscillatory component graphed in Figure 3.67. If there are more than two time components to be fitted, new residuals are computed by subtracting the two fitted components, the next component is fitted, and so forth.

In the next pass, each component is fitted again by subtracting all other fitted components and fitting a loess curve. For example, in a second pass through the melanoma data, we subtract the oscillatory component from the first pass and fit the trend component to the residuals. Then we subtract this new trend component from the data and fit the oscillatory component to the residuals.

Several passes can be made through all components until the results stabilize, which typically happens after a small number of passes. The reason for multiple passes is that in some cases, different components can compete for the same variation in the data. The potential for competition increases as any two values of ℓ get closer. The multiple passes are needed for the components to settle down and decide which component gets what variation. For the melanoma data, additional passes beyond the first produce fits nearly identical to those from the first pass, so there is virtually no competition at all, and Figures 3.65 and 3.67 show what amount to the final fits.

Visualizing the Final Residuals

Figure 3.68 graphs the residuals from the two components of the fitting to the melanoma data. No major effect appears. One minor peculiarity is that the three largest residuals are preceded by the three smallest residuals. Figure 3.69 is a normal q-q plot of the residuals. The distribution of the data appears well approximated by the normal. For example, there are no outliers or more pervasive leptokurtosis. This is comforting because the loess fitting did not employ the bisquare robustness feature. Were such robustness needed, we would compute bisquare weights at the end of each pass and use them in each fitting of the next pass.

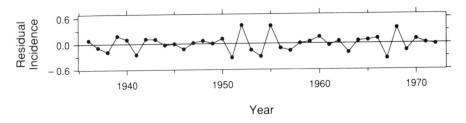

3.68   The display graphs the residuals from the fitting of two time components to melanoma incidence. The local segments are banked to $45°$.

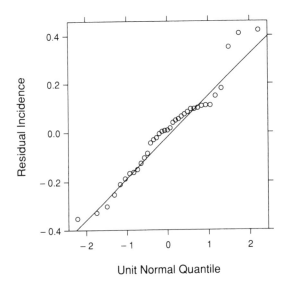

3.69 A normal q-q plot displays the incidence residuals.

For the visualizations of the data earlier in the chapter, r-f spread plots showed the relative amounts of variation in fitted values and residuals. For a time series fitting with multiple components, we want to compare the amount of variation not only in the overall fit and the residuals, but also in the different components as well. This can be done simply by graphing the components and the residuals against time as shown in the r-f spread plot of Figure 3.70 for the melanoma fits. The trend panel shows the yearly trend values minus their mean; the resulting values are centered on zero as are the values of the other two components. The trend component accounts for a large amount of the variation in the data. The oscillatory has less variation, and the residual component has the least.

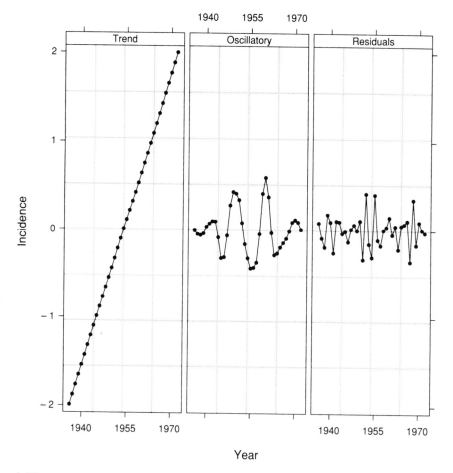

3.70 An r-f spread plot compares the variation in the three time components of melanoma — the trend component, the oscillatory component, and the residuals.

Causal Factors for the Melanoma Data

The trend component in the melanoma data has a number of possible causes. One, of course, is simply more exposure — for example, people spending more time at the beach. A second is more widespread and accurate diagnosis. A third is a population with greater susceptibility. No firm explanation of the cause is known at this time.

The oscillatory component has a firm explanation. The cycles have periods of about 12 years. Given that solar radiation is a cause of melanoma, given that the sunspots have an 11-year cycle , and given that solar activity increases with increasing sunspot number, it seems quite likely that the oscillatory component and the sunspot numbers are related. Figure 3.71 graphs both the oscillatory component and the sunspot numbers on juxtaposed panels. There is an obvious association between the two series in which the peaks and troughs of the sunspots occur somewhat earlier. This time delay, or lag, is not surprising. An increase in radiation would not necessarily trigger melanoma cases instantaneously but rather would trigger them at some point in the future. And diagnosis once symptoms appeared would not occur immediately.

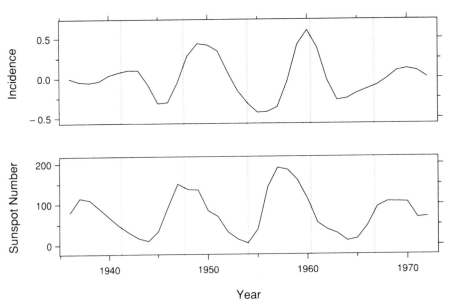

3.71 The oscillatory component fitted to melanoma incidence is compared with the sunspot numbers.

3.12   *Seasonal Components in Time Series*

Figure 3.72 displays monthly average CO_2 concentrations at the Mauna Loa observatory in Hawaii [10, 58]. One time component revealed by the graph is a persistent upward trend. This is the result of man's emissions of CO_2 into the atmosphere. The rise, if continued unabated, will cause atmospheric temperatures to rise, the polar ice caps to melt, the coastal areas of the continents to flood, and the climates of different regions of the earth to change radically [70].

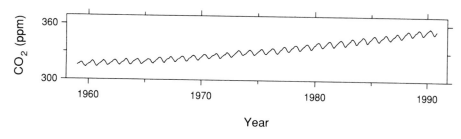

3.72   The display shows a time series, monthly CO_2 concentrations at Mauna Loa. The local segments are banked to $45°$.

The aspect ratio in Figure 3.72 has been chosen by $45°$ banking of the local segments, the line segments connecting successive monthly observations. This gives an opportunity to study local behavior, but it does not serve our assessment of the trend particularly well. If the segments of a trend curve were banked to $45°$, the aspect ratio of the graph would be close to one.

Figure 3.73 graphs the data again with an aspect ratio of one to provide a better visualization of the trend component. The graph suggests there is convexity in the trend; the rate of increase of CO_2 is itself increasing through time.

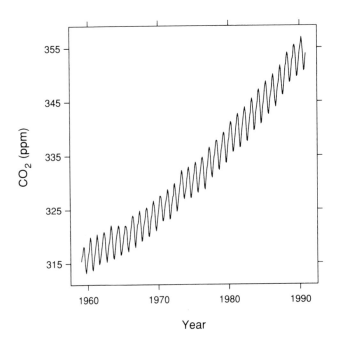

3.73 The CO_2 time series is graphed again with an aspect ratio equal to 1 to approximately bank the underlying trend to $45°$.

A second time component in the CO_2 data is oscillations with a period of one year. The cause is foliage in the Northern Hemisphere. When the amount of foliage begins to increase in the spring, CO_2 is absorbed from the atmosphere, and when the amount of foliage begins to decrease in the fall, CO_2 is returned to the atmosphere. This component has a special property. It operates like a good clock; it is a *seasonal component*. The driving mechanism, the change in foliage throughout the year in the Northern Hemisphere, is tied to the revolution of the earth around the sun. As time has marched along, peaks have occurred in late spring and troughs have occurred in the fall. Unless man's activities disrupt the mechanism, we can count on this behavior for the future, and we could accurately predict the occurrences of peaks in 100 years. Oscillations in a time series do not always keep good time. For example, the cycles in the sunspot series, a few of which are graphed in Figure 3.71, are not a particularly good clock. Over short time intervals of a few cycles, peaks can be predicted, but it is not possible to accurately predict peaks many decades into the future.

Figures 3.72 and 3.73 provide helpful visualizations of the CO_2 time components, but we can expect to see considerably more by fitting. We could proceed as we did with the melanoma data — fit the trend with a large value of ℓ and with $\lambda = 1$, and then fit the seasonal oscillations with a small value of ℓ and with $\lambda = 2$. But the excellent clock in the seasonal component gives an opportunity to take another tack that produces a better fit.

Seasonal Loess

Seasonal loess is a procedure for fitting a seasonal component. The procedure is iterative in the same way that repeated loess fitting is iterative, with several passes and with the fitting of components on each pass [18]. For seasonal loess, each pass consists of fitting two components. One is the seasonal component; seasonal loess has a special method for fitting this component. The other is a component whose sole purpose is to enable an uncontaminated fitting of the seasonal component; it captures long-period variations, which are trends and oscillations whose periods are longer than that of the seasonal period, which is 12 months for the CO_2 data. First, the seasonal component is fitted. Then the long-period component is fitted to the residuals. This is the first pass. In subsequent passes, each component is fitted to residuals from the other component. Usually, three passes are quite sufficient. If robustness is needed, bisquare weights can be computed at the end of each pass and used in each fitting of the next pass.

To fit the seasonal component, loess is applied separately to each *cycle subseries* of the residuals from the current long-period component. A cycle subseries consists of all data at one position of the cycle. For example, for the CO_2 data there are 12 subseries: the January values, the February values, and so forth. So to fit the seasonal component for CO_2 there are 12 separate loess smoothings, one for each subseries; the 12 fits are then combined to form the complete seasonal component. The details of the fitting for seasonal loess are given at the end of this section.

To carry out seasonal loess, values of ℓ and λ for the loess fits to the subseries must be chosen. For the CO_2 data, some experimentation showed that $\ell = 25$ and $\lambda = 1$ resulted in a seasonal component that was smooth and that adequately tracked the seasonal pattern in the data.

Cut-and-Stack Plots

The seasonal fit to the CO_2 data is displayed in Figure 3.74. A *cut-and-stack* display method is used to enable banking to 45°. Suppose we attempted to graph the CO_2 seasonal component on a single panel with 45° banking of the local segments. The resulting aspect ratio would be 0.017; and a single-panel graph with this aspect ratio that was 2 cm high would be 1.18 meters wide, too big for either a book page or a computer monitor. The solution is to take the single long panel, cut it into pieces, and stack the pieces up as in Figure 3.74. The seasonal component consists of 384 values, one value for each month. If the component were graphed on a single panel, the data would be displayed by 383 line segments connecting successive values. The cut-and-stack method also uses 383 segments because each cut occurs where one line segment joins the next one.

Figure 3.74 shows the seasonal cycles are all quite similar, but one change is apparent; the sizes, or amplitudes, of the seasonal oscillations increase slightly though time. The next visualization method provides a more sensitive look at this behavior.

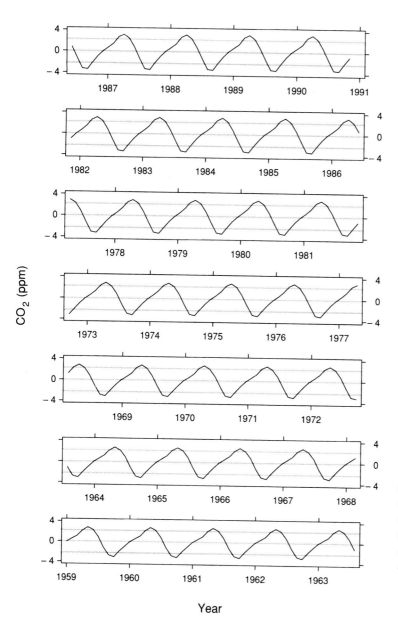

3.74 The seasonal component fitted to the CO_2 data is cut and stacked so that the curve can be banked to $45°$.

Year

Cycle Plots

Figure 3.75 is a *cycle plot*, another method for graphing a seasonal component [27]. The cycle subseries are graphed separately. First, at the left of the data region, the January values are graphed for successive years, then the February values are graphed, and so forth. For each cycle subseries, the mean of the values is portrayed by a horizontal line segment. The graph shows the overall pattern of the seasonal cycles — for example, as portrayed by the horizontal mean lines — and also shows the behavior of each monthly subseries. Thus we can readily see

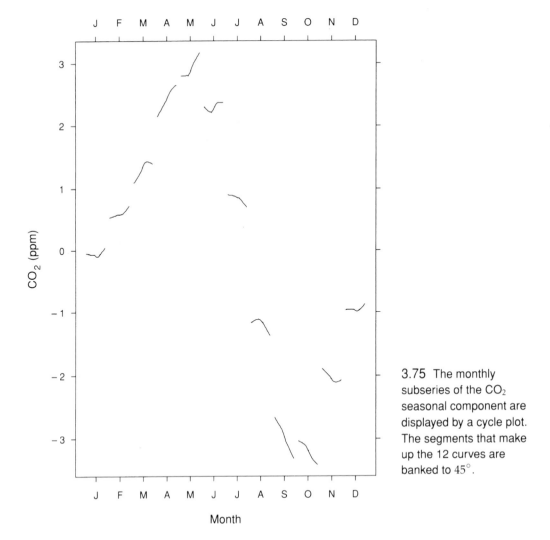

3.75 The monthly subseries of the CO_2 seasonal component are displayed by a cycle plot. The segments that make up the 12 curves are banked to $45°$.

whether the change in any subseries is large or small compared with the
overall pattern of the seasonal component.

Figure 3.75 shows interesting features. The first is the overall seasonal
pattern, with a May maximum and an October minimum. The second
feature is the patterns in the individual monthly subseries. For months
near the yearly maximum, the subseries tend to be increasing rapidly
although the overall increases are small compared with the seasonal
amplitude; the biggest increases occur for April and May. Near the
yearly minimum, cycle subseries tend to be decreasing; the biggest
decreases are for September and October. The net effect is the increase in
the amplitudes of the seasonal oscillations observed earlier. At present,
no one knows if this has been caused by human activity or whether it is
part of a natural cycle.

Fitting the Residuals from a Seasonal Component

Once a seasonal component has been fitted, other time components
can be studied by fitting the residuals from the seasonal component. The
CO_2 residuals, which still contain the trend component, are graphed in
Figure 3.76.

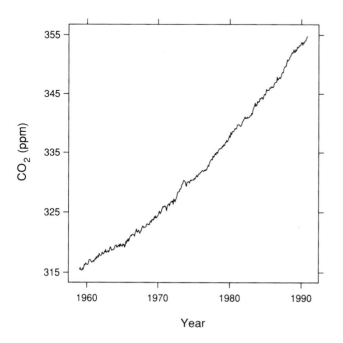

3.76 The residuals from the
seasonal component are displayed.

Figure 3.77 graphs a loess trend fit to the residuals with $\ell = 101$ and $\lambda = 1$. Figure 3.78 graphs the residuals from the trend fit. There are oscillations in the data — a rising and falling of the general level with periods of about 2 to 5 years. Figure 3.79 shows a loess fit to these residuals with $\ell = 35$ and $\lambda = 2$. Since we have fitted two time components to the residuals from the seasonal component, several passes of repeated loess fitting are in order. But as with the melanoma data, the final fits are very close to the initial.

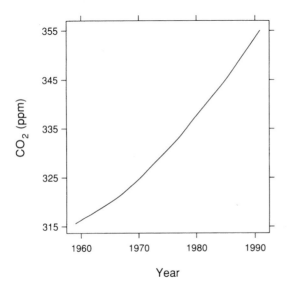

3.77 The display graphs a loess trend fit to the residuals from the seasonal component. The local segments are banked to $45°$.

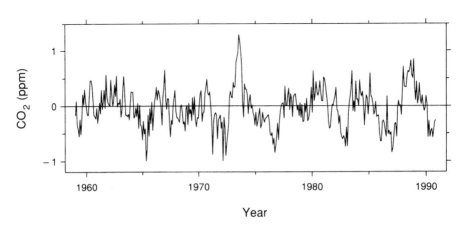

3.78 The residuals from the loess trend fit are displayed. The aspect ratio is 1/3 to enhance the perception of the oscillations in the data.

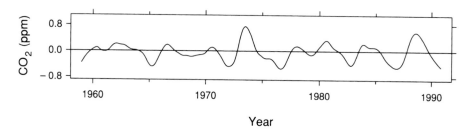

3.79 The curve is an oscillatory component fitted to the residuals from the trend fit. The local segments are banked to 45°.

The trend component in Figure 3.77 is convex; the rate of increase of CO_2 is increasing. The oscillatory component in Figure 3.79 has about 9 complete cycles over 32 years, so the average period is about 3.5 years. This variation is associated with changes in the southern oscillation index, a measure of the difference in atmospheric pressure between Easter Island in the South Pacific and Darwin, Australia. Changes in the index are also associated with changes in climate. For example, when the index drops sharply, the trade winds are reduced and the temperature of the equatorial Pacific increases. Many regions, including South America, can be drastically affected. In years when such an event occurs, the ocean warming normally begins in December, so the event has become known as El Niño, the child [59].

The final residuals from the three components fitted to the CO_2 data
— trend, 3.5-year, and seasonal — are graphed in Figure 3.80. No
striking time effect remains.

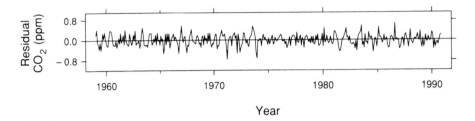

3.80 The residuals from the trend, 3.5-year, and seasonal components are displayed.
The aspect ratio is 0.1. Banking local segments to $45°$ results in an aspect ratio that is
too small.

Figure 3.81, a normal q-q plot, shows that the distribution of the
residuals is well approximated by the normal. Thus we need not fear
that outliers or more pervasive leptokurtosis is damaging our fits.

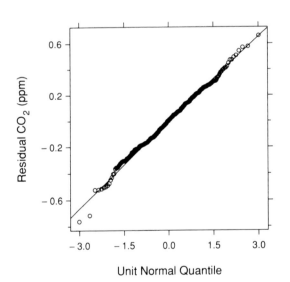

3.81 The CO_2 residuals are displayed by a
normal q-q plot.

Finally, Figure 3.82 graphs the 3.5-year, seasonal, and residual
components by an r-f spread plot. The trend component has been
omitted since, ominously, its variation is so much greater than that of the
other three. Its overall variation is 39.4 ppm, while the largest overall
variation of the other three, that of the seasonal, is only 6.6 ppm.

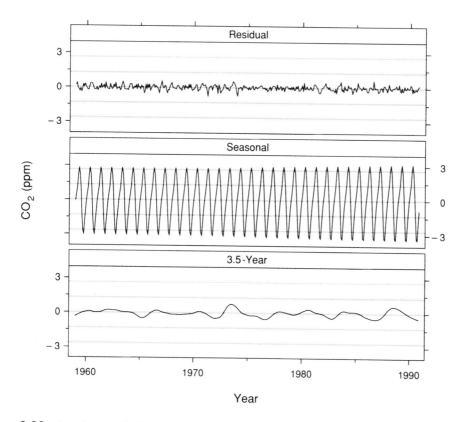

3.82 An r-f spread plot compares the variation in the 3.5-year component, the
seasonal component, and the residuals.

For the Record: The Details of Seasonal Loess

In seasonal loess, the long-period component is fitted to prevent variation with periods greater than that of the seasonal from leaking into the seasonal. The long-period component is not thought of as an output of the procedure; its purpose is just to facilitate the production of the seasonal component.

Let the time series be Y_t for times $t = 1$ to n. Suppose the number of observations in each period, or cycle, of the seasonal component is p. For example, if the series is monthly with a yearly periodicity, then $p = 12$. Suppose also that the choices of the parameters for the seasonal fitting are $\ell = \ell_{(s)}$ and $\lambda = \lambda_{(s)}$. As we will see, all other loess parameters used in seasonal loess are chosen automatically.

As stated earlier, seasonal loess is an iterative procedure, with several passes. On each pass, the seasonal component and the long-period component are fitted. Suppose $S_{t,k}$ and $L_{t,k}$ are the seasonal and long-period components at the end of the kth pass.

The result of the first stage of pass $k + 1$ is an updated seasonal component. First, residuals, $Y_t - L_{t,k}$, are computed. (On the first pass, no long-period component is available, so no subtraction is carried out.) Each cycle subseries of the residual series is fitted by loess with $\ell = \ell_{(s)}$ and $\lambda = \lambda_{(s)}$. Each loess fit is evaluated at all time points of the subseries and at two additional points: one time step ahead and one time step behind. For example, suppose that the series is monthly, that $p = 12$, and that the January subseries ranges from January 1943 to January 1997. Then the loess fit for January is evaluated at all time points from January 1942 to January 1998. The collection of fitted values for all of the subseries is a series, $C_{t,k+1}$, consisting of $n + 2p$ values that range from $t = -p + 1$ to $n + p$. Next, $C_{t,k+1}$ is filtered by a moving average of length p, followed by another moving average of length p, followed by a moving average of length 3, followed by a loess fit with $\lambda = 1$ and ℓ equal to the smallest odd integer greater than or equal to p. The output, $F_{t,k+1}$, is defined at time positions $t = 1$ to n because the three moving averages cannot extend to the ends, so in all, p positions are lost at each end. The fitted seasonal component from this pass is $S_{t,k+1} = C_{t,k+1} - F_{t,k+1}$ for $t = 1$ to n. $F_{t,k+1}$ is subtracted to help prevent long-period variation from entering the seasonal component.

The result of the second stage of pass $k + 1$ is an updated long-period component. First, residuals, $Y_t - S_{t,k+1}$, are computed. Then the residuals are fitted by loess with $\lambda = 1$ and

$$\ell = \frac{1.5p}{1 - 1.5\ell_{(s)}^{-1}}$$

rounded to an integer. The fitted long-period component from this step $L_{t,k+1}$, is the loess fit evaluated at the time points $t = 1$ to n.

As with repeated loess fitting, bisquare can be used in seasonal loess by computing bisquare weights at the end of each pass and using them in the next pass. The weights after pass k are computed using the residuals, $Y_t - S_{t,k} - L_{t,k}$. Bisquare was not used for the CO_2 data because the residuals have a distribution that is well approximated by the normal.

In some cases, the change in the level of each subseries can be nearly flat through time but not quite constant. In other words, the seasonal component changes, but only very gradually. In such a case, it can make sense to take $\lambda_{(s)} = 0$, a value of λ not yet encountered in our account of loess fitting. This means a constant in time is fitted locally rather than a linear or quadratic function of time. While such a value of λ can make sense for time series applications, it almost never makes sense for the applications in which the factor is not time.

Other loess smoothing parameters in the above description of seasonal loess have been given values that work quite well in most applications. But aficionados of fitting seasonal components can experiment with these parameters as well.

3.13   Direct Manipulation: Labeling by Brushing

For some bivariate data sets, each observation has a label. Figure 3.83 is a scatterplot of log brain weight against log body weight for a collection of animal types. In this case, the label for each bivariate observation is an animal name.

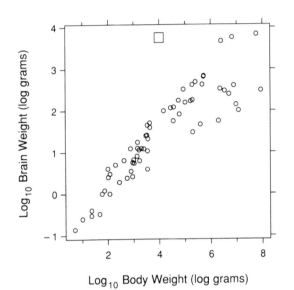

3.83 Log brain weight is graphed against log body weight for various animal types. The rectangle on the graph is the brush.

In the course of visualizing labeled data, it is often helpful to selectively label points identified as interesting from their location on a scatterplot. This typically cannot be achieved simply by labeling all points because the labels overlap and obscure one another. Because our selection of points to be labeled is based on visual identification, direct manipulation is ideal for labeling.

Brushing is a basic tool of direct manipulation that can be used for labeling and, as we shall see in later chapters, for other direct manipulation methods as well [6]. The rectangle at the top of the data region in Figure 3.83 is the *brush*, the central object in brushing. There are two important aspects of the control that the data analyst has of the brush. One is that it is moved around the screen by moving a mouse. The second is that it can be made any size or shape; in Figure 3.83, it has been made small and square.

The problem of labeling points on a scatterplot is solved quite nicely by brushing. When the brush covers one or more points, the label for each covered point appears. This is illustrated by Figure 3.84; we can now see that the animal with the largest brain weight is the blue whale.

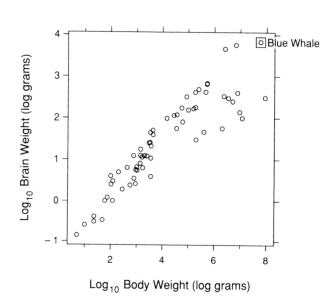

3.84 Brushing with the labeling operation in the transient mode shows one label.

There are three modes in which the labeling operation can be carried out — *transient, lasting,* and *erase.* If the mode is *transient,* the label for a covered point disappears when the brush no longer covers it. This is illustrated by Figure 3.85. The brush has been moved from the blue-whale point to the point of an animal type with a slightly bigger body than the blue whale, but with a much smaller brain, clearly a dumb animal compared with the whale. As soon as the brush leaves the blue-whale point, the blue-whale label disappears. As soon as the brush touches the new point, the new label appears showing it is the genus Brachiosaurus.

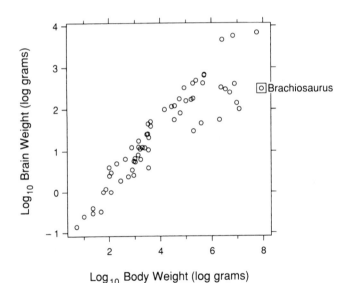

3.85 Brushing in the transient mode shows another label.

If the mode is *lasting,* the label remains even after the brush is removed from the point. This is illustrated by Figure 3.86. The brush has touched two points, and the labels remain even after the brush is moved from the points.

If the mode is *erase,* a lasting label is removed when the brush touches it. This is illustrated by Figure 3.87; the lasting Brachiosaurus label created in Figure 3.86 has been removed by covering the genus' point.

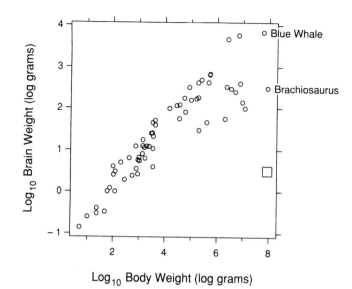

3.86 Brushing in the lasting mode has resulted in two lasting labels.

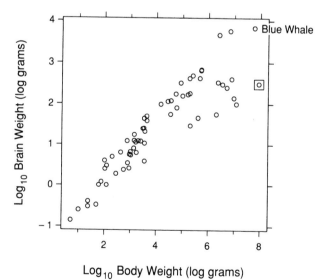

3.87 Brushing in the erase mode has removed one of the lasting labels.

Finally, in Figure 3.88, brushing in the lasting mode has been applied to all points on the scatterplot. The result, a mess, shows why the simple procedure of drawing all labels at the outset does not work.

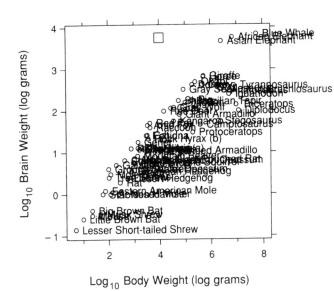

3.88 Brushing in the lasting mode has been used to draw the names of all animal types.

3.14 Visualization and Probabilistic Inference

Rote Data Analysis

The experimenters who collected the ganglion data that were analyzed at the beginning of this chapter related CP ratio to area by fitting a least-squares line [60]. Probabilistic inference was carried out using a standard t-interval method that is based on an assumption that the deviations of the response from the line are a homogeneous random sample from a normal population distribution. Suppose this assumption is true. If we subtract the population slope from the slope estimate and then divide by a standard estimate of the population standard deviation of the slope estimate, the result has a t-distribution. This t-statistic can be used to form confidence intervals and to test the null hypothesis that the slope is zero. The experimenters quote the results of the hypothesis test in their account:

> The linear relation between the C/P ratio and retinal area is highly significant (slope $= 0.107 \pm 0.010$; $P < 0.001$)...

Such a quotation of a p-value is part of the ritual of science, a sprinkling of the holy waters in an effort to sanctify the data analysis and turn consumers of the results into true believers.

The rote data analysis of the experimenters has produced nonsense. The visualizations earlier in the chapter showed that a line does not fit the data. That ends matters right there. The standard t-interval method is not valid. The sampling variability that it prescribes for the estimate is not the actual variability. Once the lack of fit is appreciated, it is possible to make correct statements about variability, but in this example it makes no sense to characterize the probabilistic properties of a function estimate that does not fit the data.

The visualizations of the chapter also showed that a quadratic polynomial fits CP ratio without lack of fit, but there is monotone spread. So even with the right function, the t-interval method is inapplicable because the residuals are not homogeneous.

Finally, the visualizations showed that by taking the logarithm of CP ratio, the underlying pattern is linear, the spread no longer depends on location, and the distribution of the residuals is well approximated by the normal distribution. For this analysis, we can venture the standard methods to make probabilistic inferences.

Combining Prior Information and Data

Visualization is an effective framework for drawing inferences from data because its revelation of the structure of data can be readily combined with prior knowledge to draw conclusions. By contrast, because of the formalism of probablistic methods, it is typically impossible to incorporate into them the full body of prior information.

Even when we have checked all assumptions that underlie a probabilistic inference, we must be prepared to ignore its results if knowledge not accounted for in the inferences appears to provide a better explanation of the behavior of the data. The fly data analyzed in Section 3.8 are one example. The actual temperatures of the incubators in the fly experiment are the causal factor, not the nominal temperatures. Fortunately, the experimenters report much information about the actual temperatures, and they wisely encourage us to incorporate this knowledge into our conclusions from the experiment:

> Errors in this study may arise from fluctuating temperatures. . . . Nominal temperatures in accompanying tables and figures are to be considered with these remarks in mind.

The visualization suggested a temperature anomaly at 23°C and 25°C — a deviation from the overall linear pattern. But the information that the actual temperatures varied by substantial amounts, particularly the large variation at 23°C, combined with the information from the visualization, makes it quite clear that the deviations in the actual temperatures could easily account for the anomaly at 23°C and 25°C. In other words, combining the results of the visualization with the knowledge of the actual temperature variation leads to a conclusion that the dependence of facet number on actual temperature is likely linear.

R. A. Fisher analyzed these data with probabilistic methods [38]. In an exceedingly uncharacteristic moment of poor insight, he used the nominal temperatures and ignored the information about actual temperature variation offered up by the experimenters. He tested the null hypothesis that the underlying pattern in facet number is linear in nominal temperature. To do so, he chose a method of analysis — the analysis of variance — that is based on an assumption of normal distributions with the same standard deviation. Our visualization shows that this is a reasonable assumption for the nominal temperature distributions. Fisher concluded that the null hypothesis of a linear dependence of facet number on temperature is rejected because the p-value of the test is small. He reports:

> The deviations from linear regression are evidently larger than what would be expected, if the regression were really linear . . . There can therefore be no question of the statistical significance of the deviations from the straight line, although the latter accounts for the greater part of the variation.

It is certainly true that a small p-value would be expected if the underlying pattern were not linear. But a small p-value could also result from other causes. One of them is a fluctuation in actual temperature, the likely cause [9].

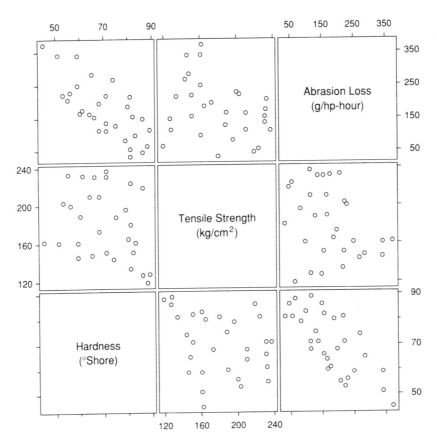

4.1 A scatterplot matrix displays trivariate data: measurements of abrasion loss, hardness, and tensile strength for 30 rubber specimens.

4 Trivariate Data

Figure 4.1, a scatterplot matrix, shows data from an industrial experiment in which thirty rubber specimens were rubbed by an abrasive material [31]. Measurements of three variables — abrasion loss, hardness, and tensile strength — were made for each specimen. Abrasion loss is the amount of material abraded from a specimen per unit of energy expended in the rubbing; tensile strength is the force per unit of cross-sectional area required to break a specimen; and hardness is the rebound height of a steel indenter dropped onto a specimen. The goal is to determine the dependence of abrasion loss on tensile strength and hardness; thus abrasion loss is a response, and hardness and tensile strength are factors. Each panel of the scatterplot matrix in Figure 4.1 is a scatterplot of one variable against another. For example, the upper left panel is a scatterplot of abrasion loss on the vertical scale against hardness on the horizontal scale. This scatterplot also appears in the lower right panel, but with the axes reversed.

The rubber data are trivariate data: measurements of three quantitative variables. Geometrically, the 30 values of abrasion loss, hardness, and tensile strength are 30 points in a three-dimensional space. Visualization, whether on a computer screen or on paper, uses a two-dimensional physical medium. The tools in this chapter enable us to visualize the three-dimensional structure within this two-dimensional medium.

A Coordinate System for Panels

Each panel of a scatterplot matrix, or any other multi-panel display, will be referenced by its column and row numbers; the left column is column one and the bottom row is row one. In Figure 4.1, the upper left panel is (1,3) and the lower right panel is (3,1). This convention amounts to a coordinate system for the panels where the column number is the horizontal coordinate and the row number is the vertical coordinate.

4.1   *Coplots of Data*

The hardnesses of the rubber specimens range from 45 °Shore to
89 °Shore. Consider those specimens whose hardnesses lie in the range
45 °Shore to 62 °Shore. There are nine such specimens; their data are
displayed in Figure 4.2 by the "+" plotting symbols. Geometrically, we
have sliced through the three-dimensional space of the data with two
planes that intersect the h axis perpendicularly at 45 °Shore and
62 °Shore, and have selected the specimens that lie between the two
planes. On the (2,3) panel of Figure 4.2, the "+" symbols show how
abrasion loss depends on tensile strength conditional on hardness lying
between 45 °Shore to 62 °Shore. There is a nonlinear conditional
dependence.

The concept of *conditioning* illustrated in Figure 4.2 is a fundamental
one that forms the basis of a number of graphical methods developed in
the past [71, 78, 81]. And it forms the basis for the *conditioning plot*, or
coplot, a particularly powerful visualization tool for studying how a
response depends on two or more factors.

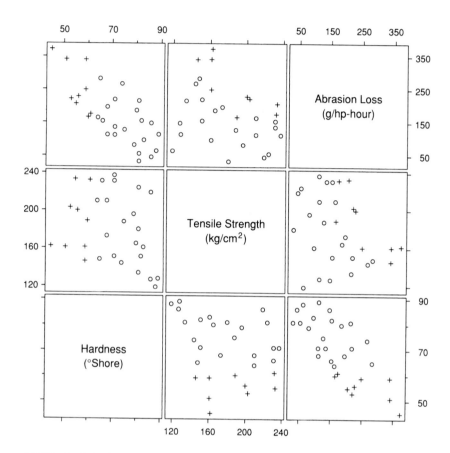

4.2 The "+" plotting symbols encode the data for those specimens with hardness less than 62 °Shore.

The Coplot Display Method

The display method of the coplot presents conditional dependence in a visually efficient way. Figure 4.3 illustrates the method using the rubber data. The panel at the top is the *given panel*; the panels below are the *dependence panels*. Each rectangle on the given panel specifies an interval of values of hardness. On a corresponding dependence panel, abrasion loss is graphed against tensile strength for those observations whose values of hardness lie in the interval. If we start at the (1,1) dependence panel and move in graphical order — that is, from left to right in the bottom row, then from left to right in the next row, and so forth — the corresponding intervals of the given panel proceed from left to right and from bottom to top in the same fashion. The intervals were determined by the equal-count algorithm that was used for slicing in Chapter 3. The use of the algorithm for conditioning will be discussed shortly.

In Figure 4.3, a loess curve has been added to each dependence panel. Bisquare is used in the fitting to protect against outliers that might be present in the data. At this early stage of the analysis, outliers cannot be ruled out, so we take the conservative route of using robust fitting just in case they are there.

The aspect ratio of the dependence panels is critical. In Chapter 3, the aspect ratio was chosen on many displays to bank curves to 45°. In those examples, there was just a single panel. On coplots there are many panels, but they all have the same scales, so we simply apply 45° banking to the entire collection of segments. Suppose all of the symbols and line segments on the dependence panels of Figure 4.3 were graphed on a single panel. The aspect ratio that would result from applying 45° banking to the line segments is the aspect ratio used in Figure 4.3. In other words, the method of 45° banking does not depend on whether we happen to juxtapose subsets of the data on different panels or graph everything on the same panel. And as with single-panel displays, if 45° banking results in an aspect ratio that is too large or too small to maintain the resolution of labels and plotting symbols, we simple use the closest aspect ratio that allows sufficient resolution.

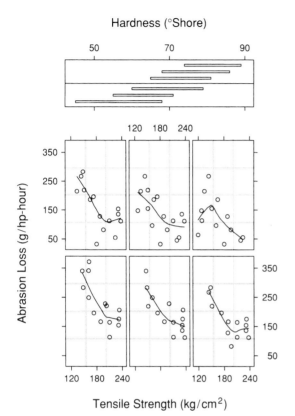

4.3 A coplot graphs abrasion loss against tensile strength given hardness. The parameters of the six robust loess curves are $\alpha = 3/4$ and $\lambda = 1$. The aspect ratio of the data rectangle of the dependence panels has been chosen to produce $45°$ banking of the collection of line segments that make up the curves.

Figure 4.3 shows a wealth of information about the dependence of abrasion loss on tensile strength. Except for panel (3,2), each conditioning on hardness has a nonlinear pattern: a broken-line, or hockey-stick, function. Below 180 kg/cm², the pattern is linear; above this value, it is also linear, but with a different slope. On the five panels, the slopes below the breakpoint are negative and nearly equal. Above the breakpoint, the five slopes are nearly equal to zero. In other words, the patterns shift up and down, but do not appear to change otherwise by a significant amount. This suggests that for the most part there is no *interaction* between the two factors; the effect of tensile strength on abrasion loss is the same for most values of hardness. But Panel (3,2) shows a major departure from the hockey-stick pattern. As tensile strength decreases, the handle of the stick begins to form but then, suddenly, for the lowest three values of tensile strength, the pattern turns precipitously downward.

Coplots intervals must be chosen to compromise between two competing criteria — number of points and resolution. On the one side, their lengths must be sufficiently great that the dependence panels have enough points for effects to be seen; if there are too few points on a dependence panel, noise in the data typically prevents points from coalescing into a meaningful pattern. On the other side, the lengths must be small enough to maintain reasonable resolution; if a conditioning interval is too big, there is a risk of a distorted view if the nature of the dependence changes dramatically as the value of the conditioning factor changes within the interval. The intervals in Figure 4.3 were selected by the equal-count algorithm. The inputs to the algorithm are the number of intervals and the target fraction of values to be shared by successive intervals. In Figure 4.3, the number of intervals is 6 and the target fraction is 3/4. These two values were the result of experimentation with a variety of values in an attempt to steer a middle course between resolution and number of points.

Figure 4.4 conditions on tensile strength; abrasion loss is graphed against hardness for six intervals of tensile strength chosen, again, by the equal-count algorithm with a target fraction of overlap equal to 3/4. For each conditioning on tensile strength, the dependence of abrasion loss on hardness has, for the most part, a linear pattern. Furthermore, the patterns have roughly the same slope and change only in the intercepts. This supports the observation in Figure 4.3 that, for the most part, there is little or no interaction between hardness and tensile strength. And again, there is a departure from the overall pattern for a small number of points. In panel (1,1), the observations with the three or so largest values of hardness drop well below the linear pattern established by the other observations. The scatterplot matrix in Figure 4.1 shows that the three observations with the smallest values of tensile strength take on the three largest values of hardness. Thus the aberrant behavior on the two coplots is caused by the same three observations, which sit by themselves in a corner of the factor space.

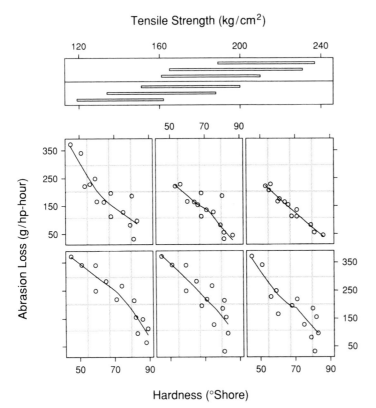

4.4 Abrasion loss is graphed against hardness given tensile strength. The parameters of the robust loess curves are $\alpha = 3/4$ and $\lambda = 1$. The curves are banked to $45°$.

Ethanol Data

Figure 4.5 is a scatterplot matrix of data from an experiment that studied exhaust from an experimental one-cylinder engine fueled by ethanol [12]. The response, which will be denoted by NO_x, is the concentration of nitric oxide, NO, plus the concentration of nitrogen dioxide, NO_2, normalized by the amount of work of the engine. The units are μg of NO_x per joule. One factor is the equivalence ratio, E, at which the engine was run. E is a measure of the richness of the air and fuel mixture; as E increases there is more fuel in the mixture. Another factor is C, the compression ratio to which the engine is set. C is the volume inside the cylinder when the piston is retracted, divided by the volume when the piston is at its maximum point of penetration into the cylinder. There were 88 runs of the experiment.

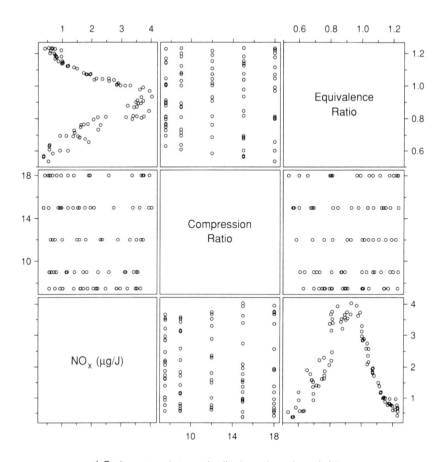

4.5 A scatterplot matrix displays the ethanol data.

The (3,2) panel in Figure 4.5 shows that C and E are nearly uncorrelated and that C takes on one of five values. The (3,1) panel shows a strong nonlinear dependence of NO_x on E with a peak near $E = 0.9$. The (2,1) panel does not reveal a relationship between NO_x and C, but it is possible that a dependence is being masked by the strong effect of E.

Figure 4.6 is a coplot of NO_x against C given E. The equal-count method has been used to select the intervals; the target fraction of overlap is 1/4. The coplot shows that NO_x does, in fact, depend on C; for low values of E, NO_x increases with C, and for medium and high values of E, NO_x is constant as a function of C. In all cases, the underlying pattern appears linear; for low values of E, the slope is positive and for high values, it is zero.

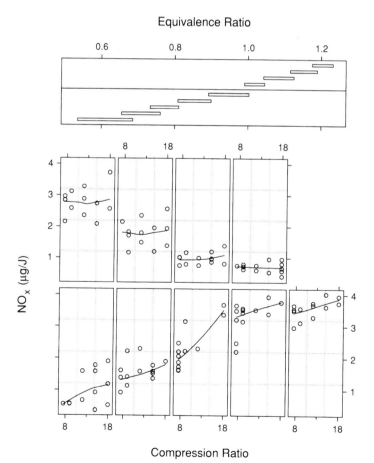

4.6 A coplot graphs NO_x against compression ratio given equivalence ratio. The parameters of the robust loess curves are $\alpha = 1$ and $\lambda = 1$. The curves are banked by an aspect ratio of 2.5; banking to $45°$ results in an aspect ratio that is too large.

Figure 4.7 is a coplot of NO_X against E given C; since C takes on only one of five distinct values, each dependence panel corresponds to one of these distinct values. The coplot shows that the peak concentration of NO_X occurs near $E = 0.9$ for all five values of C. But the value of NO_X at the peak increases slightly as C increases. This coplot and the previous one in Figure 4.6 show that the effect of C on NO_X depends on the value of E, and vice versa, so there is an *interaction* between the factors. This contrasts with the rubber data where no major interaction was detected.

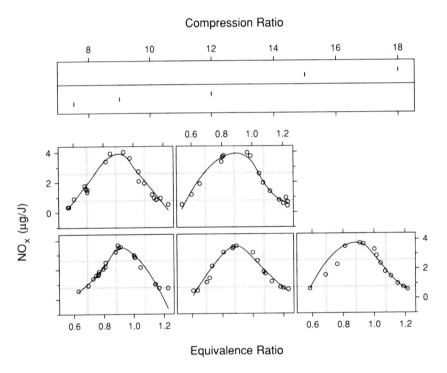

4.7 A coplot graphs NO_X against equivalence ratio given compression ratio. The parameters of the robust loess curves are $\alpha = 3/4$ and $\lambda = 2$. The curves are banked to $45°$.

Figure 4.7 shows that the amount of residual variation about the underlying pattern is small. But several observations appear to wander from the underlying pattern by considerably more than the majority of the points. For example, on panel (3,1), two points lie well below the curve. Thus, on the scale of this residual variation, there appear to be outliers, or more pervasive leptokurtosis.

4.2 Direct Manipulation: Conditioning by Brushing

Conditioning analyses can also be carried out by brushing, the direct manipulation tool introduced in Chapter 3. Brushing has a number of *operations* that are applied either in the transient, lasting, or erasing modes. One operation, described in Chapter 3, is labeling. Another, *enhanced linking*, can be used to condition.

Figure 4.8 is a scatterplot matrix of the rubber data. The brush is in the (1,2) panel, and is small and square. First, we turn on the enhanced linking operation of brushing by a menu selection. Next, we change the size and shape of the brush and cover a set of points as shown in

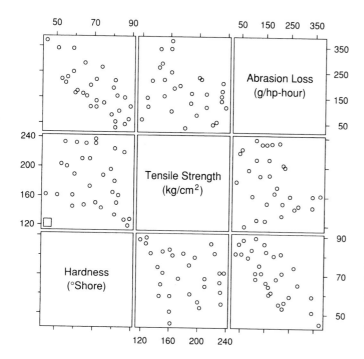

4.8 A scatterplot matrix displays the rubber data. A brush is sitting in the (1,2) panel waiting for instructions to carry out conditioning.

Figure 4.9. The points inside the brush are highlighted as well as all points on the other scatterplots that correspond to these points. The shape and positioning of the brush is vital to producing a conditioning analysis. Its vertical extent spans the range of values of tensile strength, and its horizontal extent spans an interval of low values of hardness. The highlighted points on the (2,3) panel are a scatterplot of abrasion loss against tensile strength conditional on low values of hardness.

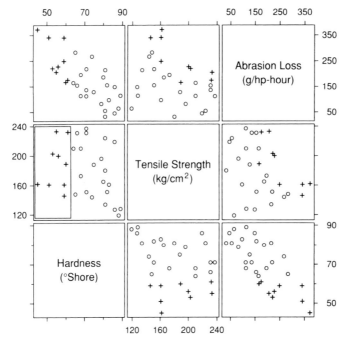

4.9 Brushing with the enhanced linking operation in the transient mode produces a conditioning on low values of hardness.

We can move the brush to the right on the (1,2) panel to condition on other intervals. This is illustrated in Figure 4.10. The mode is transient in this application, so the old highlighting disappears when the brush is moved, and a new set of points is selected for highlighting. Moving the brush left and right on the (1,2) panel provides conditioning on a continuum of hardness intervals. Furthermore, we can quickly change the width of the brush, making it smaller to increase the resolution of the conditioning, or making it larger to decrease the resolution, and then resume the brushing left and right with the new width. Also, moving the brush to the (2,1) panel allows conditioning on tensile strength. This is illustrated in Figure 4.11; the highlighted points on the (1,3) panel show the dependence of abrasion loss on hardness for tensile strength in an interval of low values.

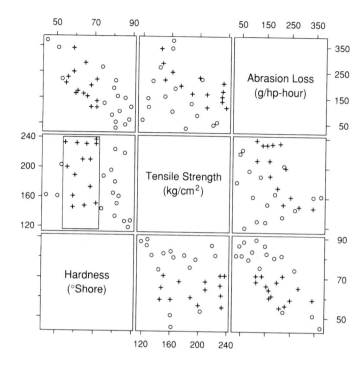

4.10 The brush has been moved to the right to condition on a different interval of hardness.

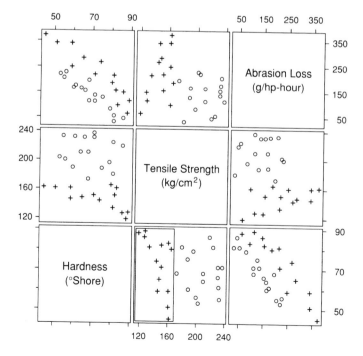

4.11 The brush has been moved to the (2,1) panel to condition on tensile strength.

The term "enhanced linking" is used for the brushing operation just shown because the scatterplot matrix by itself provides some visual linking of effects on different panels just through visual scanning along rows and along columns. This issue of visual perception is taken up in more detail in Chapter 5.

4.3   Coplots of Fitted Surfaces

In Chapter 3, fitting was introduced to aid the visualization of the dependence of a response, y, on a single factor, x. The two methods were least-squares fitting of parametric families and loess curve fitting. And bisquare iterations were added to these two methods when outliers or more pervasive leptokurtosis was present.

The same approach can be used to study the dependence of y on two factors, u and v. Suppose the data are u_i, v_i, and y_i for $i = 1$ to n. The fitted function is now a surface, $\hat{g}(u, v)$, a function of two variables. To visualize the data, we graph both the fitted function and the residuals,

$$\hat{\varepsilon}_i = y_i - \hat{g}(u_i, v_i) .$$

If the underlying pattern in the data is simple, parametric fitting might be satisfactory. If the underlying pattern is too complex for a parametric fit, then loess can be used.

Parametric Fitting

Least-squares fitting for trivariate data is a simple extension of the method for bivariate data. Suppose the underlying pattern of the dependence of y on u and v is linear. To fit a linear parametric family by least-squares, we find values of a, b, and c that minimize

$$\sum_{i=1}^{n} (y_i - a - bu_i - cv_i)^2 .$$

This minimizes the sum of squares of the residuals.

Bisquare fitting is also a simple extension. The first step is to fit by least-squares. Then, residuals and bisquare robustness weights, r_i, are computed, and the function is fitted again using weighted least-squares with weights r_i. For a linear parametric family, the weighted least-squares fit minimizes

$$\sum_{i=1}^{n} r_i(y_i - a - bu_i - cv_i)^2 \, .$$

This weighted fitting is then iterated until the fit converges.

Loess

For two factors, loess fitting is similar to the one-factor case; details are given at the end of this section. The loess parameter α controls the amount of smoothness of the fitted surface; as α increases, the smoothness of the surface increases. The loess parameter λ controls the degree of the local fitting. If $\lambda = 1$, the fitting is locally linear, so linear polynomials,

$$a + bu + cv \, ,$$

are fitted. If $\lambda = 2$, the fitting is locally quadratic, so quadratic polynomials,

$$a + bu + cv + duv + eu^2 + fv^2 \, ,$$

are fitted. And bisquare iterations can be added when robustness is needed.

Distance, however, must be given additional consideration for two factors. For the case of one factor, x, the neighborhood weight, $w_i(x)$ given to (x_i, y_i) for the fit at x is based on the distance of x_i from x. Since x and x_i are points lying on a line, it is natural to use $|x - x_i|$ as the distance between them. For two factors, the value at which the fit is computed is now a point (u, v) in the plane, and the measurements of the factors are other points (u_i, v_i) in this plane. We could simply take distance from (u, v) to (u_i, v_i) to be Euclidean,

$$\sqrt{(u - u_i)^2 + (v - v_i)^2} \, .$$

This might be sensible in cases where u and v describe geographical location and thus have the same units. But in most applications of loess, the units of the factors are different. For example, for the rubber data, the units of the factors are kg/cm^2 for tensile strength and °Shore for hardness. Euclidean distance depends on the choice of these units. If we changed from kg/cm^2 to g/cm^2, all values of tensile strength would be multiplied by 10^3, and relative values of the Euclidean distances would change drastically. We can remove the dependence on units by dividing each factor by a measure of spread, then using Euclidean distance for the standardized variables. One way to standardize would be to divide each factor by its sample standard deviation. But as we saw in Chapter 2, the sample standard deviation is not robust; it can be badly distorted by just a few outliers that are much smaller or much larger than the majority of the data. To protect against this, we will use a *trimmed sample standard deviation*. The values of the factor are sorted from smallest to largest, the smallest 10% and the largest 10% are dropped, and the sample standard deviation is computed from the remaining 80% of the values.

Coplots of a Fit to the Ethanol Data

For the ethanol data, the coplots in Figures 4.6 and 4.7 showed that the dependence of NO$_X$ on C and E is too complex to be adequately fitted by a simple parametric family. Thus we will use a loess fit, $\hat{g}(C, E)$, to describe how NO$_X$ depends on C and E. Figure 4.7 showed that bisquare is needed in the fitting because some observations deviate substantially from the underlying pattern compared with the deviations of the majority of the observations. Figure 4.7 also showed that conditional on C, NO$_X$ as a function of E has a large amount of curvature with a peak near $E = 0.9$. Because of the curvature, we must take $\lambda = 2$. But Figure 4.6 showed that given E, the underlying pattern in the data is linear in C. By using a feature of loess called *conditionally linear fitting*, we can produce a fitted surface that is linear in C given E. As E changes, the slope and intercept of the fit change, but it is always linear in C given E. The details of conditionally linear fitting are given at the end of this section. Finally, a value of α equal to 1/3 resulted from trying different values to find one that produced no lack or surplus of fit; this will be discussed further in Section 4.4.

Coplots can also be used to visualize fitted surfaces. Figure 4.12 is a coplot of the robust loess fit, $\hat{g}(C, E)$, to the ethanol data. As with coplots of data, the given panel is at the top and the dependence panels are below. Consider the (1,1) dependence panel. E has been set to a specific conditioning value, 0.535. Then $\hat{g}(C, 0.535)$ has been evaluated for equally spaced values of C ranging from the minimum value of C in the data to the maximum. On the panel, the values of $\hat{g}$ are graphed against the equally spaced values of C. The same method is used on the other dependence panels, but for different conditioning values of E. There are 16 equally spaced conditioning values ranging from the minimum value of E in the data to the maximum; the given panel shows the 16 values.

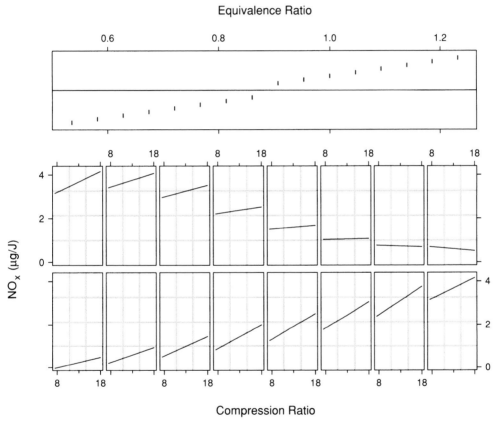

4.12 A coplot graphs the robust loess fit against compression ratio given equivalence ratio. The curves are banked by an aspect ratio of 2. Banking to 45° results in an aspect ratio that is too large.

Figure 4.12 shows that given E, $\hat{g}$ is linear in C, the result of specifying the loess fit to be conditionally linear in C. As the conditioning values of E increase from the lowest values, the slopes of the lines first increase until E is about 0.8, and then decrease to zero. Thus, as we saw in the coplots of the data, there is a strong interaction between C and E.

Figure 4.13 is a coplot of the robust loess fit against E for 16 conditioning values of C. Figure 4.13 shows that $\widehat{g}$ varies in a highly nonlinear way as a function of E given C. The maximum of $\widehat{g}$ increases by about 1 $\mu g/J$ as the conditioning values of C go from the minimum to the maximum; the value of E at which this maximum occurs is always close to 0.9.

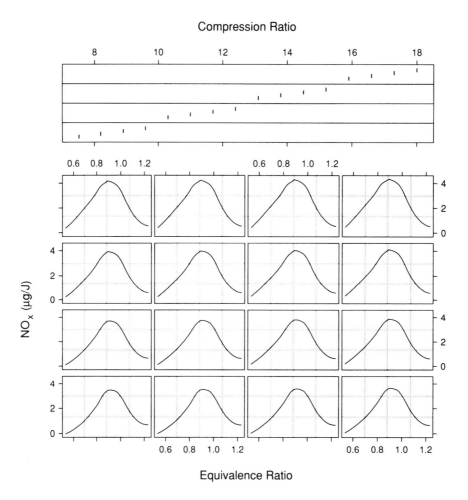

4.13 A coplot graphs the robust loess fit against equivalence ratio given compression ratio. The curves are banked to 45°.

Figure 4.14 illustrates further how the coplots of the fit, $\hat{g}(C,E)$, have been constructed. The circles are the observed values of C and E. The fit is a surface lying above this plane of (C,E) values. Figure 4.14 shows 16 horizontal line segments drawn at the 16 conditioning values of E; each of these segments ranges in the horizontal direction from the minimum value of C in the data to the maximum. For the coplot of Figure 4.12, the surface is graphed along the 16 horizontal segments. Figure 4.14 also has 16 vertical segments, drawn in the same manner, but showing the conditioning on C. For the coplot of Figure 4.13, the surface is graphed along the 16 vertical line segments.

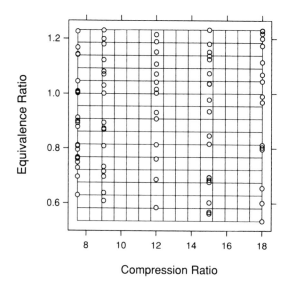

4.14 The coplots of the robust loess surface display the surface along the 16 horizontal and 16 vertical line segments shown here.

The coplots have provided an effective visualization of the loess surface fitted to the ethanol data. But we must reserve judgment about whether this has shed light on the structure of the data. We must validate the fit by visualizations of the residuals, making sure that the fit has been true to the data. In other words, we must convince ourselves that the coplots have not provided a thorough understanding of nonsense. Validation of the fit will be discussed in Section 4.4.

Coplots of a Fit to the Rubber Data and Cropping

There are only 30 observations of the rubber-specimen variables and three of them are aberrant. Because there is so little data, we will begin the fitting with a parametric family that is as simple as is reasonable. And we will use bisquare fitting in the hope that it will prevent the aberrant observations from distorting the fit to the remaining.

The coplots of the rubber data in Figures 4.3 and 4.4 showed a dependence on tensile strength that has a hockey-stick pattern with a break at 180 kg/cm², and a dependence on hardness that is linear. Furthermore, there appeared to be little or no interaction between the factors. We need a mathematical description of this dependence. Let t denote tensile strength. Let

$$[t - 180]^- = \begin{cases} t - 180 & \text{for } t < 180 \\ 0 & \text{otherwise.} \end{cases}$$

Similarly, let

$$[t - 180]^+ = \begin{cases} t - 180 & \text{for } t > 180 \\ 0 & \text{otherwise.} \end{cases}$$

The hockey-stick pattern is

$$\gamma[t - 180]^- + \delta[t - 180]^+ .$$

γ is the slope for $t < 180$ and δ is the slope for $t > 180$. Let h denote hardness. The observed dependence of abrasion loss on hardness and tensile strength is described by the function

$$g(h, t) = \mu + \beta h + \gamma[t - 180]^- + \delta[t - 180]^+ .$$

We will begin by forcing δ to be zero since it appeared to be zero on the coplots. Thus the parametric family has three free parameters: μ, β, and γ. The bisquare fit of the family is

$$\hat{g}(h, t) = 602 - 6.74h - 3.37[t - 180]^- .$$

Great care must be exercised in selecting the region of the factor space over which we study a fitted surface. For the ethanol data, the fit was visualized over the smallest box that contains the observations of the two factors, the data rectangle. This was reasonable because most of the rectangle is populated with observations. The rubber data are quite a different case. Figure 4.15 graphs the observations of hardness and tensile strength. The data rectangle has regions not populated with data. Visualizing the fit over the data rectangle would show behavior not supported by the data.

Figure 4.15 has two pairs of parallel lines. We will study the fit only over the intersection of the two regions between the two pairs of lines. This *cropping* of the data rectangle, which will be discussed in detail in Chapter 5, was carried out visually to produce a region well populated throughout with data. The cropped region does not include the upper left corner of the data rectangle. Because the data there are isolated and aberrant, we cannot expect to determine the dependence of the response on the factors in that corner with much precision. Note that the cropping does not imply that data are discarded outside of the cropped region; we still use all of the data in the bisquare fitting.

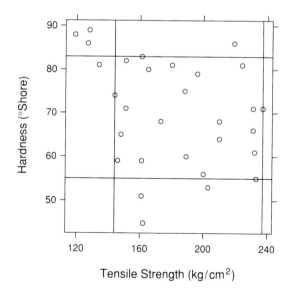

4.15 The rectangle formed by the intersection of the region between the two vertical lines and the region between the two horizontal lines is the cropped region for evaluating the bisquare fit to the rubber data.

Figures 4.16 and 4.17 are coplots of the fit for values of hardness and tensile strength over the cropped region. In Figure 4.16 there are four equally-spaced conditioning values of hardness; the minimum conditioning value is the smallest value of hardness in the cropped region, and the maximum conditioning value is the largest value of hardness in the cropped region. A similar statement holds for Figure 4.17.

The four hockey-stick curves in Figure 4.16 are parallel and move up or down as we move from one dependence panel to another. This is also true of the four lines in Figure 4.17. These parallel patterns occur, of course, because the parametric function fitted to the data contains no term that allows for an interaction. The residuals for this fit will be visualized in Section 4.4 to determine whether the fit accurately reflects patterns in the data.

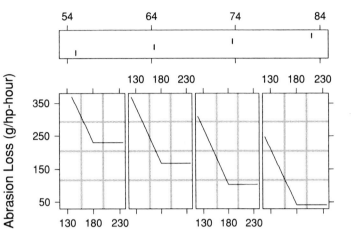

4.16 A coplot graphs the fitted abrasion loss surface against tensile strength given hardness. The segments of the fits below 180 kg/cm^2, the breakpoint, are banked to 45°.

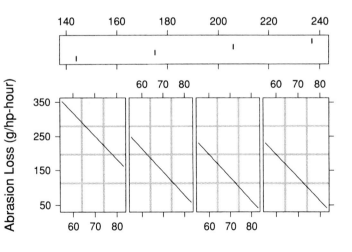

4.17 A coplot graphs the fitted abrasion loss surface against hardness given tensile strength. The lines are banked to 45°.

For the Record: The Details of Loess Fitting

Let the measurements of the two factors be denoted by $x_i = (u_i, v_i)$. If standardization is carried out as described above, then the x_i are the standardized values. Let $x = (u, v)$ be a point in the space of the factors at which the loess surface is to be computed. Again, if the measurements of the factors are standardized, x lies in the standardized space of the factors.

Suppose first that $\alpha \leq 1$. As with one factor, q is αn truncated to an integer, and the neighborhood weight given to the observation (x_i, y_i) for the fit at x is

$$w_i(x) = T\left(\frac{\Delta_i(x)}{\Delta_{(q)}(x)}\right) \ ,$$

where $\Delta_i(x)$ is the distance from x_i to x. For $\alpha > 1$, the $w_i(x)$ are defined in the same manner, but $\Delta_{(q)}(x)$ is replaced by $\Delta_{(n)}(x)\sqrt{\alpha}$.

After the neighborhood weights are computed, the local fitting is carried out. If locally linear fitting is used, a linear surface is fitted to the data using weighted least squares. This means that we find values of a, b, and c that minimize

$$\sum_{i=1}^{n} w_i(x)(y_i - a - bu_i - cv_i)^2 \ .$$

Let $\hat{a}$, $\hat{b}$, and $\hat{c}$ be the values that achieve the minimization. Then the loess fit at $x = (u, v)$ is

$$\hat{a} + \hat{b}u + \hat{c}v \ .$$

If locally quadratic fitting is used, a quadratic surface is fitted to the data in a similar manner using weighted least-squares. In other words, the terms 1, u, v, uv, u^2, and v^2 are fitted locally.

If bisquare is added to loess fitting, an initial loess estimate is computed using the above procedure. Then bisquare iterations are carried out using bisquare weights, r_i, until the surface converges. For the local fit at x, the weight for (x_i, y_i) is $r_i w_i(x)$, the bisquare weight times the neighborhood weight.

If a loess fit, $\widehat{g}(u, v)$, has been specified to be conditionally linear in u, then given any value of v, say $v = \cdot$, $\widehat{g}(u, \cdot)$ is a linear function of u. Similarly, if the fit is conditionally quadratic in u, $\widehat{g}(u, \cdot)$ is a quadratic function of u. Suppose first that $\lambda = 1$. To make the fit conditionally linear in u, we simply ignore the measurements of u in computing the distances, $\Delta_i(u, v)$, from $x = (u, v)$ to $x_i = (u_i, v_i)$. In other words, only the measurements of v are used in the computation of distance. Given $v = \cdot$, the distances $\Delta_i(u, \cdot)$ are the same for all u, so the function fitted locally at $(u, \cdot)$, which is linear, remains the same as u changes, and thus this linear fit is equal to $\widehat{g}(u, \cdot)$. Suppose now that $\lambda = 2$. The same method makes it conditionally quadratic in u — the u_i are ignored in computing the distances. For $\lambda = 2$, the fit can be made conditionally linear in u by dropping the term u^2 in the local fitting. In other words, the terms 1, u, v, uv, and v^2 are fitted instead of 1, u, v, uv, u^2, and v^2. Again, of course, the u_i are ignored in computing distance.

In later chapters, loess will be used to fit data with more than two factors. Except for one issue, the above discussion holds with obvious modifications. The exception is the definition of $w_i(x)$ for $\alpha > 1$. For p factors, $\Delta_{(q)}(x)$ is replaced by $\Delta_{(n)}(x)\sqrt[p]{\alpha}$.

4.4 Graphing Residuals

The overall strategy for graphing residuals for trivariate data is the same as that for bivariate data. First, residual dependence plots are made to check for lack or surplus of fit. If a problem is detected, we can either alter the fit or simply use the visualization of the residuals as part of the characterization of how the response depends on the factors. Other residual displays explore the distribution of the residuals. An s-l plot can detect monotone spread; if it occurs, we can attempt to remove it by a power transformation of the response. A normal q-q plot of the residuals compares the distribution of the residuals with the normal distribution. An r-f spread plot shows how much of the variation in the response is explained by the fit, and how much remains in the residuals.

Searching for Lack of Fit with Residual Dependence Plots

A good first step to probe lack of fit is to graph the residuals against each of the factors. This is done in Figures 4.18 and 4.19 for the fit to the rubber data. The three negative outlying residuals correspond to the three aberrant observations. Their abrasion losses are lower than expected based on the pattern of the other data, so their residuals are negative. But otherwise no lack of fit is revealed by these residual dependence plots.

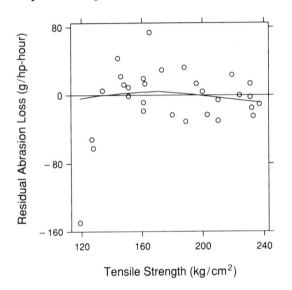

4.18 The residual dependence plot graphs the abrasion loss residuals against tensile strength. The parameters of the robust loess curve on the graph are $\alpha = 1$ and $\lambda = 1$.

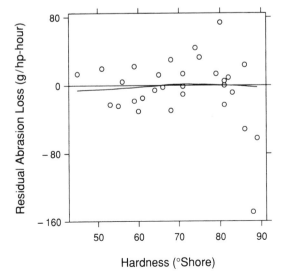

4.19 The residual dependence plot graphs the abrasion loss residuals against hardness. The parameters of the robust loess curve are $\alpha = 1$ and $\lambda = 1$.

Figure 4.20 is a coplot of the residuals against tensile strength given hardness. The intervals of hardness are the same as those used in the coplot of the data, Figure 4.3. The coplot reveals a remaining dependence in the residuals, which signals lack of fit. The underlying pattern on panels (1,1), (2,1), (3,1), and (1,2) has a negative slope that results largely from positive residuals at tensile strengths below 180 kg/cm², the breakpoint of the hockey-stick fit. This means the slope of the fit below the breakpoint is not sufficiently negative. Despite the bisquare fitting, the three outliers have caused lack of fit by forcing a reduction in the steepness of the fitted slope below the breakpoint. This is disappointing since bisquare is normally impervious to a small fraction of outliers. But in this example, the three outliers have conspired together at a location that exerts substantial leverage on the fit. It is a good lesson. No fitting method is perfect. This is one reason why we must subject residuals to intensive visualization.

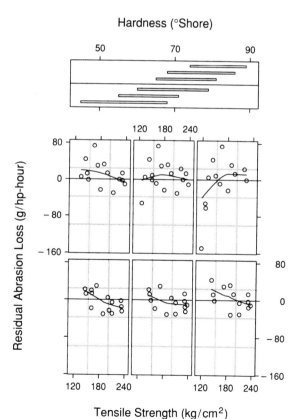

4.20 The abrasion loss residuals are graphed against tensile strength given hardness. The parameters of the robust loess curves are $\alpha = 1$ and $\lambda = 1$. The aspect ratio of the dependence panels is 2 to accommodate the outlying negative residual.

Figure 4.21 is a coplot of the residuals against hardness given tensile strength. Again, the intervals are the same as those used in the coplot of the data, Figure 4.4. More lack of fit is revealed — an interaction between hardness and tensile strength. As tensile strength increases, the underlying pattern has an increase in slope. The effect is convincing, though small compared to the overall variation in abrasion loss, which is why we did not detect it on the original coplots of the data. This represents another example of the magnifying effect of residual plots, which was discussed in connection with the Playfair data in Chapter 3. There is another quite interesting aspect to the pattern of the interaction — the three aberrant observations appear to be conforming to it, but in a more extreme way.

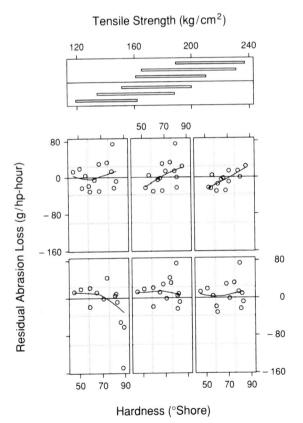

4.21 The abrasion loss residuals are graphed against hardness given tensile strength. The parameters of the robust loess curves are $\alpha = 1$ and $\lambda = 1$. The aspect ratio of the dependence panels is 2 to accommodate the outlying negative residual.

The visualization has given us substantial qualitative insight into the behavior of the rubber data. There is a hockey-stick pattern of dependence on tensile strength and a linear dependence on hardness. For most of the data, there appears to be a mild interaction between hardness and tensile strength in which the hardness slope increases somewhat as tensile strength increases. Three observations in one corner of the factor space show aberrant behavior that might represent a conforming to the interaction pattern. For some purposes, this qualitative description might be enough, for example, if the 30 runs that generated the rubber data were just a pilot experiment to plan a more thorough one.

Suppose, however, that we want a quantitative description of the dependence of abrasion loss on hardness and tensile strength. Then we must continue the fitting. It is unrealistic to suppose that we could account with much accuracy for the dependence in the region of the factor space occupied by the three aberrant observations. We will drop them. Since the residual coplot in Figure 4.21 showed an interaction, we must add an interaction term to the parametric family that we fit to the data. One possibility is the product term ht. But the residual coplot in Figure 4.20 showed the fit was adequate above the tensile strength breakpoint of 180 kg/cm^2, and the product term would affect the fit at all values of tensile strength. Instead, we will add $h[t - 180]^-$, which has no effect above the breakpoint, but allows for an interaction below it. With this term, the effect of h given t is still linear, as the residual coplot in Figure 4.21 suggests it should be, but with a changing slope. The bisquare fit to the reduced data with the added term is

$$\widehat{g}(h, t) = 531 - 5.78h - 7.76[t - 180]^- + 0.055h[t - 180]^- .$$

For this fit, the slope of $\widehat{g}(h, t)$ as a function of h increases as t increases up to 180 kg/cm^2, and then remains constant.

Figures 4.22 and 4.23 are coplots of the residuals for this new fit. No convincing dependence is revealed; the new fit appears adequate.

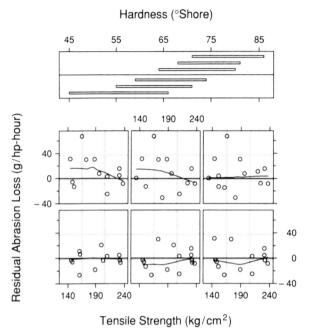

4.22 The residuals for the interaction fit to the reduced rubber data are graphed against tensile strength given hardness. The parameters of the robust loess curves are $\alpha = 1$ and $\lambda = 1$, and the target fraction of overlap of the intervals is 3/4.

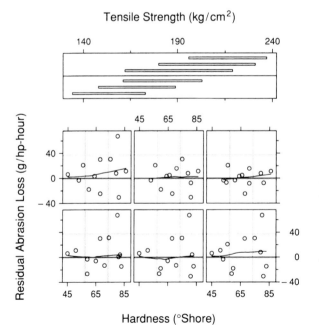

4.23 The residuals for the interaction fit to the reduced rubber data are graphed against hardness given tensile strength. The parameters of the robust loess curves are $\alpha = 1$ and $\lambda = 1$, and the target fraction of overlap of the intervals is 3/4.

Figures 4.24 and 4.25 are coplots of the new fit with the same conditioning values as the coplots of the first fit in Figures 4.16 and 4.17. The interaction is visible, although small, as expected.

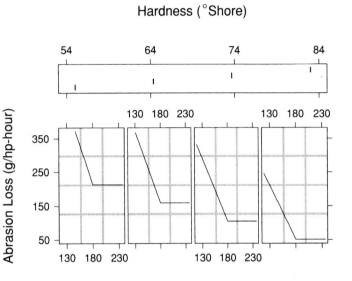

4.24 A coplot graphs the fitted abrasion loss surface against tensile strength given hardness. The segments of the broken lines below 180 kg/cm^2, the breakpoint, are banked to 45°.

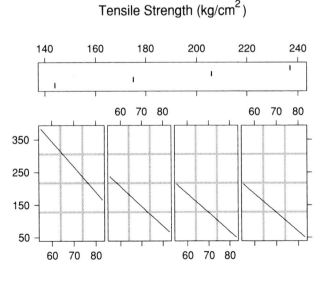

4.25 A coplot graphs the fitted abrasion loss surface against hardness given tensile strength. The lines are banked to 45°.

The Distribution of the Residuals

Figure 4.26 is an s-l plot for the fit to the reduced rubber data. The loess curve has a slight negative slope, but in view of the small number of observations, the magnitude of the effect is too small for us to believe there is significant monotone spread. Figure 4.27 is a normal quantile plot of the residuals; there is mild skewness toward large values. Figure 4.28 is an r-f spread plot. Despite the difficulties with the data, the response has been closely fitted for the reduced data.

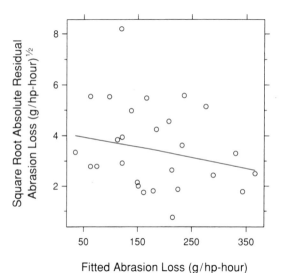

4.26 An s-l plot checks for monotone spread in the abrasion loss residuals. The parameters of the robust loess curve on the plot are $\alpha = 2$ and $\lambda = 1$.

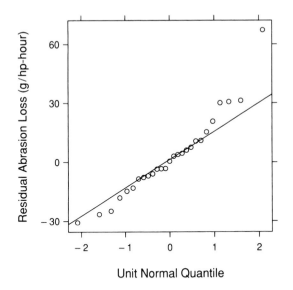

4.27 The distribution of the abrasion loss residuals is displayed by a normal q-q plot.

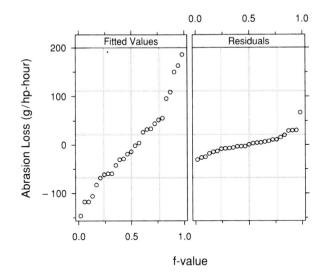

4.28 An r-f spread plot compares the spreads of the residuals and the fitted values minus their mean for the interaction fit to the reduced rubber data.

Ethanol Residuals

Fumblings every bit as extensive as those for the rubber data produced the ethanol fit graphed in the coplots of Figures 4.12 and 4.13. The tortuous path will not be described here. The robust fit, whose loess parameters are $\alpha = 1/3$ and $\lambda = 2$, appears to be adequate. Four residual dependence plots were used to check for lack of fit — two scatterplots of the residuals against the two factors, a coplot of the residuals against C given E, and a coplot of the residuals against E given C. No lack of fit was revealed. Increasing the value of α introduces lack of fit. This is illustrated in Figure 4.29. The residuals are graphed against E for a fit with α increased to $1/2$. There is a slight positive bump at $E = 0.9$, the approximate location of the ridge in the NO_x surface. Thus the fit is not reaching the top of the ridge. While the lack of fit is small, there is no reason to introduce it because, as the coplots in Figures 4.12 and 4.13 showed, the surface with $\alpha = 1/3$ is quite smooth.

Figure 4.30 is an s-l plot. No monotone spread is revealed. Figure 4.31 is a normal quantile plot of the residuals. There is leptokurtosis, but in this case bisquare has done its job. Figure 4.32 is an r-f spread plot. The fit accounts for much of the variation in the NO_x concentrations.

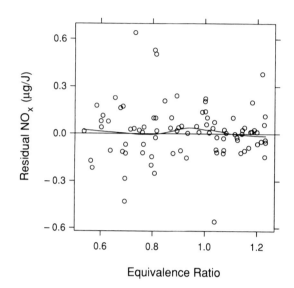

4.29 The residuals from a smoother robust loess fit to NO_x are graphed against equivalence ratio. The parameters of the robust loess curve on the graph are $\alpha = 1/2$ and $\lambda = 1$.

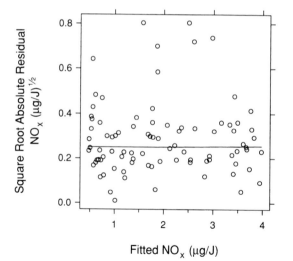

4.30 An s-l plot checks for monotone spread in the residuals for the robust loess fit to NO_x. The parameters of the robust loess curve on the plot are $\alpha = 2$ and $\lambda = 1$.

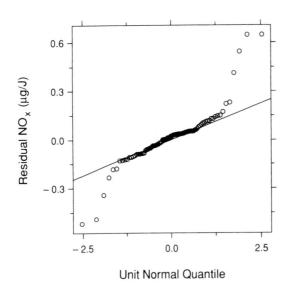

4.31 A normal q-q plot compares the normal distribution with the distribution of the residuals for the robust loess fit to NO_x.

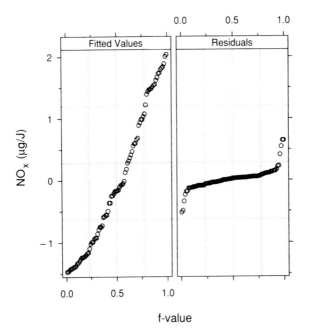

4.32 An r-f spread plot compares the spread of the residuals and the fitted values minus their mean for the robust loess fit to NO_x.

In the original analysis of these data, the experimenter fitted log
concentration by a high-order polynomial and used least-squares [12].
The leptokurtosis in the residuals makes it clear that least-squares is
inappropriate. And Figure 4.33 shows that taking logs induces
monotone spread; the figure is an s-l plot for a loess fit to log
concentration using the same parameters as the fit to concentration, and
using bisquare. The spread of the residuals decreases with increasing
location, exactly what one would expect when logs are taken in a case
where there is uniform spread for a fit to the data without
transformation. The mistreatment of these data by the experimenter and
others who analyzed them will be taken up at the end of this chapter.

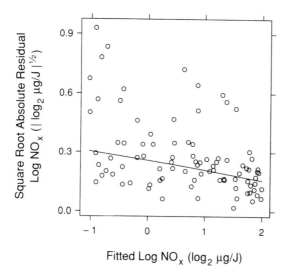

4.33 An s-l plot checks for monotone spread
for a robust loess fit to log NO$_x$. The
parameters of the robust loess curve on the
plot are $\alpha = 2$ and $\lambda = 1$.

4.5   More on Coplots and Fitting

Judging the slopes of line segments on a graph is a critical visual task of graphical perception that yields information about the rate of change of one variable as a function of another [20]. The purpose of banking to $45°$ is to maximize the efficiency of such slope judgments. An experiment, whose data we will now analyze, led to the first formulation of the $45°$ principle [25, 26].

The left panel of Figure 4.34 has two line segments. Suppose we must judge the ratio of the slopes of the segments; more specifically, suppose we judge the ratio of the slope of the lower right segment to the slope of the upper left segment as a percent. Suppose the guess from a quick visual assessment is 40%. The true value is 50%, so our absolute error is $|40\% - 50\%| = 10\%$. What might determine the accuracy with which we make such a judgment?

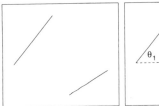 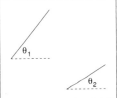

4.34 The figure illustrates the judgment of slopes of line segments, an important task in the visual decoding of information from graphical displays.

Experiment

In the experiment, 16 subjects judged the relative slopes of 44 line-segment pairs. All slopes were positive, and the subjects judged what percent one slope was of another, just as we did for the segments on the left panel of Figure 4.34. The true percents ranged from 50% to 100%. Subjects judged this complete set 12 times, and the order of the line-segment pairs was randomized separately within each of the 12 replications. For each subject's judgment,

$$|\text{true percent} - \text{judged percent}|$$

was computed; then, for each line-segment pair, these absolute values were averaged across subjects and replications. The resulting 44 values of this response variable, a, measure the absolute error of judging the relative slopes of the line segments.

There are three factors in the experiment, all of which measure geometric aspects of the segments. To describe them, we need the notation in the right panel of Figure 4.34; θ_1 and θ_2 are the *orientations* of the two line segments. The first factor is p, the actual value of the percent being judged. The second factor is

$$d = |45° - (\theta_1 + \theta_2)/2| ,$$

the distance of the mid-orientation, $(\theta_1 + \theta_2)/2$, of the two segments from 45°. Values of p and d determine the orientations of the segments; that is, if we specify both d and p, we specify the orientations of the segments, and therefore the ratio of the slopes. In the experiment, d and p were systematically varied. Another factor is the resolution, $r = \theta_1 - \theta_2$, of the two orientations, which is related to p and d by

$$r = \arcsin \left[\frac{100 - p}{100 + p} \cos(2d) \right] .$$

The important variable in the experiment is d. When $d = 0$, the segments are banked to 45°. And in making a graph, we control d by the aspect ratio. The hypothesis of the experiment was that for fixed p, the absolute error, a, increases as d increases; in other words, a increases as the segments get further from the position prescribed by 45° banking. As d increases for a fixed p, r decreases. The hypothesis is based on the notion that it is harder to judge a slope ratio p as the visual separation of the segments decreases.

Exploring the Data

For the 44 line-segment pairs in the experiment, there are 44 values of a, d, p, and r. Figure 4.35 is a scatterplot matrix of the data; the values of p have been jittered to cure a problem of exact overlap. The (3,2) panel shows the 44 combinations of p and d that were used in the experiment. There are 11 distinct values of p and each one is repeated four times, although this cannot be appreciated from the figure because of the jittering. The values of d range from $0°$ to $37°$.

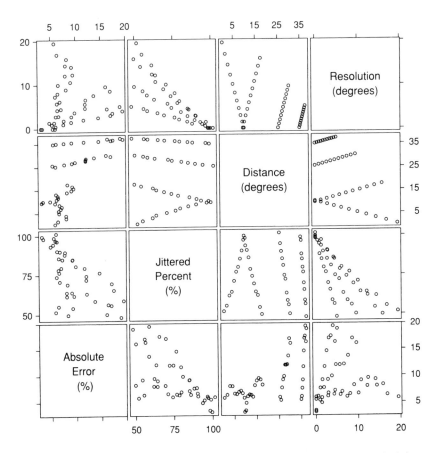

4.35 A scatterplot matrix displays the data from the experiment on judging slopes.

Figures 4.36 is a coplot of a against d given p. Because there are so few points on each dependence panel, loess curves have not been added. The conditioning values of p are the 11 distinct values of the measurements of p. Most panels have patterns with positive slopes, and for the smaller values of p, the patterns are slightly curved. Thus the hypothesis of the experiment — an increase of a as d increases — appears to be true. As p gets larger, the slope of the underlying pattern approaches the horizontal. (Note how we are making slope judgments in studying these data.) This means there is an interaction between p and d; the effect on a of increasing d is greater when p is low than when it is high.

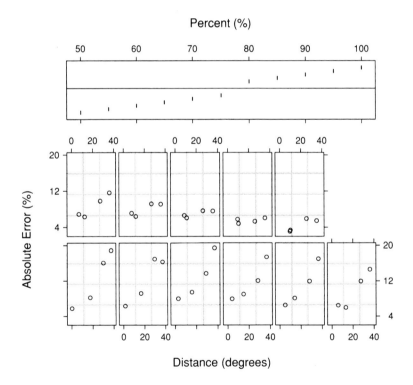

4.36 A coplot graphs absolute error against distance from $45°$ given percent. The aspect ratio has been chosen to bank the line segments between successive observations (not drawn) to $45°$.

Figure 4.37 graphs a against r given p. The patterns are linear with no apparent curvature, and the slopes of the patterns, which are negative, do not appear to change, which means there is no interaction between p and r in explaining a. To probe the linearity and lack of interaction further, the coplot in Figure 4.38 graphs a against p given r. The equal-count method has been used to select the conditioning intervals; the number of intervals is 8 and the fraction of overlap is 1/4. Again, the patterns appear linear and there is no interaction, confirming the effect seen in Figure 4.37.

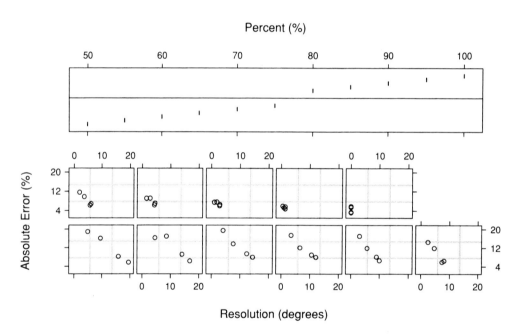

4.37   A coplot graphs absolute error against resolution given percent. The line segments between successive observations (not drawn) are banked to 45°.

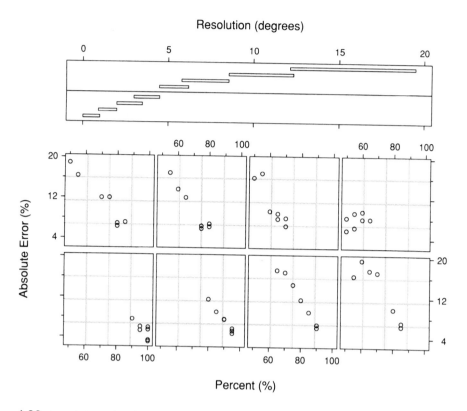

4.38 A coplot graphs absolute error against percent given resolution. The underlying patterns on the panels are banked by an aspect ratio of one.

As discussed earlier, the orientations of the line segments in the experiment are determined by p and d. They are also determined by p and r; in other words, we can fit a to p and d, or to p and r. The coplots suggest that we should use r because the dependence has a simpler structure: a function linear in p and r. By contrast, an equation relating a to p and d would be more complicated, in part, because there is both curvature and an interaction between p and d. Once we have determined the dependence of a on p and r, we can use the equation that relates r to p and d to determine the dependence of a on p and d, and thus understand the interesting factor, d.

Fitting

The coplot of a against r given p in Figure 4.37 shows that the residual variation about the underlying pattern is small. But as in previous data sets in this chapter, there appear to be a few observations that deviate by substantially more than the others, which suggests outliers among the residuals. Thus we will use bisquare to fit a linear function of p and r to a. The resulting fit is

$$a = 53 - 1.2r - 0.48p .$$

For this fit, an increase of 1% in p results in a decrease of 0.48% in a, and an increase of $1°$ in r results in a decrease of 1.2%.

Graphing Residuals

Figures 4.39 and 4.40 are residual dependence plots that graph the residuals against the factors. Figure 4.40 shows there is lack of fit, a convincing undulation that produces nearly all positive residuals for values of r between about $3°$ and $4°$, and a preponderance of negative residuals between $5°$ and $10°$. The graphs also reveal outliers for two observations with small values of p and values of r near $5°$. Figure 4.41 is an r-f spread plot. Despite the lack of fit, the fitted function explains much of the variation in the absolute errors.

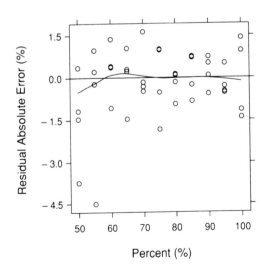

4.39 A residual dependence plot graphs residual absolute error against percent. The parameters of the robust loess curve on the plot are $\alpha = 1/2$ and $\lambda = 1$.

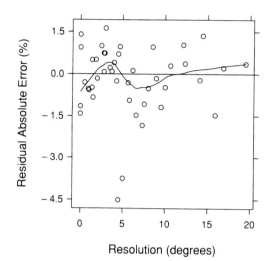

4.40 A residual dependence plot graphs residual absolute error against resolution. The parameters of the robust loess curve on the plot are $\alpha = 1/2$ and $\lambda = 1$.

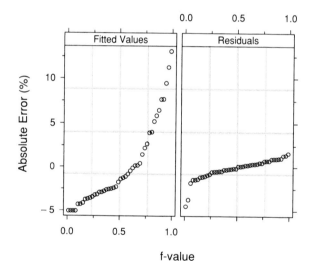

4.41 An r-f spread plot compares the spreads of the residuals and the fitted values minus their mean for the bisquare fit to absolute error.

We will ignore the lack of fit in this case. The r-f spread plot has shown that the residual variation is exceedingly small, so any resulting improvement would not have an appreciable effect on the fitted surface. It is likely that we would need loess to remove the lack of fit; thus the cost of a negligible change in the surface would be the loss of the extreme simplicity of the linear fit. For this scientific application, the nonlinear surface is not worth the cost.

Visualizing the Dependence on Distance

The response, a, has been fitted by a function of p and r,

$$a = 53 - 1.2r - 0.48p .$$

But it is d, the distance from $45°$, that is of chief interest. However, r is related to p and d by

$$r = \arcsin \left[\frac{100 - p}{100 + p} \cos (2d) \right] .$$

Substituting for r in the fitted equation, we have

$$a = \widehat{g}(d, p) = 53 - 1.2 \arcsin \left[\frac{100 - p}{100 + p} \cos (2d) \right] - 0.48p .$$

Figure 4.42 graphs this fitted function by a coplot of a against d given p. For all values of p, a does not change by much as d increases from $0°$ to about $10°$. In other words, small deviations from $45°$ banking do not appreciably degrade the judgment of orientation. But once d gets above $10°$, the error increases rapidly for some percents, particularly those close to 50%. However, for percents close to 100%, the absolute error is very small and d has little influence. Percents near 100% are judged very accurately because it is easy for our visual system to recognize that the segments lie on nearly parallel lines.

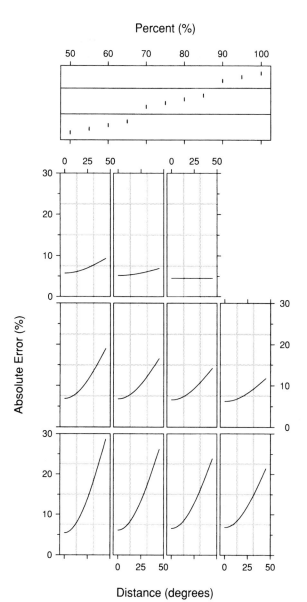

4.42 The surface fitted to absolute error by bisquare is graphed against distance given percent. The curves are banked to 45°.

4.6   *Level Plots of Data*

NGC 7531 is a spiral galaxy in the Southern Hemisphere. When looked at from the earth, the galaxy fills a very small area on the celestial sphere. If the only motion of NGC 7531 relative to the earth were the rapid recession due to the big bang, then over the entire region, the velocity relative to the earth would be constant and equal to about 1600 km/sec. But the actual motion is complex. The galaxy appears to be spinning, and there are other motions that are not well understood. The velocity at different points of the galaxy varies by more than 350 km/sec.

Figure 4.43 shows locations where 323 measurements were made of the galaxy velocity [15]. The values have been jittered to reduce overlap. The two scales, whose units are arc seconds, are east-west and south-north positions, which form a coordinate system for the celestial sphere based on the earth's standard coordinate system. Note that east and west are reversed because we are looking at the celestial sphere from the inside. The measurement locations lie along one of seven lines, or slits, that intersect in the center of the measurement region; of course, this does not appear to be exactly the case in Figure 4.43 because the points are jittered.

The goal in analyzing the galaxy data is to determine how the velocity measurements vary over the measurement region; thus velocity is a response and the two coordinate variables are factors. We want to determine regions in the plane where velocity is low, regions where it is high, and regions where it is approximately equal to any one of the values between the two extremes of 1409 km/sec and 1775 km/sec. There is no compelling need to study the data by conditioning on one coordinate and graphing against the other. This would endow the coordinates with an importance they do not have. The geocentric coordinate system imposed on the sky by man is clearly of no importance to the energy arriving now from the galaxy, which began its transit about 50 million years ago. Any other set of perpendicular axes could equally well serve as a coordinate system.

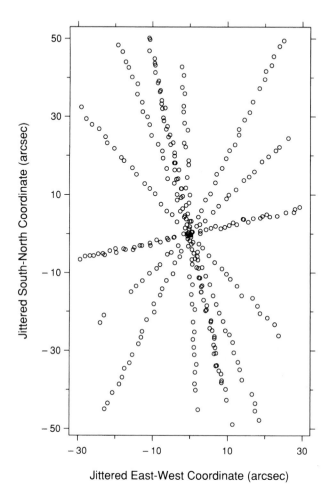

4.43 The plotting symbols show the locations of 323 measurements of the velocity of NGC 7531 relative to the earth. The aspect ratio has been chosen to make the number of data units per cm the same on both scales.

Level Regions

Figure 4.44 is a *level plot*, a visualization that shows regions with different levels of velocity. The format is that of a coplot, but instead of conditioning on a factor, as in a coplot, the conditioning is on the response. Velocity is broken up into different *levels*, the intervals shown in the *level panel* at the top of the figure. The intervals have been chosen using the equal-count method with the fraction of overlap equal to 1/4. The 5 × 3 array of panels below shows *level regions*; each region is made up of those measurement locations where velocity is within one of the levels. The velocity levels increase as we move in graphical order through the level-region panels.

The (1,1) panel of Figure 4.44 shows that the region for the lowest velocity level lies in the northeast. As the levels increase, the regions move to the south and west, first as long narrow regions that are convex upward, then nearly straight regions, and then convex downward regions. Finally, the region for the highest level lies in the southwest.

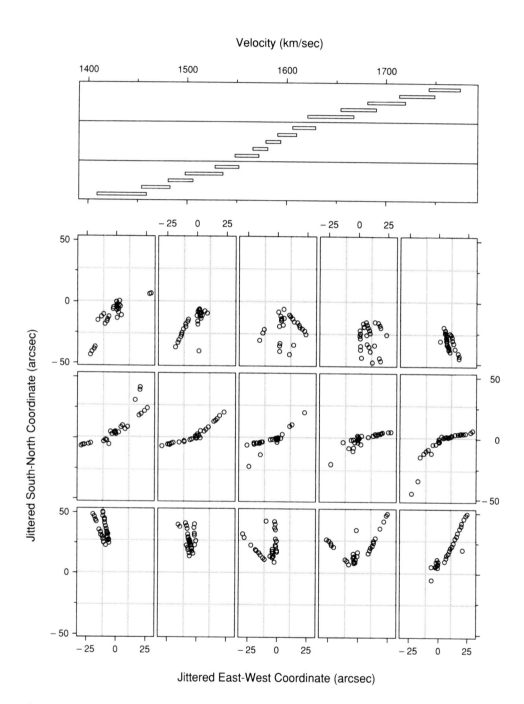

4.44 A level plot displays level regions of galaxy velocity. The aspect ratio of the level-region panels has been chosen to make the number of data units per cm the same on both scales.

4.7   Improvisation

One aspect of the structure of the galaxy data provides a special opportunity for further visualization. The measurements, as we have seen, lie along seven slits that intersect at the origin; for each slit separately, we can graph velocity against position along the slit. This, of course, is not a general method, but an improvisation, a visualization that is possible because of the special structure of this trivariate data set. Data analysis is difficult. Serendipity should be exploited.

Each slit can be described by the angle of a clockwise rotation to the horizontal; the seven angles are 12.5°, 43°, 63.5°, 92.5°, 102.5°, 111°, and 133°. Each location of a velocity measurement has a slit angle, the angle of the slit on which it lies. And each location has a radial position along the slit, which we will take to be distance of the location from the origin, multiplied by −1 if the east-west coordinate is negative and by 1 if it is nonnegative.

Figure 4.45 graphs velocity against radial position for each slit; this is achieved by a coplot in which slit angle is the conditioning variable. The underlying patterns of the seven sets of data in Figure 4.45 are varied and highly nonlinear. The overall amount of deviation of the data from the patterns is not large, but a number of observations deviate by considerably more than the others, which suggests leptokurtosis.

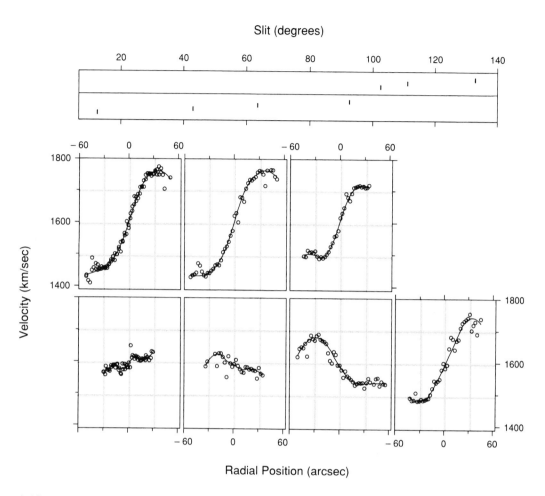

4.45 A coplot graphs galaxy velocity against radial position given slit angle. The parameters of the robust loess curves are $\alpha = 1/2$ and $\lambda = 2$. The curves are banked to $45°$.

Fitting and Graphing Residuals

The next step in analyzing the galaxy data is to fit a surface. The level plot in Figure 4.44 and the coplot in Figure 4.45 show a complicated pattern with substantial curvature. We cannot expect a parametric surface to adequately track such a pattern. Loess fitting is needed. Because of the substantial curvature, λ must be two. Extensive experimentation led to a choice of $1/4$ for α; this value struck a reasonable balance between lack and surplus of fit. Graphs of the fit and the residuals, to be shown shortly, will demonstrate this. As suggested by the coplot in Figure 4.45, the residual variation is leptokurtic, so bisquare is needed. Finally, to preserve the actual distance in the coordinate system of the celestial sphere, the loess fitting omits the standardization of the measurements of the two factors by their 10% trimmed standard deviations.

The slit structure of the galaxy data can also be used to see how well the loess surface fits the data. Figure 4.46 is a coplot of the data; the curves are the fitted surface evaluated along the slits. The fit is excellent and does almost as well as the robust loess curves fitted separately to the data of each panel in Figure 4.45.

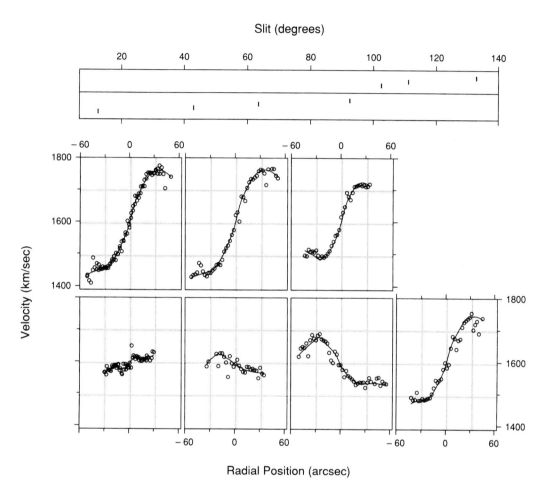

4.46 The coplot of the data graphs velocity against radial position given slit angle. The curves are the robust loess surface evaluated along the slits. The curves are banked by taking the aspect ratio of the dependence panels to be the same as that of Figure 4.45.

Figure 4.47 is a coplot of the residuals. There is lack of fit, a remaining
dependence of the location of the residuals on radial position. In panel
(4,1), there is a slight downward slope, and in panel (3,2), most of the
residuals for radial positions less than zero are positive and most for
radial positions greater than zero are negative. While we have detected
lack of fit, its magnitude is quite small; we will endure it rather than
endure the decrease in the smoothness of the surface that would result
from curing it. Figure 4.47 also suggests there is nonhomogeneous
spread; for example, in panel (4,1), there is a sudden change in the
spread of the residuals at the origin.

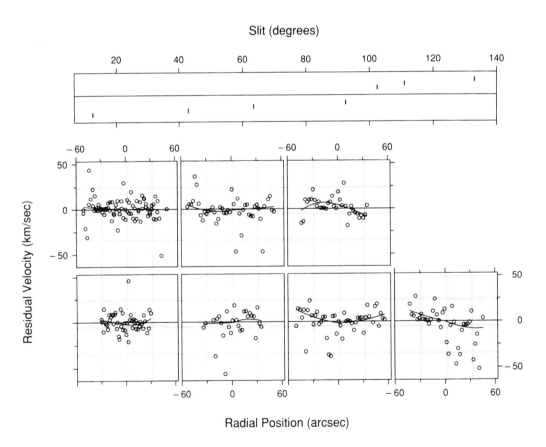

4.47 The velocity residuals are graphed against radial position given slit angle. The parameters of
the robust loess curves are $\alpha = 1$ and $\lambda = 2$.

Figure 4.48, a normal quantile plot of the residuals, reveals significant leptokurtosis. Figure 4.49 is an r-f spread plot; the surface explains a major portion of the variation in the velocities. In the next three sections we will show further visualizations of the fit.

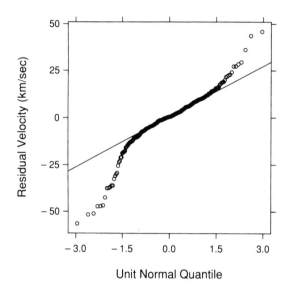

4.48 A normal q-q plot compares the distribution of the velocity residuals with the normal distribution.

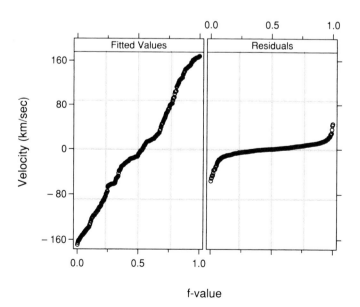

4.49 An r-f spread plot compares the spread of the residuals and the fitted values minus their mean for the robust loess fit to the galaxy velocities.

4.8   Contour Plots of Surfaces

For decades, the *contour plot* has been a workhorse display for
rendering surfaces [54]. Figure 4.50 is a contour plot of the loess fit to the
galaxy velocities. The levels of the black contours range from
1440 km/sec to 1760 km/sec in steps of 20 km/sec; for the black and
gray contours combined, the step size is 5 km/sec and the range is
1435 km/sec to 1760 km/sec. The two curve types enhance the
perception of properties of the surface. The complete collection of curves
conveys local properties, and the black curves by themselves convey
global properties.

The contouring in Figure 4.50 is based on an evaluation of the surface
on a grid whose east-west coordinates are 101 equally spaced values
from $-25''$ to $25''$ and whose south-north coordinates are 181 equally
spaced values from $-45''$ to $45''$. Thus there are $101 \times 181 = 18281$ grid
points that move in steps of $0.5''$ along each coordinate axis. The grid
lies slightly inside the rectangle that just contains the measurement
locations of the data; such cropping for displaying a fit to data is
discussed in Chapter 5.

The contours in Figure 4.50 are roughly symmetric about a line that
runs from the region in the northeast where the velocities are lowest to
the region in the southwest where the velocities are highest. From north
to south along this line, the intersecting contours increase monotonically.
The contours for the lowest velocities have a convex upward shape; as
velocity increases, the convexity decreases until, for velocities around
1580 km/sec the contours are nearly linear. Then, as velocity increases
further, the contours turn convex downward.

Suppose the only motions of NGC 7531 relative to the earth were a
rotation and a recession. Then the velocity surface would be linear, and
the contours in Figure 4.50 would be linear, parallel, equally spaced, and
perpendicular to the projection of the axis of rotation onto our viewing
plane. The actual contours bend and are not equally spaced. But in a
small region centered near $(0'', 0'')$, with a diameter of about $10''$, they
do appear to be linear, parallel, and equally spaced. This suggests that at
the core of the galaxy the dominant motion is a rotation.

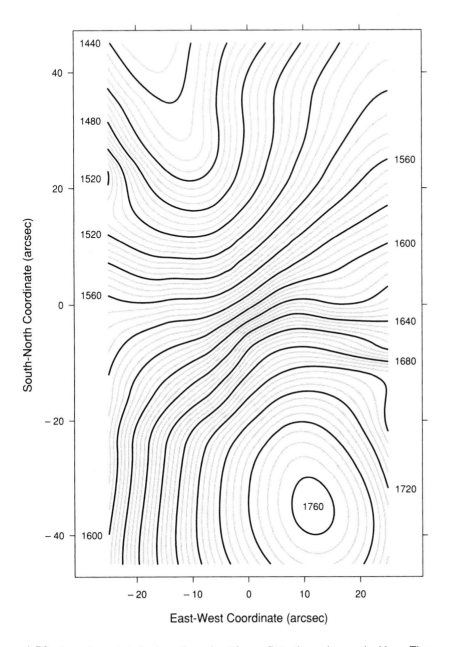

4.50 A contour plot displays the robust loess fit to the galaxy velocities. The aspect ratio has been chosen to make the number of data units per cm the same on both scales.

An Algorithm for Drawing Contours

There are many procedures for drawing the contours of a function but most of them proceed in the same basic way [32, 46, 63, 72, 83]. The function is evaluated at a collection of points in the plane, usually a rectangular grid, and then approximate contours are computed by interpolation using this evaluation.

One algorithm for computing contours is illustrated in Figure 4.51, which shows the computation of the 0.5 contour of the function

$$g(u, v) = u^2 + v^2 + uv .$$

The actual contour is an ellipse centered at (0,0).

The first step in the algorithm is to evaluate g for a rectangular grid of points covering the region of study. A grid is shown in the top left panel of Figure 4.51; there are 10 rows of points and 10 columns, so altogether there are 100 points. The grid gives rise to a collection of horizontal and vertical line segments that connect the grid points. These segments are drawn in the top right panel of Figure 4.51. Consider all grid segments for which the function value at one endpoint is greater than 0.5, and the function value at the other endpoint is less than 0.5. Since our function is continuous, the contour for $g(u, v) = 0.5$ must cross each of these segments somewhere in the interior of the segment. If the function is 0.5 at an endpoint, then, of course, the contour also crosses the segment, but at the endpoint. In the top right panel of Figure 4.51, the *crossed segments* for $g(u, v) = 0.5$ are marked with dots.

The next step is to determine locations on crossed segments where the function is 0.5, or approximately so. If the function is equal to 0.5 at an endpoint, then the endpoint is such a location. If the function is greater than 0.5 at one endpoint and less at the other, we use linear interpolation to determine a location. A line is put through the two function values at the endpoints; the location is the position where the line is equal to 0.5. On the top right panel of Figure 4.51, the dots show the 0.5 locations that arise from this method.

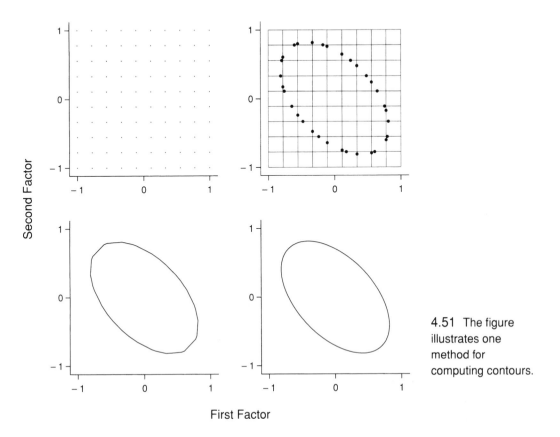

4.51 The figure illustrates one method for computing contours.

First Factor

Second Factor

The final step in the contour algorithm is to connect the 0.5 locations of the crossed segments. A connection is illustrated in the bottom left panel of Figure 4.51. Doing the connection by computer might seem trivial, but it can be tricky because certain ambiguities can occur. One connection algorithm is given at the end of this section.

For most contour procedures, the only choice that needs to be made is the density of the grid. Greater density is typically better than less. If the grid is too coarse, more ambiguities can occur and the connection method can become confused. Also, contours that should be smooth can look jagged. For example, the contour in the bottom left panel of Figure 4.51 suggests the elliptical shape of the contour, but because the grid is coarse, there are unpleasant corners. A more sophisticated algorithm could round corners, but in this example, and in many others like it in practice, the simple solution is to increase the density of the grid. The same contour for a 50×50 grid is shown in the bottom right panel of Figure 4.51; the result is a curve that now appears smooth.

For the Record: A Connection Algorithm

One approach to connection is local in the sense that the connection of dots on a rectangle of the grid is not based on the locations of any other dots. Suppose the contour value is $c = 0$. Consider a rectangle with no dot at an endpoint of a segment. There are four possibilities, which are illustrated in Figure 4.52 — no dots, two dots on opposite sides, two dots on adjacent sides, and four dots. The figure shows the connection method for no dots and two dots. The four-dot case is ambiguous because there are several possibilities: two line segments with positive slopes connecting points on adjacent sides, two line segments with negative slopes connecting points on opposite sides, and so forth. And ambiguities can occur when dots are at endpoints.

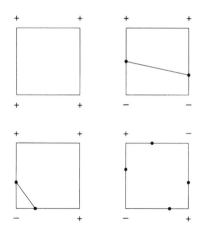

4.52 The figure illustrates the four possibilities for crossings when the contour level is zero and when the function is not zero at an endpoint. The connection method is shown except in the lower right panel, which is an ambiguous case.

Grosse developed an elegant method for resolving the ambiguous cases [46]. Consider first, the four-dot case in the lower right panel of Figure 4.52. Let

$$g(u, v) = a + bu + cv + duv$$

be the bilinear function put through the values of the function at the endpoints. The fit is exact since there are four parameters and four values being fitted. Suppose we used this bilinear function as the interpolant to determine the positions of the dots. The results would be the same as the method described above. In other words, as an interpolant, the bilinear function does linear interpolation along the segments of each rectangle.

But the bilinear is defined inside the rectangle. This means it has contours. And these contours, which are hyperbolas, have a special property: they cross the rectangle either as in the upper left panel of Figure 4.53 or as in the lower left. In Grosse's method, the bilinear contours are used to determine the connection. If they cross as in the upper left, the dots are connected as shown in the upper right. If they cross as in the lower left, the dots are connected as shown in the lower right. But here is the best part. The bilinear function does not need to be fitted to determine the connection. There is a very simple rule: the dots with the two smallest horizontal coordinates are connected, and the dots with the two largest horizontal coordinates are connected.

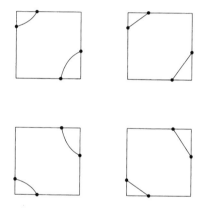

4.53 The figure shows how the connection is determined by Grosse's method for the ambiguous case of Figure 4.52.

Grosse's method of bilinear approximation can also be applied when one or more values at the endpoints are zero. The possibilities, and the connections to which the method leads, are shown in Figure 4.54.

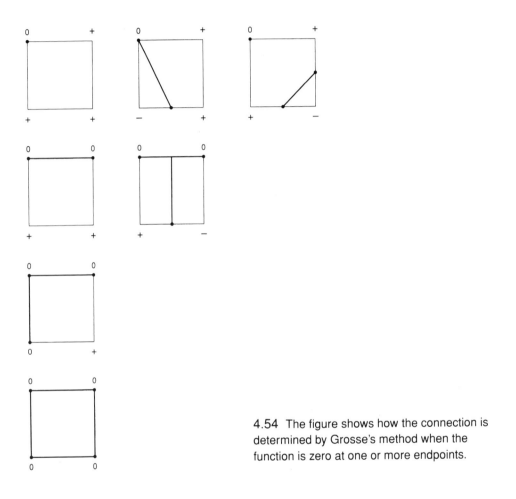

4.54 The figure shows how the connection is determined by Grosse's method when the function is zero at one or more endpoints.

4.9   *Level Plots of Surfaces*

Contour plots can succeed. The contour plot of the velocity surface in Figure 4.50 is one example. But there are two problems. The first is fundamental to the method. If a surface is very nearly flat in some region of the factor space compared with the steepness in other regions, the definition of a contour as a curve becomes unstable. If the surface is flat in a region — that is, equal to a constant over a region with positive planar area — the contour for the constant value is no longer a curve. Consider the bottom panel of Figure 4.54. The function is zero at all four endpoints. The connection method gives an answer, a rectangle, but if the function is zero on and inside the rectangle, the ideal visualization would show a contour containing both the rectangle and its interior. Sophisticated contouring methods solve the problem by ignoring it; contours do not enter flat or nearly flat regions.

A second problem is one of visual perception. On a contour plot we cannot effortlessly perceive the order of the contours from smallest to largest. We must resort to the slow process of reading the contour labels. For a simple surface such as the velocity surface this suffices. But for more complicated surfaces with many peaks and valleys, it does not.

Another method solves both problems — a level plot. This method was introduced in Section 4.6 for displaying data, but it can also be used for displaying fitted surfaces. For functions, there are two versions of the plot. One, described in this section, renders the level regions by juxtaposing them in black and white; this is the same display method used for level plots of data. The second version, described later in Section 4.12, uses color and superposes the level regions.

A level plot in Figure 4.55 displays the loess fit to the galaxy data. First, the surface was evaluated on the same 101×181 grid used for the contour plot of the surface in Figure 4.50. The grid points and the values of the loess surface on the grid form a trivariate data set. The level plot of the surface is simply a level plot of these data, constructed as described in Section 4.6, but with one difference: instead of using levels from the equal-count method, the 48 levels are of equal length. The levels range from 1431 km/sec, the minimum value of the surface over the grid, to 1763 km/sec, the maximum surface value. The levels overlap only at their endpoints, but in other applications it can make sense to have greater overlap or to have no overlap and gaps between the levels.

Figure 4.55 shows the same behavior of the individual contours as the contour plot in Figure 4.50 — a change from upward convexity to downward convexity as velocity increases. But in Figure 4.55 we can also detect erratic behavior over small areas. As velocity increases through panels (3,2) to (6,2), the level regions in the vicinity of $(-20'', 20'')$ shift rapidly and become disconnected; this is an indication of a rapid local fluctuation. In panels (7,5) and (8,5) there is another rapid fluctuation near $(20'', -20'')$, but not as pronounced as the first. Figure 4.43, the graph of the measurement locations, shows that these two locations are at the ends of the $133°$ slit. The display of the data along the slits in Figure 4.45, and the display of the residuals along the slits in Figure 4.47, do not indicate any peculiar behavior on the $133°$ slit or any lack of fit. But the ends of the $133°$ slit do lie in regions with little other data, so the fluctuations are most probably simply the artifacts that result from applying loess to regions that are sparse in data.

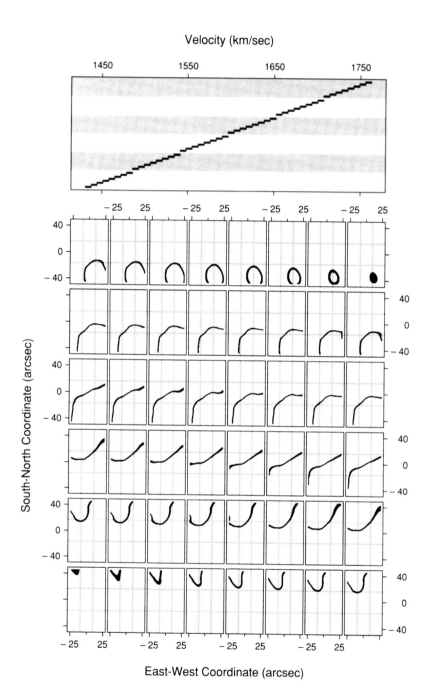

4.55 A level plot displays the loess fit to the galaxy velocities. The aspect ratio of the level-region panels has been chosen to make the number of data units per cm the same on both scales.

On a level plot of a function, each level region is rendered by placing a dot at a grid point if the function value at the point lies in the level corresponding to that region. The grid needs to be sufficiently dense to produce level regions that characterize the actual level regions of the function; thus greater density is better than less until the limit of resolution of the display device is reached.

One important aspect of a level plot is that when there are contours that are well defined curves, we see them as the boundaries of the level regions. But when curves do not adequately describe the behavior of the function, we can still perceive the behavior. For example, if a function is constant over a region, the region appears as part of the level region for the level that contains the constant. A second important aspect of a level plot is that the arrangement of the panels in graphical order provides a mechanism for perceiving order that does not require table look-up. However, the drawback of rendering level regions on juxtaposed panels is a reduction in our ability to perceive the relative locations of level regions. In Section 4.12, superposition will be used.

4.10   3-D Wireframe Plots of Surfaces

A *3-D plot* of a fitted surface shows the surface as if it were an object in real 3-D space. Aspects of the display method allow us to see the surface-object in depth. Figures 4.56 to 4.59 are four 3-D plots of the velocity surface fitted to the galaxy data The rendering in this case is a simple although effective method — a wireframe with hidden line removal [42, 79]. In Section 4.13 we will discuss more sophisticated schemes.

To carry out the wireframe rendering, the surface is first evaluated on a grid. The grid values together with the values of the surface form a set of points in three-dimensional space. The 3-D plot renders line segments that connect these points. Two aspects of the rendering, perspective and occlusion of features in the background by features in the foreground, provide the 3-D effect [68]. And the box drawn around the surface not only shows axes but contributes to our perception of depth; this is the reason for drawing all visible line segments of the box rather than just three to indicate axes.

In Figures 4.56 to 4.59, the scale lines have arrows to indicate increasing values of the variables. There are no tick marks because scale reading, or table look-up, of numerical values from 3-D plots is often poor. To carry out table look-up for features detected on a 3-D plot, it is typically far more satisfactory to also display the surface by a level plot or by a contour plot, locate the detected features on the adjunct display, and use the scales of the adjunct display to carry out the table look-up.

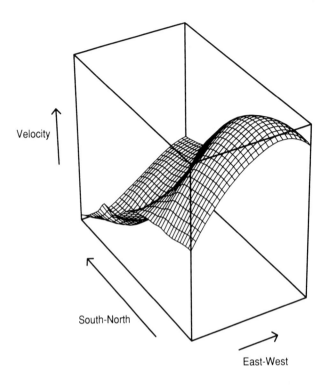

4.56 A 3-D wireframe plot displays the robust loess surface fitted to the galaxy velocities.

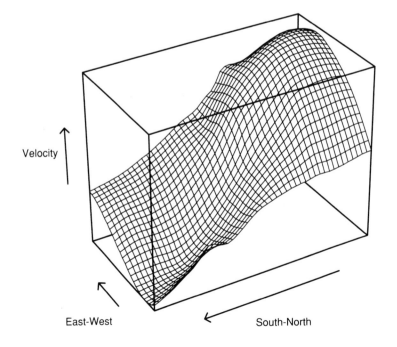

4.57 The surface in Figure 4.56 is shown again after a rotation of $90°$ about the velocity axis.

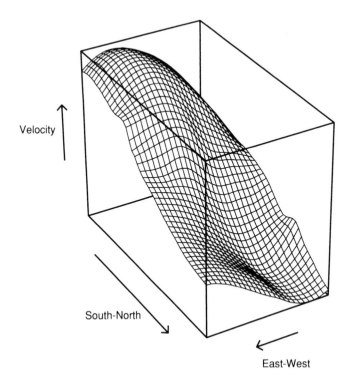

Velocity

South-North

East-West

4.58 The surface in Figure 4.56 is shown again after a rotation of 180° about the velocity axis.

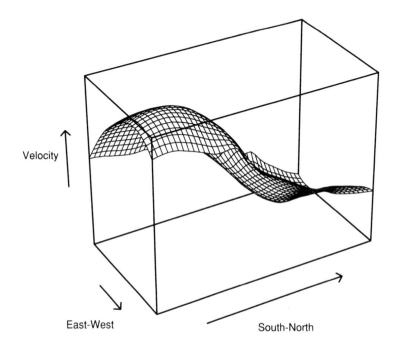

Velocity

East-West

South-North

4.59 The surface in Figure 4.56 is shown again after a rotation of 270° about the velocity axis.

Rendering Choices

There are a surprisingly large number of choices to make in wireframe rendering. We must choose the grid density. We must choose the different orientations of the surface. We must decide whether to render the surface in perspective, or by an orthogonal view, a rendering of the surface as it would look if it were far away and studied by a powerful telescope. If we choose perspective, we must specify the viewing distance; as we move closer to the box, the effect of perspective increases. We must choose the ratios of the lengths of the three box dimensions, and the overall size of the display. None of the choices can be fully automated; they typically must be made iteratively based on successive trial renderings. The following discussion defines the issues and in some cases gives rough guidelines that can provide reasonable first attempts.

If the grid density is too small, surface features are lost; if it is too large, the white space of patches closes up, and depth perception is lost. Thus the goal is to choose the density just large enough to reflect important features and no larger. It can happen that there is no good choice. If the surface has fine structure that requires a grid so dense that, given the resolution of the display device, the patches are obscured, then we need to move to the more ambitious 3-D rendering described in the Section 4.13. For the 3-D plots of the velocity surface in Figures 4.56 to 4.59, the grid is 26×46. This is less dense than the 101×181 grid used for the level plot of the velocity surface in Figure 4.55 and the contour plot of the surface in Figure 4.50; the denser grid is too dense for the 3-D plot.

Choosing several orientations is necessary in the common situation where no one view shows all features well; a single orientation that allows good perception of certain features can occlude other important features. But typically it is best to coordinate the different views by pointing the function axis in the same direction. This has been done in Figures 4.56 to 4.59. The result is views that form a revolution of the surface about the function axis. In addition, our perception is often enhanced by making the orientations of this revolution cover $360°$ in equal steps. In Figures 4.56 to 4.59, there are four orientations in steps of $90°$. The coordination and the equal steps help us maintain our understanding of which axis is which on the 3-D plots.

The relative lengths of the three box dimensions are important to perceiving the properties of the displayed surface. If the two factor variables have difference units of measurement, then the ratio of the two box lengths for the factors can simply be one. If, however, the units are the same — in particular, if the factors are spatial coordinates — then it is typically best to choose the factor lengths so that the number of data units per cm along each factor scale is the same. This has been done in Figures 4.56 to 4.59 because the factors are position on the celestial sphere. The relative length of the function, or response, box length needs to be chosen by trial and error; the choice determines a banking of surface slopes just as the aspect ratio of a two-variable graph banks the slopes of a curve. It is possible that there is a 45° principle, but the necessary research in visual perception has not yet been carried out to determine this.

A requisite amount of perspective is helpful for maintaining stable depth perception. Perspective creates foreshortening, a convergence of parallel lines that recede into the background. This foreshortening needs to be treated with great caution because, as a coming example will show, it is a distortion of the quantitative information. And the greater the amount of perspective, the greater the distortion.

Orthogonal views eliminate the distortion of perspective; parallel lines moving from the foreground to the background stay a constant distance apart, and constant-size objects have a constant image size. But orthogonal views often result in other distortions. For wireframe renderings, it is often impossible without very focused attention on small regions of the display to determine front and back, so disconcerting reversals of foreground and background are common. For the more sophisticated renderings discussed in Section 4.13, where other visual cues such as shading convey depth, an orthogonal view provides conflicting information, and the algorithms of our visual system often respond by contorting the rendered object; for example, a rectangular box around the surface can appear nonrectangular. But an orthogonal view is needed for one visualization task that will be described in the next example.

Figure 4.60 is a perspective view of the loess surface fitted to the ethanol data. The surface appears to be a tunnel with arches of constant size. Figure 4.61 is another perspective view. The tunnel now appears to have arches whose size increases as C increases. Thus the two views convey conflicting conclusions about quantitative aspects of the surface. We know from the coplot of the fitted surface in Figure 4.13 that the arch sizes do in fact change, so we are fooled in Figure 4.60. For this figure, the arches expand in size from the foreground to the background. But the foreshortening due to perspective makes the actual image size of these arches decrease from front to back, and the decrease in size just matches the actual increase, so all arches are nearly visually coincident. To understand this phenomenon, it helps to consider that when we look into a tunnel with constant arch size, foreshortening makes the actual image size of the opening at the opposite end smaller than that of the opening at the near end.

An orthogonal view is needed for looking along a direction parallel to one of the three axes to see the relative locations of the orthogonal projections of features onto the plane formed by the other two axes. A perspective view does not give orthogonal projections as Figure 4.60 has illustrated. Figure 4.62 shows an orthogonal view of the NO_x surface. The view is parallel to the C axis. Because there is no perspective distortion, we can trust what we see; for low values of E, the surface is nearly constant as a function of C, and for middle and large values of E, there is a change with C.

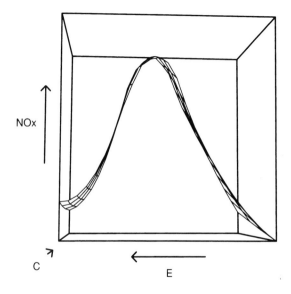

4.60 A 3-D plot displays the NO_x surface.

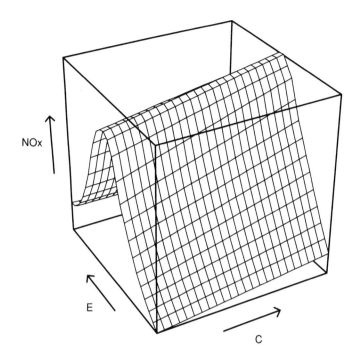

4.61 Another 3-D plot displays the NO$_x$ surface.

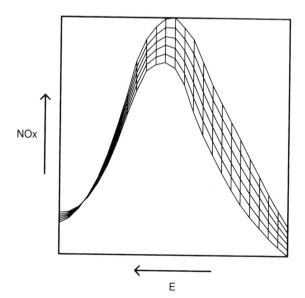

4.62 This 3-D plot of the NO$_x$ surface uses an orthogonal view.

4.11 3-D Plots of Data: Stereo

The visual impression of depth that we get from occlusion and perspective foreshortening in 3-D plots of functions does not extend readily to data. If the number of observations is small, we can endow plotting symbols with depth cues such as changing symbol size and occlusion, but for even moderate amounts of data, the result is not reliable and too often results in an inscrutable mess despite our best efforts.

Stereo viewing is a far more satisfactory method for 3-D rendering of data. Stereopsis is a powerful mechanism for depth perception. Figure 4.63 shows a stereogram of the galaxy data. For those without a stereo viewer, Chapter 2 has instructions on how to trick the eyes into fusing the two images. The method is not easy to master, but practice helps. The overall behavior of the galaxy velocities — an increase in going from the northeast corner to the southwest — is lucidly conveyed.

Motion is another powerful cue for depth perception. For trivariate data, a rotating point cloud on a computer screen provides excellent depth perception [41]. Furthermore, methods of direct manipulation allow us to control the orientation of the point cloud in a natural, perceptual way. Sadly, we cannot even approximate rotation in the static environment of a book because the animation is critical to the perception.

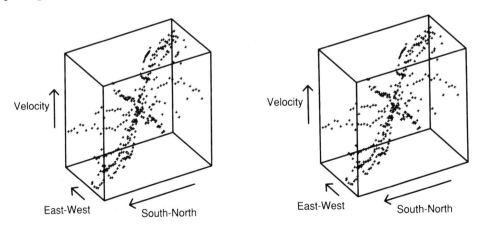

4.63 A stereogram displays the galaxy velocities.

4.12   Level Plots of Surfaces with Superposed Color

The visual displays so far presented in the book have been images created by line segments and symbols rendered in black and gray. But computer graphics allows more sophisticated rendering [42, 79]. Among the capabilities is color, which can be used to good purpose to produce level plots.

Soil Data

How things get measured is a fascinating topic. And a critical one, of course. In many domains of science, brilliance and great ingenuity abound in measurement techniques. This intellectual effort is crucial because measurement is the foundation of scientific enquiry.

Suppose we had to measure the electrical resistivity of soil. Would we simply insert two electrodes in the ground and measure the current flowing between them? That would work, but suppose now that we had to survey the resistivity at ten thousand locations over a region of one square kilometer. Just to make the problem a little more difficult, suppose we had to run a business doing this and make a profit. Resistivity measurements can be used to infer soil salinity, a vital matter for irrigated farm land. It is unlikely that we could economically stick electrodes in the ground ten thousand times.

A solution was found by the Salinity Surveys division of TESLA-10, a company in Western Australia where irrigation is necessary for farming. Their instrument, the EM31, has a transmitter coil that induces a current in the earth. The current generates a magnetic field whose intensity is measured by the EM31. The instrument is put on a trailer and towed around by a jeep, which stops at regular intervals and takes a measurement. Thus soil resistivity is measured economically by an instrument that never touches the ground.

Figure 4.64 shows the locations of 8641 measurements made by the
EM31. Each measurement location is graphed by a dot, but the density
of the dots is so great that they merge to form curves, the measurement
tracks. The vertical scale is labeled "northing" and the horizontal is
labeled "easting". These are just names for a local coordinate system set
up for convenience; they have nothing to do with compass directions.
For the most part, the vehicle towing the EM31 tracked along the easting
axis, but it also made a few runs along the northing axis.

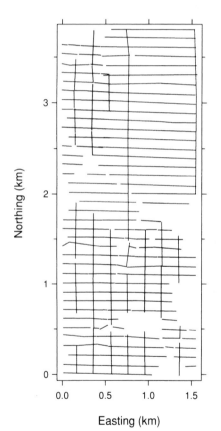

4.64 The display shows the measurement tracks for the
soil data. The aspect ratio has been chosen to make the
number of data units per cm the same on both scales.

Spatial Data

The soil data are spatial data; the factors are geographical location. Spatial data, like time series, often have different components of variation. Time series have time components, and spatial data have spatial components. The spatial components can be trends, or long-distance variation; they can be slow oscillations, or middle-distance variation; or they can be rapid ups and downs, or short-distance variation. The galaxy measurements analyzed in previous sections are also spatial data: velocities at spatial locations on the celestial sphere. The visualizations showed that the variation in velocity consists of a broad trend plus nearly random variation about the trend. Shortly, the visualization of the soil data will show many spatial components, from long-distance to short-distance variation.

Improvisation

We can improvise, exploiting the measurement tracks to visualize the raw data. In Figure 4.65, resistivity is graphed against the northing coordinate for the eight tracks that run along the northing axis. On the display, convention has been ignored, and the factor, the northing coordinate, is graphed on the vertical axis as it is in Figure 4.64. This makes it easier to match the panels of Figure 4.65 with the tracks in Figure 4.64. As the numbers at the tops of the panels increase, the tracks move from left to right along the easting axis. In Figure 4.66, resistivity is graphed against the easting coordinate for the 40 tracks that run along the easting axis. The easting coordinate is on the horizontal scale, also to conform with Figure 4.64; as the panel numbers increase, the tracks move from bottom to top in Figure 4.64.

Figures 4.65 and 4.66 show that the soil data have many spatial components of variation. Rapid local variations and slow oscillations are quite evident. There are also broad trends; for example, panels 29 to 36 of Figure 4.66 reveal an incline running along the entire easting axis.

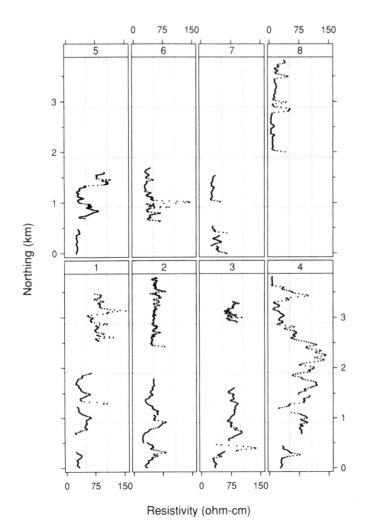

4.65 Resistivity is graphed against the northing coordinate for the eight tracks that run along the northing axis.

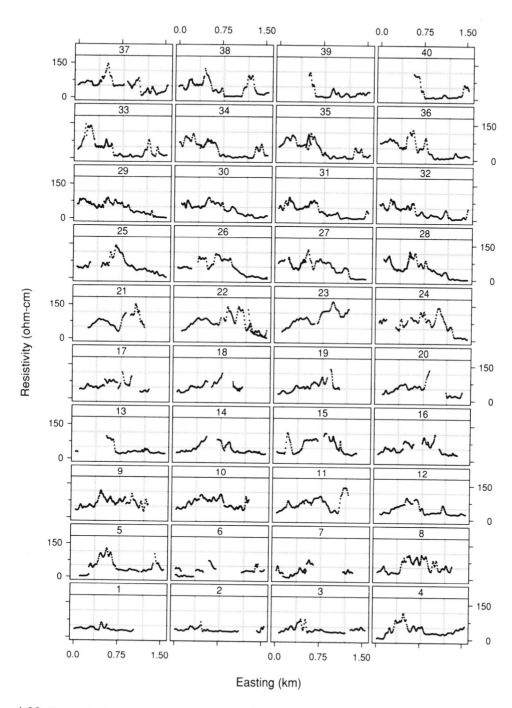

4.66 Resistivity is graphed against the easting coordinate for the 40 tracks that run along the easting axis.

Fitting

For the soil data, one important goal is to understand trends in the data to determine the broad areas where the overall level of salinity is high. We will do this with a loess trend fit with parameters $\alpha = 1/4$ and $\lambda = 2$. To preserve the natural metric of the spatial factors, the easting and northing coordinates will not be standardized by dividing by the 10% trimmed standard deviations. Also, bisquare will not be added because the visualization of the measurements in Figures 4.65 and 4.66 does not suggest outliers or other destructive behavior.

Figure 4.67 is a level plot of the loess fit evaluated on an 85×234 grid with 15m spacing ranging from 150m to 1410m along the easting axis and from 150m to 3645m along the northing axis. The grid is set slightly inside the rectangle formed from the extremes of the measurement locations. Such cropping is discussed in Chapter 5. The level plot has 28 equal intervals of resistivity that range from the minimum of the function values over the grid to the maximum; the only overlap of the intervals occurs at the endpoints.

Figure 4.67 shows that the lowest levels of resistivity occur near the upper right corner of the measurement region. From this depression, the level regions spread out to the extremes of the region, and then move inward to form two peaks, the highest one very near the center of the region.

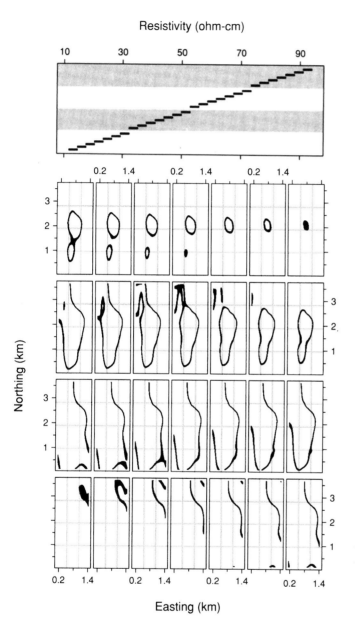

4.67 A level plot displays the loess fit to the soil data. The aspect ratio of the level-region panels has been chosen to make the number of data units per cm the same on both scales.

Superposed Level Regions in Color

The level plot in Figure 4.67 shows the level regions by juxtaposing them on different panels with the same scales. Using color, the level regions can be superposed. This is illustrated in Figure 4.68. In this case there are only 10 intervals, ranging from the minimum to the maximum function value. The wide use of level plots in color might suggest that the method is easy, but it is easy only if one is satisfied with a poor choice of colors such as a rainbow encoding. As Tufte puts it [75], "the mind's eye does not readily give an order to ROYGBIV."

There are two desiderata in choosing a color encoding of the quantitative values of a function. First, we typically want effortless perception of the order of the values. For example, effortless perception means we do not have to constantly refer to a key. Second, we want clearly perceived boundaries between adjacent levels. Achieving these two desiderata is difficult because they play against one another; it is easy to achieve one or the other, but hard to achieve both simultaneously.

The color encoding in Figure 4.68, which we will call THVL (two hues, varying lightness), represents a good compromise [54, 75]. First, there are two hues. Because the end product in this case is on a book page, the hues are cyan and magenta, which are two of the four colors standardly used in printing on paper — cyan, yellow, magenta, and black. The lightness of the colors decreases as the encoded values move away from a central value. From the middle to the extremes, the cyan ranges from 20% cyan to 100% cyan in steps of 20% cyan, and the magenta ranges from 20% magenta to 100% magenta in steps of 20% magenta. Using two hues and changing just their lightness provides the effortless perception of order. But there is a bound on the number of intervals that can be used if the desideratum of distinct boundaries is to be achieved. Because of the delicacy of color reproduction, only 10 have been used in Figure 4.68. At a computer screen it is possible to drive the number up to 15 or so, but using a significantly greater number typically results in a perceptual merging of some of the adjacent colors. Actually, more than 10 colors are used in Figure 4.68, but the additional ones occur just at boundaries of level regions and are only barely perceptible. This *anti-aliasing*, which is described later in a section for the record, gives the boundaries a smooth look. The smoothing was necessary because the display started out as an image on a computer screen; the low resolution of screens results in jagged boundaries unless anti-aliasing methods are used.

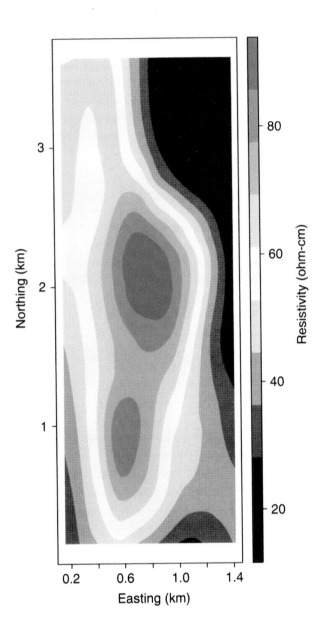

4.68 The fitted resistivity surface is displayed by a level plot with ten level regions superposed in color. An anti-aliasing method based on approximate area sampling gives the boundaries of the level regions a smooth appearance. The aspect ratio of the level-region panels has been chosen to make the number of data units per cm the same on both scales.

Superposing level regions in color rather than juxtaposing them in black and white has one benefit. We are better able to perceive the relative locations of the level regions, and this often conveys the overall gestalt of the surface more effectively. But the disadvantage is the limit to the number of colors and therefore the resolution of the display. A level plot with juxtaposed regions in black and white provides both a clear visual delineation of each level region and a clear perception of order even for a large number of intervals. For example, Figure 4.67 has 28 intervals, almost three times the number for Figure 4.68.

For the Record: Anti-Aliasing

In the anti-aliasing method of Figure 4.68, the surface is computed over a rectangular grid. In Figure 4.68, the grid is 85 by 234, the same grid used in Figure 4.67. Then, the surface is interpolated to a much denser grid, set up so that each pixel contains four grid points. For each pixel, we could average its four function values, find the interval among the 10 that contains the average, and color the pixel with the color for the interval. This would produce jagged boundaries on an output device, such as a computer screen, that does not have sufficient resolution.

One method for anti-aliasing jagged boundaries is area sampling [42]. The rendering in Figure 4.68 uses an approximate area sampling scheme. Let $c(y)$ be a function that takes values of a surface, y, into a color-description space, which is normally three-dimensional [42, 79]. Suppose that $c(y)$ takes on only the 10 colors of the color bar on the right in Figure 4.68. In the approximate area sampling method, the four colors of $c(y)$ for a pixel are averaged in the color space, and the pixel is filled with the average color. In other words, instead of averaging the four function values and applying c, we apply c to the four function values and average the colors. If the space is RBG, we simply average the intensities of the four reds, the four blues, and the four greens. Sometimes, though, the averages can produce colors that contrast with their neighbors, in which case we must alter the colors of the averages to maintain a smooth transition; an example will be given shortly. For most pixels, the four colors are the same, so the average is one of the 10 values of $c(y)$. But if a pixel is at a boundary between level regions, the colors are not the same, and the pixel receives, typically, a color that is not one of the 10. In Figure 4.68 the overall gestalt appears to have only the 10 colors of $c(y)$ because there is so little filling with other colors, but the small amount of additional coloring produces smooth boundaries by providing a smooth perceptual transition from one region to the next.

The $c(y)$ for the 10 colors of the bar in Figure 4.68 can be defined in a particularly simple way on a one-dimensional scale. Let $c(y)$ range from -100 to 100. A positive number describes a percentage of cyan and a negative number describes a percentage of magenta. The colors of the bar range from -100 to 100 in steps of 20, except there is no zero. The average of any four colors on the scale is one of the numbers -100 to 100 in steps of 5, except for the values ± 5 and ± 15. The averages work quite well in this case except for the transition from magenta to cyan; the values -10, 0 (white), and 10 are too light. The following alteration was used in Figure 4.68: -10 is 13% magenta and 7% cyan; 0 is 10% magenta and 10% cyan; and 10 is 13% cyan and 7% magenta.

4.13 Direct Manipulation and Shading for 3-D Plots of Surfaces

Our visual system is a marvelous device. It provides a perception of depth by processing visual information with extraordinary algorithms [61, 68]. There is the information in the disparity of the two views provided by the two eyes. There is pictorial information, the information in a photograph that allows depth perception; this includes perspective foreshortening and occlusion. Another pictorial cue is the shading of a surface that results from the light sources that illuminate it. And there is the information in motion, both the motion of viewed objects and the motion of the head.

The wireframe renderings presented in Section 4.10 provide depth perception through perspective foreshortening and occlusion. For relatively simple surfaces — for example, the galaxy surface that was displayed in Section 4.10 — wireframe rendering provides an adequate perception of depth. But for more complicated surfaces, a graphics environment that provides both direct manipulation and shading can increase our perception of effects. Figure 4.69 shows a rendering of the resistivity surface with foreshortening, occlusion, and shading; the view was chosen by initial exploration of the surface in a direct manipulation environment.

Shading can provide a substantial increase in our perception of depth. But shading requires many decisions [42, 79]. There is the reflective properties of the surface. It can have a dull matte finish or a shiny finish. The latter results in specular reflection, or shiny areas on the surface. There is the color of the surface. There is the number, color, intensity, and location of point light sources. There is the color and intensity of ambient light. Figure 4.69 has ambient light and three point sources. The color of the lighting is white, and the surface is gray and shiny. The lengths of the northing and easting box lengths have been chosen to make the number of data units per cm the same on both scales.

The chief benefit of direct manipulation is an ability to control the orientation of a surface in a natural way, moving it around as we might a real object held in our hands. This nicely replaces the static method described in Section 4.10 of showing multiple views that form a rotation about the function axis of $360°$. Furthermore, motion can strengthen our perception of depth.

Figure 4.69 provides a vivid portrayal of properties of the resistivity surface. The two principal features are the depression and rise to a plateau in the background, and the two peaks in the foreground and midground.

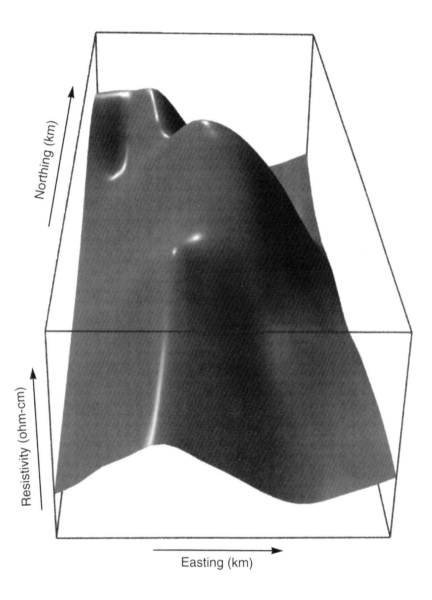

4.69 The fitted resistivity surface is rendered with perspective foreshortening, occlusion, and shading. No tick marks and tick mark labels are drawn since table look-up from this display would be ineffective. (The units are nevertheless shown to remind us of the definitions of the variables.) But the orientation of the surface matches the positioning of the color level plot in Figure 4.68, so as discussed in Section 4.10, the level plot can be used for table look-up. We simply match features found here with those of the level plot, and then use the level plot for the table look-up.

4.14   *Coplots vs. Factor-Plane Methods*

The visualization tools in this chapter can be divided into two
groups: conditioning methods and factor-plane methods. The first
group — coplots and brushing — employed conditioning on a factor.
For the second group — level plots, contour plots, and 3-D plots — the
plane of the two factors appeared in the visualization with the factors as
coordinate axes.

Conditioning methods are particularly informative when it is natural
to study conditional dependence, and when the behavior of the
information is characterized in a straightforward way by conditional
statements. This was the case for the rubber data, the ethanol data, and
the perception data. Factor-plane methods are not nearly as informative
in such cases. For example, for the ethanol data, it is informative to
understand the effect of compression ratio with equivalence ratio held
constant, and to understand the effect of equivalence ratio with
compression ratio held constant.

But if conditional behavior is neither particularly interesting nor
simple, then factor-plane methods can do better. One test is to ask
whether it is just as interesting to see the surface along line segments that
are oblique to the coordinate axes of the factors as it is to see the surface
along segments parallel to the axes. If the answer is "yes", factor-plane
methods are likely to be more useful. This is frequently the case for
spatial data. If the answer is "no," coplots are likely to be more useful.
The galaxy and soil data are two examples where the answer is "yes", so
factor-plane methods were used to visualize the data, although special
structure in both data sets was exploited by conditioning methods.

4.15   *Visualization and Probabilistic Inference*

Sometimes, when visualization thoroughly reveals the structure of a
set of data, there is a tendency to underrate the power of the method for
the application. Little effort is expended in seeing the structure once the
right visualization method is used, so we are mislead into thinking
nothing exciting has occurred. The rubber data might be such a case.

The intensive visualization showed a linearity in hardness, a nonlinearity in tensile strength, an interaction between hardness and tensile strength, and three aberrant observations in a corner of the factor measurement region. It might be thought that anyone analyzing these data would uncover these properties. This is not the case. In the original treatment, the analysts got it wrong [31]. They operated within a paradigm of numerical methods and probabilistic inference for data analysis, and not intensive visualization. They missed the nonlinearity. They missed the interaction. They missed the outliers. In other words, they missed most of the structure in the data.

The ethanol data were treated no better. In the original analysis by the experimenter, a high-order polynomial was fitted to log concentration by least-squares, and probabilistic inference used standard methods that are based on homogeneous errors with a normal distribution [12]. The visualization in Section 4.4 makes it clear that such probabilistic inferences are clearly not valid; the error distribution is strongly leptokurtic and on a log scale, there is monotone spread. In another study of these data, the mistake of taking logs was not made, but the leptokurtosis of the residuals was missed [23]. In a third study, the analyst used numerical statistical methods to find transformations of the response and factors that supposedly removed the interaction between the factors [69]. But the visualization of the data in this chapter shows that it is absurd to try this. When the equivalence ratio is large, concentration is constant as a function of compression ratio; for other values of equivalence ratio, concentration varies linearly as a function of compression ratio with a positive slope. Monotone transformations of the three variables, the only transformations that make sense for such factor-response data, cannot alter this equality and inequality, and therefore cannot remove the interaction. Finally, an analysis with no visualization of the data made the biggest error [17]. It was concluded that NO_x does not depend on C. Our visualization here manifested a dependence.

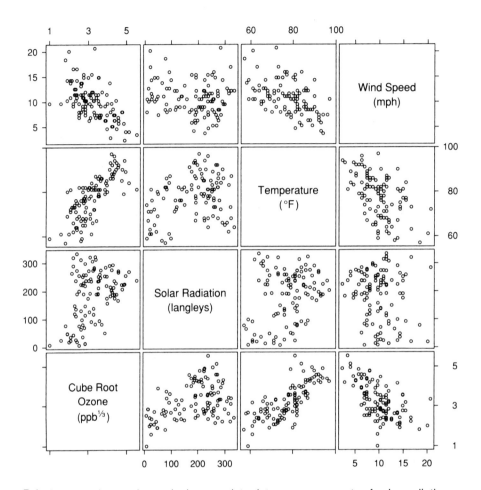

5.1 A scatterplot matrix graphs hypervariate data: measurements of solar radiation, temperature, wind speed, and cube root ozone concentration on 111 days at sites in the New York metropolitan region.

5 Hypervariate Data

Figure 5.1 is a scatterplot matrix of measurements of four environmental variables from an air pollution study [13]. The variables, all measured at ground level, are wind speed, temperature, solar radiation, and cube root ozone concentration. Ozone is one of the nasty constituents of photochemical smog, and its concentration is the standard indicator of the severity of such smog. If its level is high, a smog alert is called. Ozone is not emitted directly into the atmosphere. Rather, it is a product of chemical reactions that require solar radiation and emissions of primary pollutants from smoke stacks and automobile tail pipes. When the ventilation of the atmosphere is low, the chemical reactions bring ozone to high levels. Low ventilation tends to occur when wind speeds are low and temperatures are high because on hot, calm days in the summer the atmosphere cannot cleanse itself. The goal in analyzing the environmental data is to determine how ozone depends on the other variables, so cube root concentration is the response and the other variables are factors.

The environmental data in Figure 5.1 lie in a four-dimensional space. In Chapter 2 we visualized univariate data, which lie on a line; in Chapter 3 it was bivariate data, which lie in the plane; and in Chapter 4 it was trivariate data, which lie in three-space. The data in these cases lie in spaces with physical reality. We exploit this reality to visualize the data. The environmental data are hypervariate; they have too many variables for visual reality. We must peer cognitively, not perceptually, into hypervariate space by looks at subspaces of dimension three or fewer. In classical statistics, the word "multivariate" means two or more variables, and was coined because probabilistic methods have a natural breakpoint between one dimension and two. For visualization, we need the term "hypervariate" to acknowledge the visual breakpoint between three and four dimensions.

The measurements in Figure 5.1 were made on 111 days from May to September of 1973 at sites in the New York City metropolitan region; there is one measurement of each variable on each day. Solar radiation is the amount from 0800 to 1200 in the frequency band 4000–7700Å, and was measured in Central Park, New York City. Wind speed is the average of values at 0700 and 1000, and was measured at LaGuardia Airport, which is about 7 km from Central Park. Temperature is the daily maximum, and was also measured at LaGuardia. Ozone is the cube root of the average of hourly values from 1300 to 1500, and was measured at Roosevelt Island, which is about 2 km from Central Park and 5 km from LaGuardia. The cube root transformation symmetrizes the distribution of the concentrations; on the original scale, they are significantly skewed toward large values.

To streamline the discussion we will use the following notation: O_3 = cube root ozone concentration, R = radiation, T = temperature, and W = wind speed.

5.1   Scatterplot Matrices

An award should be given for the invention of the *scatterplot matrix*, but the inventor is unknown — an anonymous donor to the world's collection of visualization tools. Early drafts of *Graphical Methods for Data Analysis* [16] contain the first written discussion of the idea, but it was in use before that. The inventor may not have fully appreciated the significance of the method or may have thought the idea too trivial to bring it forward, but its simple, elegant solution to a difficult problem is one of the best visualization ideas around.

As with other multi-panel displays in this book, we will refer to a panel of the scatterplot matrix by column and row number; the left column is column one and the bottom row is row one. For example, in Figure 5.1, the upper left panel is (1,4) and the lower right is (4,1).

Visual Linking

One way to visualize hypervariate data is to graph each pair of variables by a scatterplot. But just making the scatterplots without any coordination often results in a confusing collection of graphs that are hard to visually integrate.

The important idea of the scatterplot matrix is to arrange the graphs in a matrix with shared scales. As a result, we can visually *link* features on one scatterplot with features on another, which greatly increases the power of the visualization. Along each row or column of the matrix, one variable is graphed against all others with the scales for that one variable lined up along the horizontal or the vertical. By scanning a row or column we can link effects on different scatterplots.

Visual linking in Figure 5.1 allows us to detect important effects in the environmental data. Panel (2,1), a scatterplot of O_3 against R, has an upper envelope in the form of an inverted "V". There are two interesting properties. First, the highest values of O_3 occur when R is between 200 and 300 langleys. Second, for the very highest values of R, O_3 stays at low levels. Visual linking provides an explanation of both of these properties. First, we can focus on the points with the highest O_3 values in the (2,1) panel, and then scan to the right to panels (3,1) and (4,1). The linking shows that the high O_3 results when T is high and W is low; these are days with low ventilation. Next, we can focus on the points in the (2,1) panel with the highest values of radiation and scan up to the (2,3) and (2,4) panels. We see that for the very highest values of R, T tends not to be high and W tends not to be low, so O_3 does not rise to high levels.

Panels (3,1) and (4,1) of Figure 5.1 show there is a strong association between T and O_3 and between W and O_3. The reason, as stated earlier, is that W and T are both indicators of ventilation. But the (4,3) panel shows that W and T are related and thus are measuring ventilation, to some extent, in the same way.

Visual linking is the reason, despite the redundancy, for including both the upper and lower triangles in the scatterplot matrix; the upper left triangle has all pairs of scatterplots, and so does the lower right triangle. Suppose that only the upper left triangle were present in Figure 5.1. To see temperature against everything else, we would have to scan the first two graphs in row three, turn the corner in the (3,3) panel, and go up to row four to see the remaining scatterplot. The three temperature scales would not be lined up, which would interfere with the linking.

5.2   Coplots of Data

The scatterplot matrix of the environmental data shows a strong
association between O_3 and T and between O_3 and W. It seems likely
that each of these factors explains variation in the data not explained by
the others. There is less evidence that R explains variation in O_3 given T
and W. For example, we saw that the upper envelope on the scatterplot
of O_3 against R was explainable by the behavior of T and W. But the
photochemistry that results in O_3 requires radiation, and the laws of
chemistry must be obeyed, so we know in principle that radiation is a
causal factor. But this does not mean that for the environmental data, the
solar radiation measurements are good predictors of O_3. Perhaps only a
minimum amount of radiation is needed, and beyond that, production is
not sensitive to the amount. Or it may be that the Central Park
measurements do a poor job of characterizing the amount of radiation
that actually falls on the air mass.

We need a way to see the dependence of O_3 on radiation given
temperature and wind speed. A hypervariate coplot, an extension of the
coplot display method of Chapter 4 to three or more factors, can provide
such a conditional visualization. Figure 5.2 shows such a coplot. O_3 is
graphed against R given W and T. Each dependence panel is a scatterplot
of O_3 against R for days with both W and T in specified intervals. The
given panels, which are at the top and right of the graph, show the
intervals. The four scatterplots in any row of the 4×4 array of
dependence panels have the same conditioning interval of values of W;
as the rows go from bottom to top, the intervals of W increase. Similarly,
the four scatterplots in any column have the same conditioning interval
of values of T; as the columns go from left to right, the intervals of T
increase.

Each panel in Figure 5.2 has a loess curve to help us visualize the
dependence pattern. The fitting of the curves uses bisquare; as with
coplots for two factors, it is prudent to use robust fitting for initial looks
at the data to protect against distortion that might occur if there happen
to be outliers.

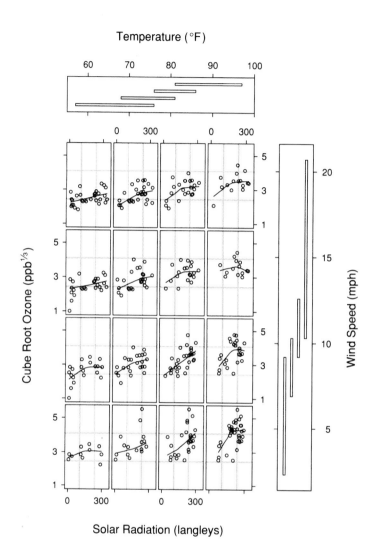

5.2 A coplot graphs O_3 against R given T and W. The robust loess curves, whose parameters are $\lambda = \alpha = 1$, are banked by an aspect ratio of 2. Banking to $45°$ results in an aspect ratio that is too large.

The coplot of Figure 5.2 is repeated in Figure 5.3 to enhance the following discussion. The conditioning intervals of Figure 5.3 have been chosen using the equal-count method with a target fraction of overlap equal to $1/2$. Thus, the number of values of the conditioning factor in each interval is roughly constant. The interval counts for T are 46, 51, 51, and 51. For W, they are 49, 50, 47, and 53. However, because the points on each dependence panel arise from satisfying two conditionings, one for T and one for W, the number of points on the dependence panels varies from 11 to 34. Consider the (1,1) panel, a scatterplot of O_3 against R for observations that satisfy two requirements: the values of T must be in the lowest temperature interval and the values of W must be in the lowest wind speed interval. There are 49 days with W in the wind interval and 46 days with T in the temperature interval. If it happened that all days with T in the temperature interval also had W in the wind interval, there would be 46 points on the dependence panel. But if it happened that no days with T in the temperature interval had W in the wind interval, there would be no points on the dependence panel. Any number between these two extremes is possible, and the actual value depends on how W and T vary with one another. Since low temperature and low wind speed tend not to occur together, the number of points on panel (1,1) is only 11. But on the (4,1) panel, where T is high and W is low, there are 34 points since high temperatures are associated with low wind speeds.

Figure 5.3 shows rather convincingly that radiation explains variation in the O_3 measurements beyond that explained by wind speed and temperature. As the theory of photochemistry predicts, O_3 increases with R. The patterns of dependence are generally concave. Thus, for the most part, the marginal effect of R diminishes as R increases. The shapes of the patterns vary. For each fixed value of W, the overall change as a function of R increases as T increases. This means there is an interaction between R and T — as the ventilation drops, the effect of R is greater. There is a suggestion of a similar interaction between W and R — a greater overall change as a function of R as W decreases, possibly for the two largest values of T — but there is too much noise in the data to be certain.

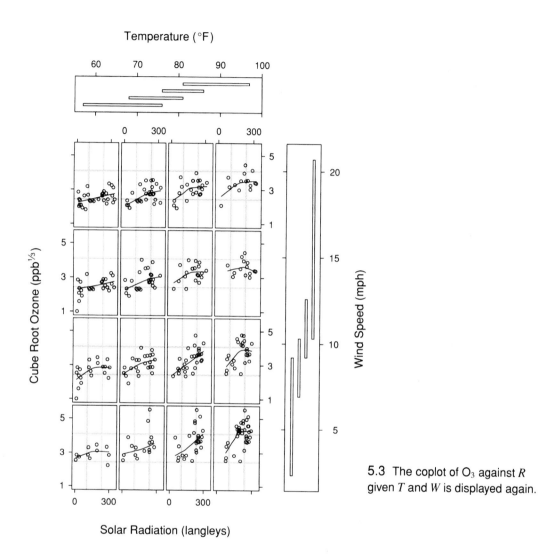

5.3 The coplot of O_3 against R given T and W is displayed again.

For three factors, there are three coplots; each factor appears once on the horizontal scale. Figures 5.4 and 5.5 are the remaining two coplots for the environmental data. Figure 5.4 shows, as expected, that as W increases, O_3 decreases. The patterns are mostly convex; the marginal effect of W diminishes as W increases. Careful examination of each column of panels does not clearly establish any interaction between W and T. The assessment must be done with care because the distribution of values of W on each panel shifts toward lower values as the conditioning

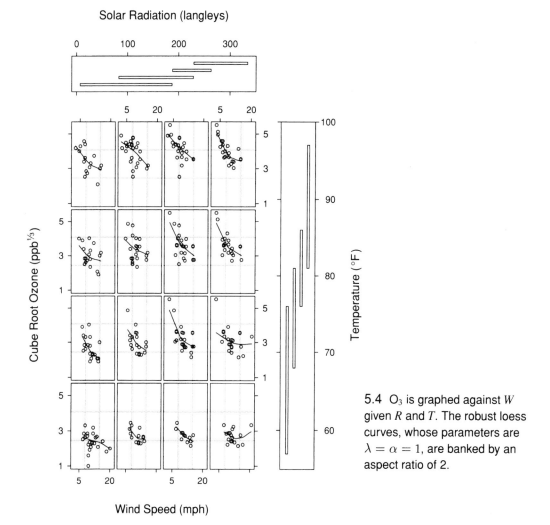

5.4 O_3 is graphed against W given R and T. The robust loess curves, whose parameters are $\lambda = \alpha = 1$, are banked by an aspect ratio of 2.

value of T increases for fixed R. But an examination of portions of curves that overlap in W does not suggest much change in shape. Also, as in the previous coplot, there is no clear indication of an interaction between R and W. Figure 5.5 shows that O_3 increases markedly with increasing T. Unlike for R and W, there is no reduction in the marginal effect for large values. The interaction between R and T is again apparent. But the change in shape of the curves with W for fixed R appears to be due more to a changing distribution of values of T on the panels than to a meaningful interaction.

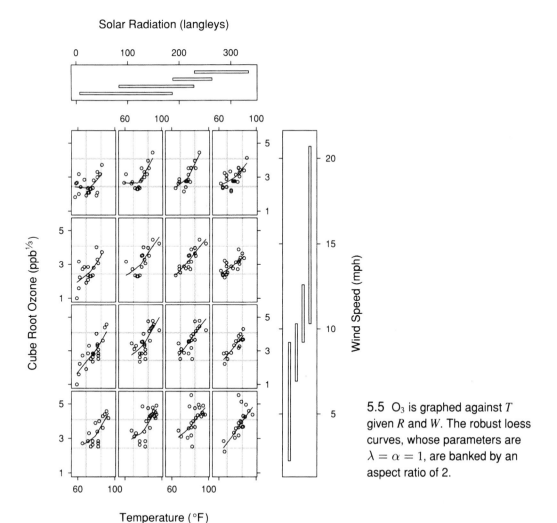

5.5 O_3 is graphed against T given R and W. The robust loess curves, whose parameters are $\lambda = \alpha = 1$, are banked by an aspect ratio of 2.

5.3   Coplots of Hypervariate Surfaces and Cropping

Fitting is essential to visualizing hypervariate data. The structure of data in many dimensions can be exceedingly complex. The visualization of a fit to hypervariate data, by reducing the amount of noise, can often lead to more insight. The fit is a hypervariate surface, a function of three or more variables. As with bivariate and trivariate data, our fitting tools are loess and parametric fitting by least-squares. And each tool can employ bisquare iterations to produce robust estimates when outliers or other forms of leptokurtosis are present.

Loess fitting provides a satisfactory fit to the environmental data. The fit is a hypervariate surface, $\hat{g}(R, W, T)$, a function of radiation, wind speed, and temperature. Extensive experimentation led to this fit, whose parameters are $\alpha = 1$ and $\lambda = 2$. Bisquare was not used since, as we shall see shortly, the residual distribution is well approximated by the normal. In Chapter 4, the ethanol data were fitted by a loess surface that was conditionally linear in compression ratio. For the environmental data, the loess fit was taken to be conditionally quadratic in W and R; this means that given T, the fit as a function of W and R is a quadratic polynomial whose coefficients change as the conditioning value of T changes. The coplots of the data in Figures 5.3 to 5.5 led to this specification; the coplots showed that the patterns of dependence on W and R are mildly curved, but the dependence on T is both greater and more complex.

Cropping

There is an insidious problem in visualizing a fit to hypervariate data — restricting our look at the fit to regions of the factor space that have sufficient data. The problem occurs for bivariate data and trivariate data as well, but it is easier to assess in these cases and solutions are simpler. For hypervariate data, the problem is treacherous because it is easy to view a hypervariate fit and not appreciate that certain portions of the fit are evaluations over regions with little or no data.

Consider first, the bivariate case. Suppose the environmental data had just one factor, wind speed. Figure 5.6 shows a loess fit to the data.

Something leaps out at us that most would regard as needing explicit justification; the curve has been extrapolated well beyond the maximum measured value of W. It would take a large leap of faith or substantial knowledge of the system under study to believe that the fit can be extended so far beyond the measurements of W. In Chapter 3, fits to bivariate data were routinely computed over a range that extended from the minimum value of the factor to the maximum. And in all cases, there were no unduly large observation gaps within the range of the data. Thus, visualized fits were supported by the data. If gaps had occurred, we would have *cropped* the visualization, showing the fits at less than the full range of the data.

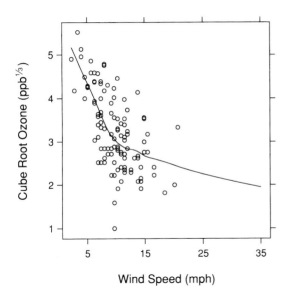

5.6 A portion of the loess fit is evaluated at values of the factor where there are no measurements. The parameters of the fit are $\alpha = 2/3$ and $\lambda = 1$.

For trivariate data, a scatterplot of the two factors shows clearly where the measurements lie in the factor space. For the ethanol data and the perception data, the fits were evaluated over the data rectangle, the rectangle which just encloses the data. In these examples, the data populated the data rectangles in all regions. But for the rubber data, the galaxy data, and the soil data, the data rectangles were cropped; in each of these examples, the fit was evaluated over a rectangle that lay inside the data rectangle. Note that cropping does not imply that data are discarded outside of the cropped region, but simply that we do not study the fit outside of the region, although dropping isolated data can also be prudent, as the rubber data illustrated.

For hypervariate data, it is a greater challenge to determine when and how to crop because the factors lie in spaces of dimension three or higher, which are harder to visualize.

For the loess O_3 fit, $\hat{g}(R, W, T)$, it is at least clear that cropping is needed. The scatterplot matrix of the data in Figure 5.1 shows that the three-dimensional box that just contains the values of the three factors has regions that are far from the measurements. In part, the problem is caused by the correlation between W and T. We could crop with a box that lies inside the data box and whose sides are parallel to those of the data box, but this parallel cropping would also eliminate regions with sufficient data. Instead, we will use the cropping shown in Figure 5.7. The two scatterplots have four pairs of parallel lines that are projections of parallel planes in the three-dimensional space of the factors. The cropped region is the intersection of the four regions between the four pairs of planes. W is cropped by moving toward the center of the data from the extremes, and T is cropped in a similar fashion. W and T are also simultaneously cropped as shown by the two oblique lines. R is not cropped. The cross section of the cropped region perpendicular to the R axis is the six-sided polygon that is formed in the interior of the right panel of Figure 5.7 by the six lines. This cropping was done visually, just as a photographer visually crops a photo for better effect.

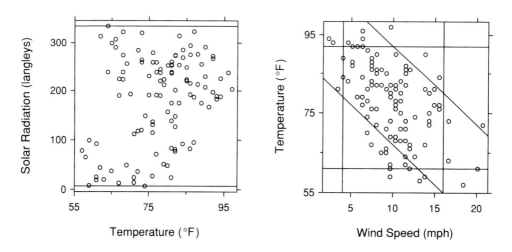

5.7 The four pairs of parallel lines indicate the cropped evaluation region for the loess fit to the environmental data.

Figure 5.8 is a scatterplot matrix of the factor measurements that lie inside the cropped region. No unduly large gaps appear; the (1,2) panel does show some small regions that are empty, but we can tolerate this. Of course, the scatterplots of the scatterplot matrix are projections, and thus could mask gaps in the three-dimensional cropped region, but rotation of the 3-D point cloud, a direct manipulation method discussed in Chapter 4, showed that the cropped region is populated throughout with data.

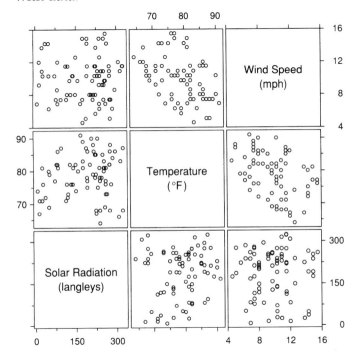

5.8 The scatterplot matrix displays those measurements of the environmental factors that lie inside the cropped region.

Displaying Hypervariate Surfaces

The strategy for displaying a fitted hypervariate surface, $\widehat{g}$, is to use conditioning. Suppose u is one of the factors. We can assign values to all other factors, and graph $\widehat{g}$ against u given these assigned, or conditioning, values. The result is a curve that can be displayed by a bivariate graph of $\widehat{g}$ against u. We must vary the conditioning values in a systematic way to visualize the surface. This can be done using the format of the hypervariate coplots of the environmental data in

Figures 5.3 to 5.5, except that the conditioning intervals are replaced by single conditioning values. The result is a hypervariate coplot of a hypervariate surface, an extension of the coplot method for displaying surfaces that was introduced in Chapter 4.

We can also graph against two factors given the others. Suppose v is a second factor. We can condition on all factors except u and v, and graph $\widehat{g}$ as a function of u and v by one of the factor-plane methods of Chapter 4, for example, by a level plot. Again, the conditioning values must be systematically varied to produce a hypervariate factor-plane display [74].

Figure 5.9 is a hypervariate coplot that displays the loess O_3 surface, $\widehat{g}(R, W, T)$, over the cropped region displayed in Figure 5.7. $\widehat{g}$ is graphed against R conditional on W and T. For each panel with a curve, T and W have been set to specific values and the curve on the panel is a graph of the fit against R. The fixed value of T for a panel is shown above the column to which the panel belongs. The fixed value of W is shown to the right of the row to which the panel belongs. For example, for the (1,5) panel, T is 61°F and W is 16 mph. The five conditioning values of W are equally spaced from 4 mph to 16 mph, the two cropping values for W. Similarly, the five conditioning values of T range from 61°F to 92°F, the two cropping values for T. The curves have been evaluated at 50 equally spaced values of R from 7 langleys, the minimum observed value of R in the data, to 334 langleys, the maximum observed value. The minimum and the maximum are the boundaries of the cropped region in the R direction. On some panels, no curves occur because the combinations of T and W put them outside the cropped region.

Figure 5.10 is a coplot of the O_3 fit against W given R and T. Figure 5.11 is a coplot of the O_3 fit against T given R and W. For these two displays, the cropping results in curves on all panels, but with varying evaluation intervals.

The three cropped coplots show general patterns that are similar to those revealed by the coplots of the data, but now the patterns are conveyed more incisively since the noise of the data has been removed. Figure 5.9 shows a nonlinear dependence of O_3 on R with a decreasing marginal effect of R. There is an interaction between R and T; as T increases for fixed W, the overall change in O_3 increases. There does not appear to be an interaction between R and W. Figure 5.10 reveals a nonlinear dependence of O_3 on W with a decreasing marginal effect of W. There are no convincing interactions. The change in shape of the curves along each column appears to be due to the change in the evaluation interval; where there is overlap in evaluation, the curves appear to have the same shape. Figure 5.11 reveals both a strong dependence of O_3 on T and the interaction between T and R that we saw in Figure 5.9.

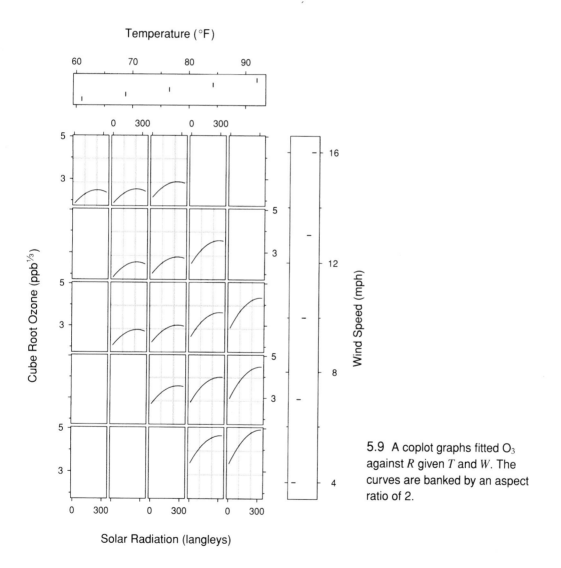

5.9 A coplot graphs fitted O_3 against R given T and W. The curves are banked by an aspect ratio of 2.

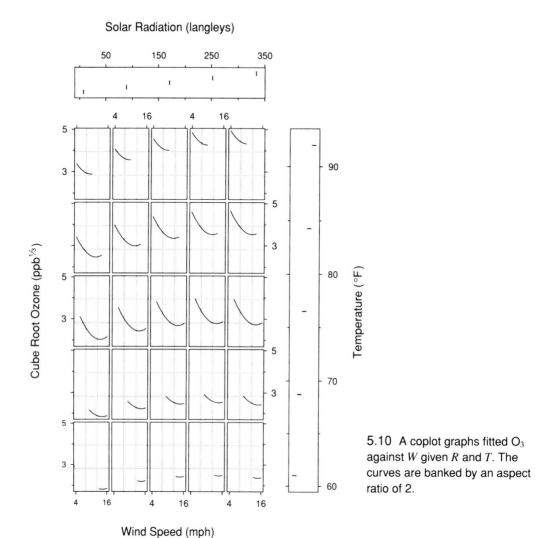

5.10 A coplot graphs fitted O$_3$ against W given R and T. The curves are banked by an aspect ratio of 2.

Solar Radiation (langleys)

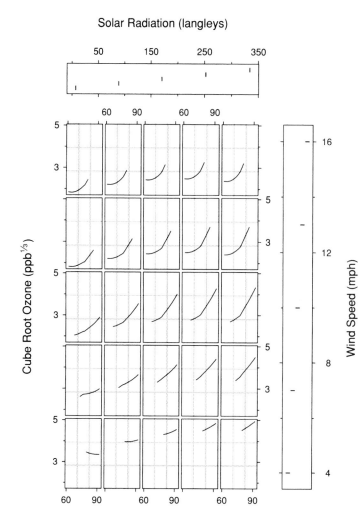

Cube Root Ozone (ppb$^{1/3}$)

Wind Speed (mph)

Temperature (°F)

5.11 A coplot graphs fitted O_3 against T given R and W. The curves are banked by an aspect ratio of 2.

Graphing Residuals

The loess O$_3$ surface appears to fit the data because six displays (not shown here) did not reveal lack of fit — three scatterplots of the residuals against the factors and three coplots of the residuals.

The analysis of the environmental data began with a transformation; taking cube roots of the ozone concentrations symmetrized their distribution. Good fortune was with us because the cube root transformation also cures monotone spread. Figure 5.12 is an s-l plot for a loess fit to concentration without transformation; the parameters are the same as those for the fit to the cube roots. There is monotone spread, an increase in the spread with the fitted values. Logs do not cure the monotone spread. Figure 5.13 is an s-l plot for a loess fit to log concentration with the same parameters as the other fits. The spread decreases as the fitted values increase. Figure 5.14 is an s-l plot for the fit to the cube roots. The spread of the residuals is uniform. The cube root has struck the proper balance.

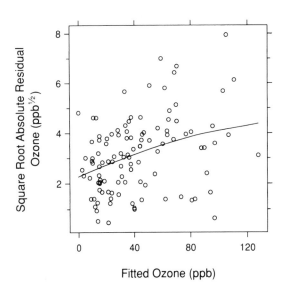

5.12 An s-l plot checks for monotone spread for the loess fit to concentration. The parameters of the loess curve on the graph are $\alpha = 1$ and $\lambda = 1$.

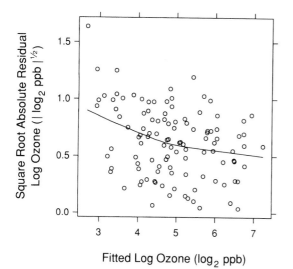

5.13 An s-l plot checks for monotone spread for the loess fit to log concentration. The parameters of the loess curve on the graph are $\alpha = 1$ and $\lambda = 1$.

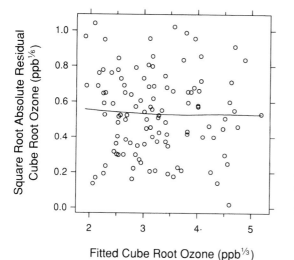

5.14 An s-l plot checks for monotone spread for the loess fit to cube root concentration. The parameters of the loess curve on the graph are $\alpha = 1$ and $\lambda = 1$.

Figure 5.15 is a normal q-q plot for the fit to the cube roots; the distribution of the residuals appears to be well approximated by the normal distribution. Because of this, bisquare was not used in the loess fit. Figure 5.16 is an r-f spread plot. The loess fit has accounted for a sizeable amount of the variation in the data.

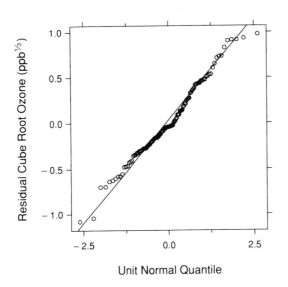

5.15 The normal q-q plot compares the normal distribution with the distribution of the residuals from the loess fit to O_3.

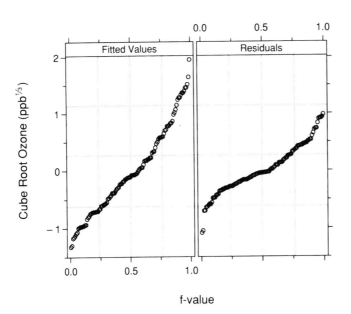

5.16 The r-f spread plot compares the spreads of the residuals and the fitted values minus their mean for the loess fit to O_3.

5.4 Multivariate Distributions

The environmental measurements are factor-response data; the goal is to determine how one variable, O_3, depends on the other three. But for many bivariate, trivariate, and hypervariate data sets, the goal is simply to determine the *multivariate distribution* of the data in the multi-dimensional space of the measurements, rather than determining how the variation in one variable depends on the variation in the others. Methods for visualizing bivariate distributions were given in Chapter 3. One example presented there is the wind speed and temperature measurements that form part of the environmental data. Another example, which we will analyze now, is data with six variables — measurements of the weights of six organs for 73 hamsters from a strain with a congenital heart problem [66]. These hypervariate data consist of 73 points in six-dimensional space.

Visualizing Univariate Distributions

One aspect of any multivariate distribution is the univariate distributions of the individual variables. Figure 5.17 uses box plots to visualize the univariate distributions of the logarithms of the hamster organ weights. Logs are taken because it is more informative to consider ratios of weights. The distributions for lung, heart, kidney, and testes have similar medians, but the liver median is much larger and the spleen median is much smaller. The spreads vary, but they do not increase or decrease with the medians. For the untransformed weights, the spreads increase with the medians, so the log transformation has removed monotone spread.

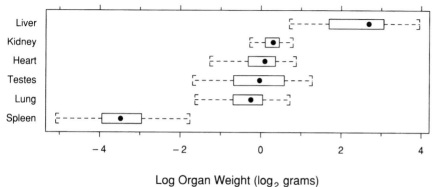

Log Organ Weight (log_2 grams)

5.17 Box plots display the univariate distributions of the log organ weights.

Visualizing Bivariate and Higher-Dimensional Distributions

Another aspect of a multivariate distribution is the bivariate distributions of all pairs of variables. Figure 5.18, a scatterplot matrix of the log organ weights, provides much information about the bivariate distributions. Lung, heart, liver, spleen, and kidney weights are correlated to varying degrees; for example, the liver and spleen weights are highly correlated. The testes weights, however, are not correlated with any of the other organ weights. That is, the testes sizes of hamsters are not related to the sizes of other body organs.

Because the scatterplot matrix allows linking by visual scanning from one panel to the next, we have the opportunity to detect aspects of multivariate distributions that involve more than just the individual bivariate distributions. But the effectiveness of linking can often be substantially increased by the enhanced linking operation of brushing, which was introduced in Chapter 4. This is the case for the log organ weights, as shown in the next section.

5.5 *Direct Manipulation: Enhanced Linking by Brushing*

The (3,4) panel of Figure 5.18, a scatterplot of log spleen weight against log liver weight, shows an outlier: the point to the northwest of the main cloud. The hamster that produced the outlier had either an enlarged spleen and a normal liver, or a small liver and a normal spleen, or perhaps even both a small liver and an enlarged spleen. The hamster has one observation on each panel of the matrix. We need to see all of these observations to help us determine if the hamster had a spleen or liver problem. Scanning to other panels from the outlying point on the (3,4) panel does not readily provide the linking because the density of the data does not let us unambiguously determine the hamster's data on the other panels. But a brush lurking in the (1,1) panel is ready to do its job.

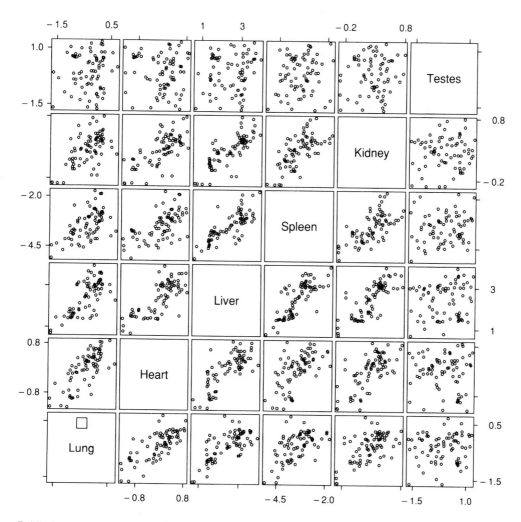

5.18 A scatterplot matrix displays the log organ weights. A brush is resting in the (1,1) panel ready to carry out enhanced linking.

In Figure 5.19, the brush is in the (3,4) panel and covers the outlier. The enhanced linking operation of brushing causes all of the data for the unusual hamster to be graphed by a "+". Row four from the bottom shows the hamster's log spleen weight is large given each of its other log organ weights; for example, its spleen is large compared with the spleens of hamsters that have about the same lung weight. But the panels of row three show that its liver weight is unusual only on the spleen plot. The hamster had an enlarged spleen.

5.6   *Improvisation*

Many of the applications of visualization in this book give the impression that data analysis consists of an orderly progression of exploratory graphs, fitting, and visualization of fits and residuals. Coherence of discussion and limited space necessitate a presentation that appears to imply this. Real life is usually quite different. There are blind alleys. There are mistaken actions. There are effects missed until the very end when some visualization saves the day. And worse, there is the possibility of the nearly unmentionable: missed effects.

One important aspect of reality is improvisation; as a result of special structure in a set of data, or the finding of a visualization method, we stray from the standard methods for the data type to exploit the structure or the finding [3, 30, 76]. A few examples have been given in earlier chapters. Here we present another.

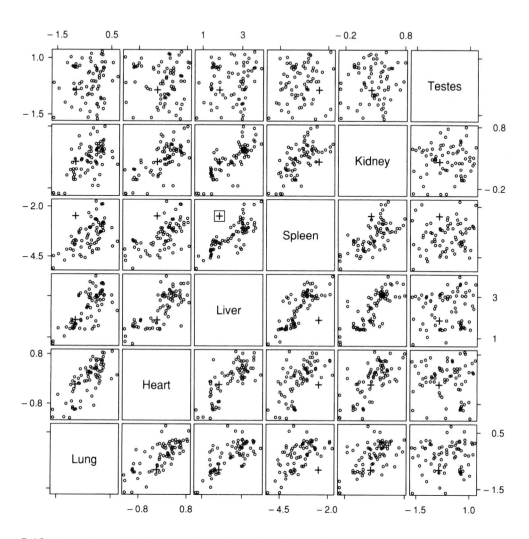

5.19 The enhanced linking operation of brushing shows all observations for one hamster.

Figure 5.20 graphs measurements of four variables — sepal length, sepal width, petal length, and petal width — for a collection of 150 irises [1]. The iris petals are the colorful parts of the flowers that we enjoy when they bloom. The sepals are the leaf-like coverings that protect the petals and other flower parts before blooming. The data, which have been jittered because of exact overlap, consist of 50 irises from each of three varieties: *Iris setosa*, *Iris versicolor*, and *Iris virginica*. Variety

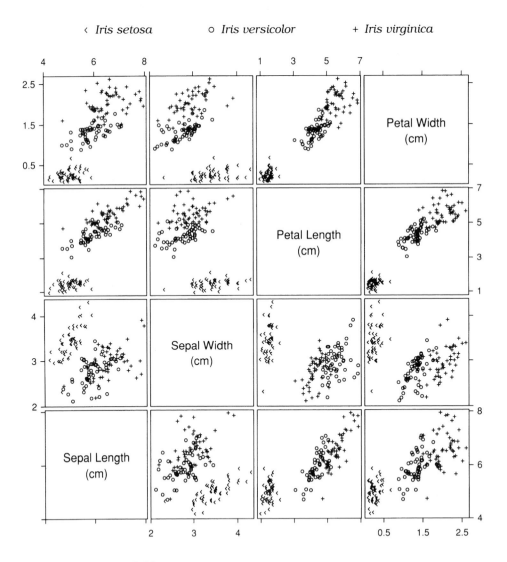

5.20 A scatterplot matrix displays the iris data.

is a categorical variable and its levels are encoded by *texture symbols*, which enhance our ability to visually separate the three sets of data [21].

Despite the jittering and the use of the texture symbols, not every plotting symbol appears with clarity because so many symbols are shown, 1800 in all. The most severe problems occur in panels (3,4) and (4,3). We cannot identify every symbol in the tight cluster that appears to contain only *setosa*. But linking provides a solution. Starting at panel (3,4) and scanning to both of the panels to the left, we can see that the observations are indeed *setosa*.

Panel (2,3) reveals an outlier: one iris in the *setosa* category with an unusually small sepal width. In this case, we can scan to find the corresponding observations on the other panels; unlike for the hamster data, we do not need the enhanced linking of brushing. First, if we scan up and down in column 2, we clearly see the observations for the unusual iris on all panels. Similarly, we can see them clearly on all panels of row 2. The positions on all other panels can be determined by scanning from both row 2 and column 2, forming cross hairs of sorts. For example, we can fix the position on panel (1,3) by scanning up from panel (1,2) and scanning to the left from panel (2,3). The scanning reveals that the sepal width is the only aspect of the iris that is unusual.

Classification

The goal in analyzing the iris data is to develop a rule based on the widths and lengths of petals and sepals that would assist in determining the variety of an iris. Panel (4,3) of Figure 5.20 shows interesting behavior that suggests there might be a simple rule. The three varieties are well separated along an axis that runs from the lower left corner to the upper right. Along this axis, *setosa* is completely separated from the others, and the amount of overlap of *versicolor* and *virginica* is small. From the lower left to the upper right along this axis, both the petal length and the petal width increase, so the axis is a measure of petal size. The petals of *setosa* are smaller than those of *versicolor*, which in turn tend to be smaller than those of *virginica*.

A simple measure of petal size is the product of length and width. Also, the ratio of length to width is a measure of petal elongation. This triggers an idea, an improvisation that arises from observing the size effect. If we take the logs of both petal length and width, the mean of the two values for each flower is another size measure: the log of the square root of the above product. And the difference of the logs is another elongation measure: the log of the above ratio. It makes sense to graph one measure against the other. But this is just a Tukey m-d plot of the log width and log length.

The m-d plot is shown in Figure 5.21. The graph reveals several interesting patterns. First, the elongation tends to decrease as the size increases; in other words, as the petals become bigger they also become

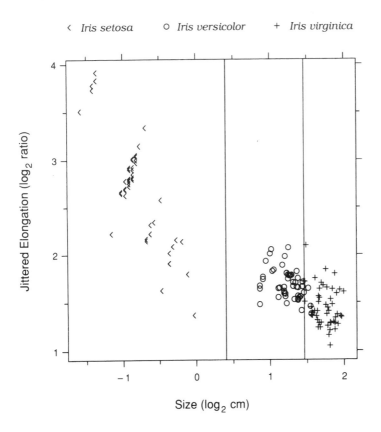

5.21 A measure of petal elongation is graphed against a measure of petal size.

less elongated. Interestingly, the pattern occurs both within and between varieties. Second, size completely separates *setosa* from the other two varieties, and it nearly separates *versicolor* and *virginica*. A classification rule is shown by the two vertical lines in Figure 5.21, which are drawn at

$$c_1 = 0.4 \log_2 \text{cm}$$

and at

$$c_2 = 1.46 \log_2 \text{cm} .$$

The variety *setosa* is chosen if size is less than c_1; *versicolor* is chosen if size is between c_1 and c_2; and *virginica* is chosen if size is above c_2. These two values minimize the errors of classification for the 150 irises in the data set. Only four of the irises are misclassified by the rule, so the petal size measure provides good assistance in variety identification, at least for this set of data.

5.7   Visualization and Probabilistic Inference

The iris data have a long and interesting history. They were originally collected by a botanist who reported them in 1935 [1]. In 1936, R. A. Fisher used the data to illustrate his mathematical method of classification [37]. After Fisher's treatment, the iris measurements became canonical data that have been used by a multitude of people as an example to illustrate other mathematical methods for analyzing multivariate data.

The irony is that visualization of the iris data reveals more about their structure than the previous long list of analyses by numerical statistical methods. For example, the reliable classification into variety simply by petal size, and the existence of an outlier, are two insights missed by these purely numerical methods of probabilistic inference. One wonders if the iris data would have become a canonical data set had they been visualized in 1936, revealing so thoroughly to all the structure of the data.

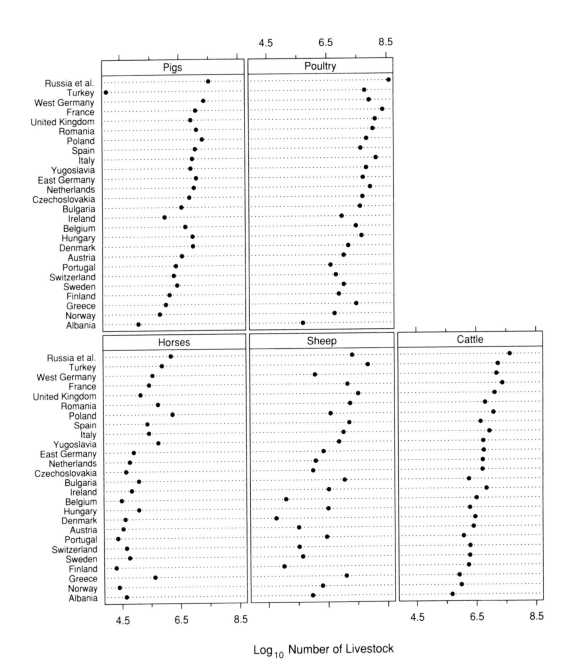

6.1 A multiway dot plot displays multiway data: log counts of five types of livestock in 26 countries.

6 Multiway Data

Figure 6.1 graphs the logarithms of livestock counts from a 1987 census of farm animals in 26 countries [14]. Logs are taken at the outset because the counts vary by about 4.5 powers of 10; if the data were graphed on the original scale, only the variability in a few large observations would be visible. Russia *et al.* is the European part of Russia and the European countries that were formerly part of the Soviet Union.

The census has a purpose that would be hard to guess — to study air pollution. The feces and urine of livestock produce ammonia, an air pollutant. The livestock counts are combined with estimates of the amounts of ammonia emitted by the wastes of different animals to provide a release rate of ammonia into the atmosphere of Europe. The counts in Figure 6.1 lead to an estimate of 5.2 megatons per year; this accounts for 81% of all ammonia emissions.

The log counts in Figure 6.1 are *multiway data*. There is one quantitative variable, log count, and two categorical variables, country and livestock type. The quantitative variable is a response, and the goal is to study how it depends on the categorical variables, which are factors. What distinguishes multiway data is the cross-classification of the categorical variables; there is a value of the response for each combination of levels of the two categorical variables. In this case, there is one log count for each combination of country and livestock type.

6.1 Multiway Dot Plots

The visualization method of Figure 6.1 is a *multiway dot plot*. There are *panels*, the individual dot plots of the display, and there are *levels*, the rows of each panel. In Figure 6.1, the livestock variable is encoded by the panels and the country variable is encoded by the levels.

The countries are assigned to the levels so that the country medians increase from bottom to top. The median of the five observations for Albania is the smallest country median. Norway has the next smallest country median, and Russia *et al.* has the largest. The panels are ordered so that the livestock medians increase in graphical order: from left to right and from bottom to top. The median for horses is the smallest, and the median for poultry is the largest.

Figure 6.1 shows that the amount of variation in the log counts for sheep is greater than that of the other livestock types; in other words, the ordering of the sheep data agrees the least well with the ordering of the country medians. The log pig counts show interesting behavior. There is an unusually low number of pigs in Turkey. Even though it is near the top in log counts overall, it has the fewest pigs. Albania has a small number of pigs as well, but its value is not nearly as deviant as that of Turkey because overall, Albania is at the bottom in log counts. And Ireland also has a small number of pigs in the sense that other countries nearby in the median ordering have more pigs.

Figure 6.2 displays the data by a second multiway dot plot, but this time the livestock variable has been assigned to the levels, and the country variable has been assigned to the panels. The display shows that for Turkey and Albania, sheep are the most abundant animal; this makes up for the lack of pigs. But for all other countries, poultry are the most abundant. The log count for pigs in Turkey is so small that it is exceeded by the log count of horses, whereas in all other countries, horses are the least abundant category.

Visual Perception

As with all display methods in this book, the display method of the multiway dot plot is based on a careful consideration of visual perception.

One visual issue is an asymmetry in the perception of the effects of the categorical variables. We can more effectively compare values within a panel than values between panels. Consider Figure 6.1 where the levels encode the country and the panels encode the livestock type.

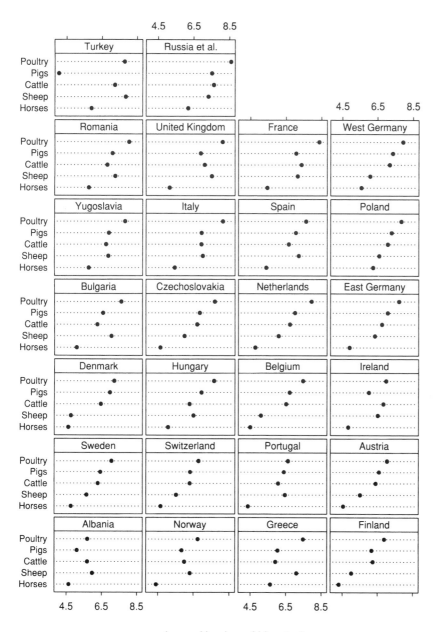

6.2 The log counts are graphed again with the livestock variable assigned to the levels and the country variable assigned to the panels.

The country values for each livestock type can be perceived as a gestalt because they are graphed along a single scale line. For example, this contributes to our ability to perceive the greater variation in the sheep data. We can, of course, readily compare these gestalts from one panel to the next; this allows us to assess how the distribution of values changes as the panel category changes. But in Figure 6.1 we cannot compare the five values for a given country as effectively. This is done far better in Figure 6.2, where the livestock type is assigned to the levels. For example, we can readily perceive that in Finland, poultry have the largest log count and horses have the smallest; this cannot be as readily perceived in Figure 6.1. Because of this asymmetry, it is often important to explore multiway data by as many multiway dot plots as there are categorical variables, with each variable assigned once to the levels.

Another visual issue is the orderings of the levels and panels by a measure of the category locations, in this case, the median. The orderings are crucial to the perception of effects. The ordering of the levels by country median in Figure 6.1 establishes gestalts on each panel that are easier to compare from one panel to the next. For example, this allows us to see that the sheep behave differently from the other livestock types. Also, the level ordering provides a benchmark for the log count for each livestock type — the values of the nearby log counts. For example, Figure 6.1 shows that the small log cattle count in Albania is not unusually small given the overall rank of Albania, but the number of pigs in Ireland is unusually small given the overall rank of Ireland.

In Figure 6.3, the log counts are displayed again with the levels ordered alphabetically and the panels ordered arbitrarily. Many of the effects readily seen in Figure 6.1 are not revealed. The sheep data no longer stand out as particularly unusual, and we cannot see that the log pig count in Ireland is low or that the log sheep count in Greece is high.

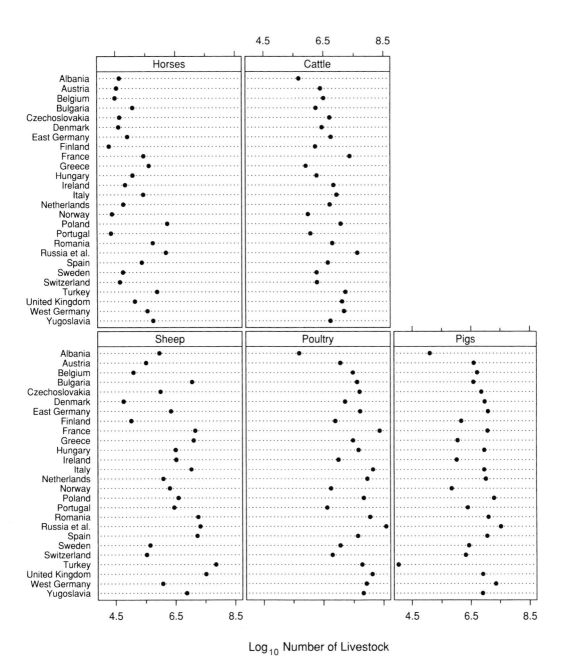

6.3 The levels and panels on this multiway dot plot of the log counts are not ordered by category median. The levels are ordered alphabetically and the panels are ordered arbitrarily.

6.2   Additive Fits

There are many mathematical functions that can be fitted to multiway data [52]. The simplest is an additive function.

An Additive Parametric Function

Let $y_{\ell c}$ denote the log count for the ℓth livestock category and the cth country category. The additive function for the log livestock counts is a parametric function of ℓ and c,

$$\mu + \alpha_\ell + \beta_c .$$

The parameter μ measures the overall value of the response. We will constrain the remaining parameters, which are the *main effects*, by

$$\sum_{\ell=1}^{5} \alpha_\ell = \sum_{c=1}^{26} \beta_c = 0 .$$

The parameters α_ℓ are the livestock main effects, and the parameters β_c are the country main effects.

The additive function does not provide for an interaction between country and livestock. The change in the function in going from livestock type i to livestock type j, $\alpha_j - \alpha_i$, is the same for all countries. Similarly, the change in the function in going from country i to country j, $\beta_j - \beta_i$, is the same for all livestock types. If the additive function provided a good fit to the data, the underlying patterns of the log counts on the panels of either Figure 6.1 or 6.2 would have the same overall shape but simply shift left and right. There would be no interaction between country and livestock type. This is clearly not the case for the log livestock counts; for example, the sheep pattern is quite different from the others. But even when an interaction is present in multiway data, fitting an additive function can be useful; the interaction becomes part of the residuals, and visualization of the residuals can give a clearer picture of the properties of the interaction than we get in exploratory graphs of the unfitted data.

Least-Squares and Bisquare

Least-squares can be used to fit an additive function to multiway data. For the log livestock counts, $y_{\ell c}$, least-squares determines values of μ, α_ℓ, and β_c that minimize

$$\sum_{\ell=1}^{5} \sum_{c=1}^{26} (y_{\ell c} - \mu - \alpha_\ell - \beta_c)^2 .$$

The minimizing values, which are the estimates of the parameters, have a simple form. The estimate of μ is the overall mean of the data,

$$\widehat{\mu} = \frac{1}{130} \sum_{\ell=1}^{5} \sum_{c=1}^{26} y_{\ell c} .$$

The estimate of α_ℓ is the mean across countries for livestock type ℓ, minus the overall mean,

$$\widehat{\alpha}_\ell = \frac{1}{26} \sum_{c=1}^{26} y_{\ell c} - \widehat{\mu} .$$

The estimate of β_c is the mean across livestock types for country c, minus the overall mean,

$$\widehat{\beta}_c = \frac{1}{5} \sum_{\ell=1}^{5} y_{\ell c} - \widehat{\mu} .$$

The fitted values are

$$\widehat{y}_{\ell c} = \widehat{\mu} + \widehat{\alpha}_\ell + \widehat{\beta}_c$$

and the residuals are

$$\widehat{\varepsilon}_{\ell c} = y_{\ell c} - \widehat{y}_{\ell c} .$$

If the initial visualization of multiway data by dot plots suggests aberrant behavior in the data, bisquare fitting can be used to fit the additive function. The robustness iterations are the same as those for the data types discussed in earlier chapters. First, the function is fitted by least-squares; in succeeding steps, robustness weights are computed and the function is re-fitted using weighted least-squares. Quite clearly, the log livestock counts contain aberrant behavior, for example, the exceptionally low log pig count in Turkey, so we will use bisquare.

Figure 6.4 graphs the bisquare estimates of the main effects. Russia *et al.* have the largest country main effect, and Albania has the smallest. Poultry have the largest livestock main effect and horses have the smallest. It seems likely that the country main effects are related to the populations and areas of the countries, but we will not check this further here. The country main effects vary by about 1.5 on the log scale, which is a factor of $10^{1.5} \approx 30$. The livestock main effects vary by about 2.5, which is a factor of 10 greater. The country main effects are spread out uniformly across their range, but the livestock main effects have one large value, one small value, and three similar values somewhat above the middle of the range.

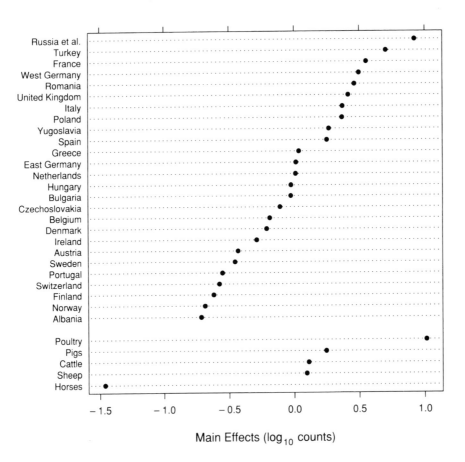

6.4 The dot plot displays the bisquare estimates of the country and livestock main effects.

The display method of the multiway dot plot, as discussed in detail earlier, orders the levels and panels by category medians. For the log livestock counts, each country median is a location measure of the five log counts for the country, and each livestock median is a location measure of the 26 log counts for the livestock type. The bisquare fitting has provided new location measures. The livestock locations are

$$\widehat{\mu} + \widehat{\alpha}_\ell$$

and the country locations are

$$\widehat{\mu} + \widehat{\beta}_c \ .$$

Figures 6.5 and 6.6 are dot plots with the panels and levels ordered by the new location measures, which, of course, is the same as ordering by the estimates of the main effects. No substantially new insight is gained, in part because the new and old orderings are similar. But the new ordering will be used for subsequent visualization of the residuals and fitted values, and having Figures 6.5 and 6.6 will be important when we are stimulated by patterns in the subsequent graphs to look back at the data.

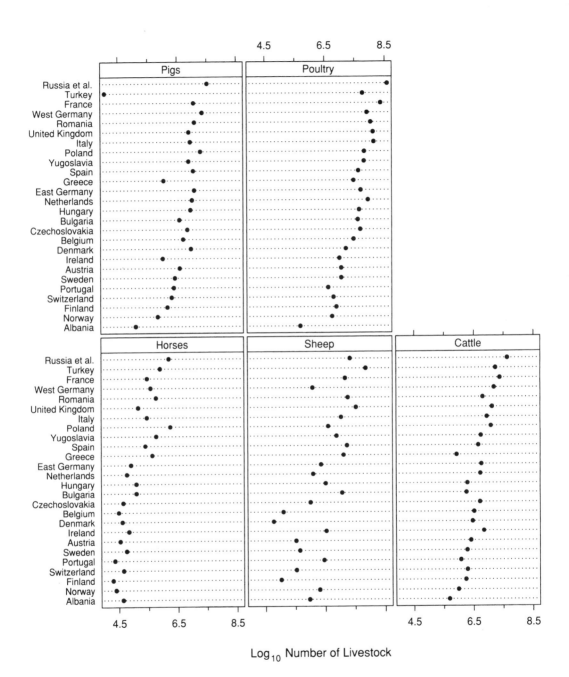

Log$_{10}$ Number of Livestock

6.5 On this multiway dot plot of the log counts, the levels and panels are ordered by the bisquare estimates of the main effects.

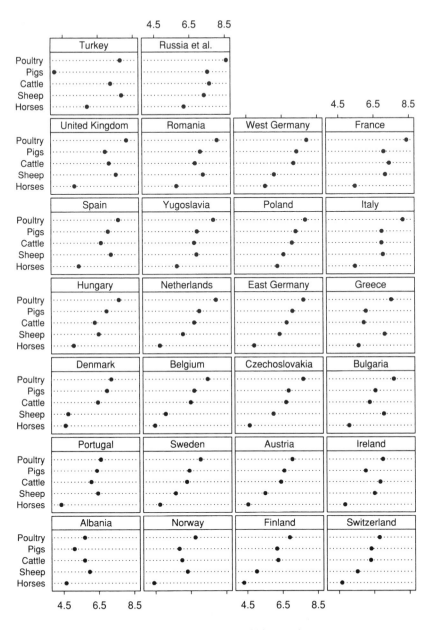

6.6 On this multiway dot plot of the log counts, the levels and panels are ordered by the bisquare estimates of the main effects.

Graphing Fitted Values and Residuals

Figures 6.7 and 6.8 graph the fitted values of the log counts. For each
dot plot, the shapes of the patterns of the points on the panels are the

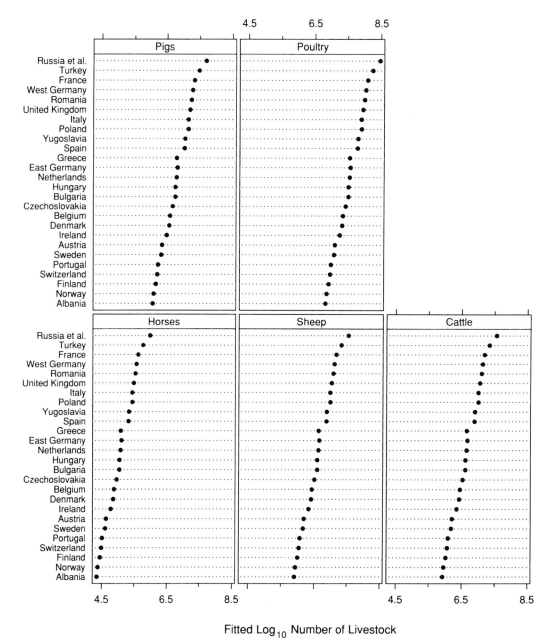

Fitted Log$_{10}$ Number of Livestock

6.7 The multiway dot plot shows the additive fit to the log counts.

same, and the patterns simply shift left and right according to the main
effects. As explained earlier, this is a feature of the additivity of the fitted
function, which results in no interaction between the two categorical
variables.

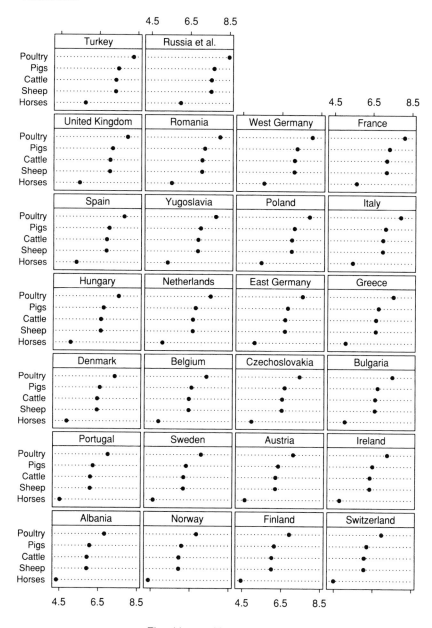

Fitted Log$_{10}$ Number of Livestock

6.8 The multiway dot plot shows the additive fit to the log counts.

The residuals are graphed in Figures 6.9 and 6.10. The scale of the residuals is log base 2 because most of them vary only by about 1 on a log base 10 scale. The residual for pigs in Turkey has been omitted because it ruins the resolution of the display; including it requires an expansion of the horizontal scale by about 70%.

A large residual indicates an over-population of the livestock type in the country, and a small residual indicates an under-population. For example, Poland has the largest horse residual, 2.7 $\log_2$ count. Given the main effect for Poland and the main effect for horses, there are more horses in Poland than one would expect by a factor of $2^{2.7} = 6.5$. In other words, Poland is horse country. Turkey and Albania have the smallest pig residuals. For both countries, the under-population of pigs is due to religious dietary laws. Turkey and Greece have the greatest over-population of sheep; anyone who has been to a Turkish or Greek restaurant knows why. Denmark has the greatest under-population of sheep, but perhaps to make up for it, the greatest over-population of pigs.

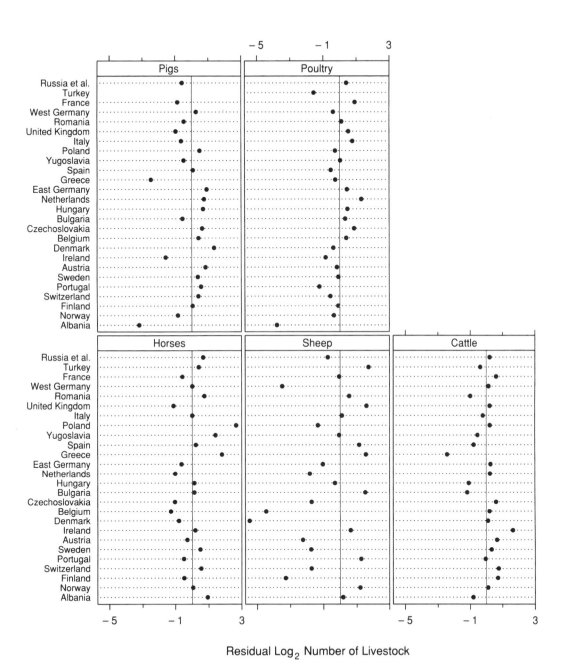

6.9 The multiway dot plot displays the residuals from the additive fit to the log counts.

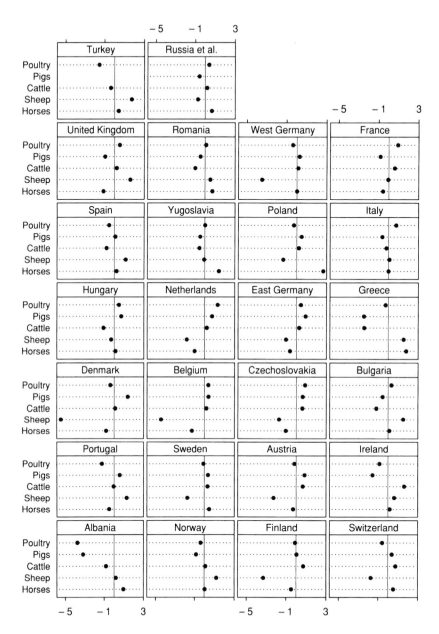

Residual Log$_2$ Number of Livestock

6.10 The multiway dot plot displays the residuals from the additive fit to the log counts.

The residuals are clearly not homogeneous. Sheep have greater
residual variation than the other livestock types. For many countries,
the sheep residual is either the largest or the smallest of the five residuals
for the country. Careful study of the multiway dot plots of the residuals
suggests a geographic influence. This is investigated in Figure 6.11; the
residuals are displayed by a level plot. The equal-count method has
been used to select the three intervals, whose fraction of overlap is 0.25.

Geography does appear to account for a part of the sheep variation.
Countries in a contiguous region covering central Europe and most of
Scandinavia have the smallest residuals; that is, they have fewer sheep
than predicted by the fitted function. As we move outward from this
region, the residuals tend to increase and are largest at the boundaries of
the region to the south and northwest. We could fit the dependence on
geographical location with loess, but we will not do so, since we have
treated the data sufficiently for our purposes.

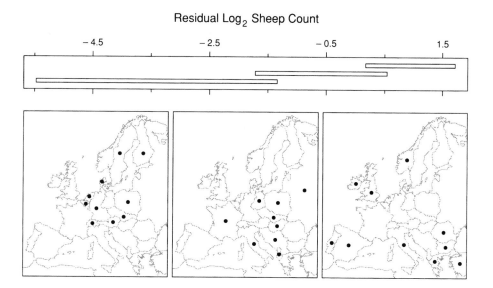

6.11 The level plot shows the dependence of the sheep residuals on geographical
location.

6.3 *Superposition and Differences*

Sorting data from smallest to largest is one of the fundamental tasks of software systems. Through the decades, as computers developed, so did sorting algorithms, with ever increasing advances in efficiency. By 1992, one might have thought that the practical limits in efficiency had been nearly reached, and that any further work would yield only small gains.

But in 1992, Jon Bentley and Douglas McIllroy became interested in qsort, a sort program in UNIX$^®$, because of reports of disastrously poor performance for several highly structured examples. For example, qsort was utterly undone by the triangular sequence

$$1, 2, \ldots, n - 1, n, n, n - 1, \ldots, 2, 1 .$$

Bentley and McIllroy promptly invented a new algorithm that solved the problems. And while they were at it, they set new speed records for general sequences, beating the old ones by a wide margin.

As part of their investigation of run-time performance, Bentley and McIllroy generated random sequences of length 10^4, and sorted them with three algorithms: their new one, the qsort program in the Berkeley version of UNIX, and the qsort program in the Seventh Edition version. They tested on two machines: a VAX 8550 and a MIPS R3000. There were six input types for the sequences: integer, float, double, pointer, record, and string. For each combination of algorithm, machine, and input type they generated and sorted 10 sequences and computed the average run time. The times are multiway data with $3 \times 2 \times 6 = 36$ observations. It makes sense to take logs at the outset since multiplicative factors are important, not absolute run times.

Figure 6.12 graphs the log run times. The algorithm factor has been assigned to the panel levels. The panels are arranged in a rectangular array with the machine factor assigned to the columns and the input factor assigned to the rows. The ordering of the levels and panels depends on the category medians as it did for the exploratory dot plots of the livestock data. The algorithm medians increase as the levels increase from bottom to top, the input medians increase from bottom to top through the rows of the panels, and the machine medians increase from left to right through the columns.

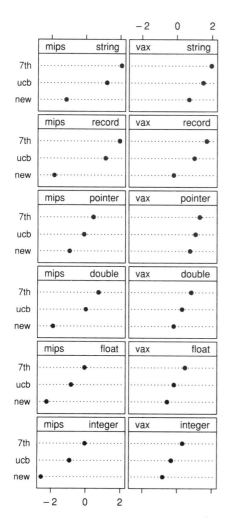

Log Run Time (log$_2$ seconds)

6.12 The multiway dot plot graphs log run times for three algorithms, two machines, and six input types.

Superposition

In Figure 6.12, the assignment of the algorithm factor to the panel levels allows us to readily assess its effect on log run time. The pattern of the three log run times on each panel can be readily perceived, and the 12 patterns can be compared. To enhance the assessment of the effect of the machine factor, we could assign it to the panel levels, but Figure 6.13 uses another method: superposition. The machine factor is encoded by the symbol type. Now its effect can be assessed for each combination of algorithm and input by comparing the two symbols on each panel level. The symbol encoding succeeds because there are only two machine categories. Superposition is used again in Figure 6.14, where the input factor is assigned to the panel levels, which allows better assessment of the effect of input.

The decrease in run time of the Bentley-McIllroy algorithm is impressive. Figure 6.12 shows that it beats Seventh Edition and Berkeley in every case. The improvement gets as large as 3.8 $\log_2$ sec, a factor of 14. The figure also shows that the size of the improvement depends on the machine and the input. The size is greater for the Mips than for the Vax. Pointers stand out as a special case; on each machine, the log run times for pointers are less spread out than for any other input.

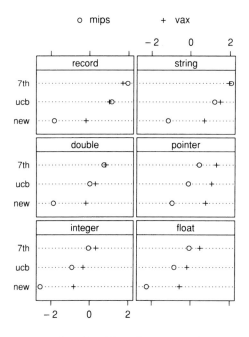

6.13 The log run times are graphed by a multiway dot plot with superposition.

Figure 6.13 shows that the effect of the machine factor for the new algorithm is much greater than for the other two. Furthermore, the machine effect for the new algorithm is stable; the log run time for the new algorithm on the Vax minus the log run time on the Mips, is always close to about $1.75 \log_2$ sec. For the other two algorithms, the machine effect depends on the input type; it is close to zero for record, string, and double, but is larger for other inputs.

Figure 6.14 shows the patterns for Seventh Edition and Berkeley have similar shapes that appear to be separated by an additive shift of Berkeley toward smaller log times. In other words, Seventh Edition and Berkeley behave very similarly except that Berkeley is somewhat faster by a constant number of $\log_2$ sec.

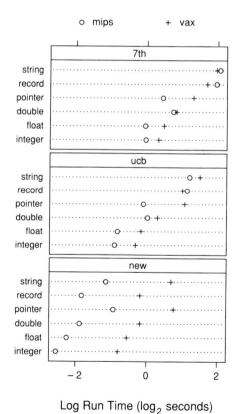

6.14 The log run times are graphed by a multiway dot plot with superposition and with the input type encoded by the panel levels.

Log Run Time ($\log_2$ seconds)

Differences

For the log run-time data, the categorical variable of chief interest is
the algorithm. The experiment was not carried out to compare the speed
of sorting on Vax and Mips machines or by input type. Machine and
input enter only because the relative performance of the different
algorithms depends on them. Furthermore, we are primarily interested,
not in the comparison of Berkeley and Seventh edition, but rather in the
magnitude of the improvement provided by the new algorithm. We can
focus on this improvement by visualizing a new data set derived from
the old — differences of log run times. The differences are graphed in
Figure 6.15. The circles display the Berkeley log times minus the new log
run times for all combinations of machine and input. Similarly, the plus
signs display the Seventh Edition log times minus the new log times.
The levels and panels have been ordered by the category means of the
differences. Means have been used instead of medians since the
exploratory visualization showed the data to be well behaved.

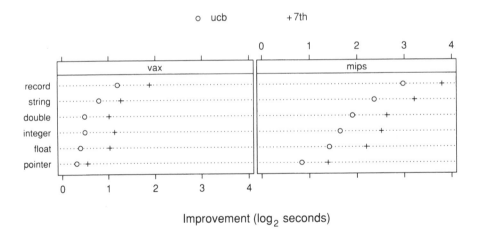

Improvement (log$_2$ seconds)

6.15 Each value graphed on this multiway dot plot is a Vax or Mips log run time minus
the log run time of the new algorithm for the same input and machine.

On each panel of Figure 6.15, the overall patterns of the two sets of
points are about the same, but simply shifted. In other words, for each
machine, the data are additive. But we do not have such additivity
across machines; the patterns for the Vax are quite different from those
for the Mips, although the order of the values for each of the four cases
— Vax-7th, Vax-Berkeley, Mips-7th, Mips-Berkeley — is nearly the same.

Figure 6.15 suggests that we fit a function that is additive in input and algorithm for each machine separately. In other words, in the fitting, we treat the data for each machine separately and fit an additive function in each case. Let m index the two machines, let i index the six input types, and let a index the two algorithms. The form of the function is

$$\mu^{(m)} + \alpha_i^{(m)} + \beta_a^{(m)} \, .$$

For each of the two machines, the input main effects

$$\alpha_i^{(m)}$$

sum to zero and the algorithm main effects,

$$\beta_j^{(m)}$$

sum to zero. Since the data appear to be well behaved, we will not employ bisquare in the fitting.

Figure 6.16 graphs the residuals; no strong effect of the variables appears to remain. In other words, there is no discernible lack of fit, so the function fits the data.

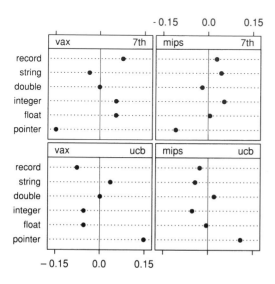

6.16 The multiway dot plot graphs the residuals from the fit to the differences.

Residual Improvement (log$_2$ seconds)

Figure 6.17 is an r-f spread plot. The residuals are contained within $\pm 0.15 \log_2$ sec, which means that on the original scale, the fitted function predicts run-time improvement to within factors of

$$2^{\pm 0.15} = 1 \pm 0.1 \ .$$

Thus the fitted function accounts for most of the variation in the data.

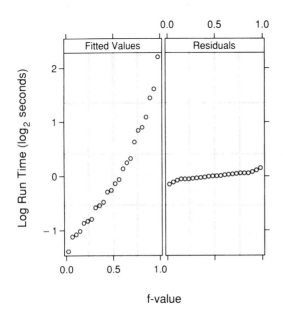

6.17 The r-f spread plot compares the spreads of the residuals and the fitted values minus their mean for the fit to the log run-time differences.

The additivity for each machine allows a simpler characterization of the improvement. For the Mips, the algorithm main effects are $-0.38 \log_2$ sec for Berkeley and $0.38 \log_2$ sec for Seventh Edition. Thus the change in the Mips fit for any input type in going from Seventh Edition to Berkeley is $-0.76 \log_2$ sec, which is a factor of $2^{-0.76} = 0.6$. In other words, on the Mips, the improvements over Berkeley are 0.6 times the improvements over Seventh Edition. A similar statement holds for the Vax with a factor of 0.7. Thus we need only consider in detail the improvement of the new algorithm over either Berkeley or Seventh Edition to understand the effect of machine and input. This is done in Figure 6.18, which displays the fit for the improvement over Seventh Edition on the $\log_2$ scale, and in Figure 6.19, which displays the fit as a factor on the original scale.

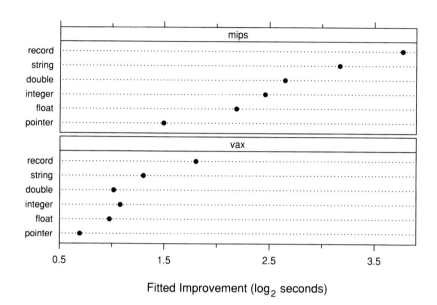

6.18 The fitted values for Seventh Edition are displayed.

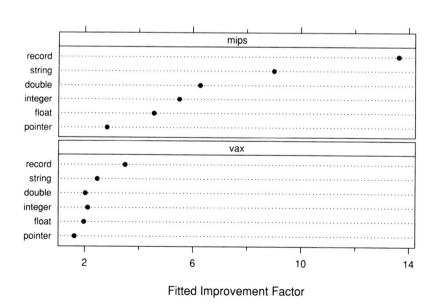

6.19 The fitted values for Seventh Edition are displayed as improvement factors.

6.4   *The Case of the Anomalous Barley Site*

The book ends as it began, with the barley data. There is a mystery — anomalous data at the Morris site. Its unraveling, to come next, provides strong testimony to the themes stressed in the book.

The Barley Data

Let us review the facts of the data. Ten varieties of barley were grown at six sites in Minnesota in each of two years, 1931 and 1932. Thus there are $10 \times 6 \times 2 = 120$ yields. The data first appeared in 1934 in the *Journal of Agronomy* [55].

The story of the data actually begins earlier, in the 1920s in England, where R. A. Fisher was establishing the foundations of statistical experimental design and modern statistical inference [38, 39]. Fisher was a brilliant scientist who also was a pioneer of mathematical genetics. His work in statistics would go on to permeate all of science and have a profound effect on the everyday lives of scientists.

Fisher's work in statistical experimental design began at the Rothamsted Agricultural Experiment Station, where he was employed for over a decade before he took the post of Galton Professor at University College London in 1933. Fisher revolutionized how people approached experiments. When he began his work, the prevailing wisdom was that only one factor should be varied at a time in a single experiment to keep investigations simple. Fisher demolished this notion. He showed by a combination of empirical and mathematical work that simultaneous variation of the levels of several factors in certain systematic ways in single experiments is far more efficient. Even more, Fisher showed how to assess the precision of estimates of factor effects. His method, now a mainstay of science, is called the *analysis of variance*, or *ANOVA*. Yates and Mather wrote in 1963 [82]:

> ... the new ideas on experimental design and analysis soon came to be accepted by practical research workers, and the methods have now been almost universally adopted, not only in agriculture but in all subjects which require investigation of highly variable material. The recent spectacular advances in agricultural production in many parts of the world owe much to their consistent use.

The barley experiment was significant because it was one of the first uses of Fisher's ideas. Fisher later reported the data from five sites, including Morris, in *The Design of Experiments* [39], which became the classic in experimental design, setting out the foundations of the subject. The fame of the book made the data famous, and they were re-analyzed by others, serving as an example for new methods of statistical science.

Exploratory Dot Plots

Figure 6.20 graphs the barley data by a multiway dot plot. The variety variable is assigned to the panel levels, the growing site is assigned to the panel rows, and the year is assigned to the columns. The order of the levels and panels is by category median. The variety medians increase from bottom to top through the levels, the year medians increase from left to right through the panel columns, and the site medians increase from bottom to top through the panel rows.

Figure 6.20 clearly shows the Morris anomaly: a reversal of the yearly effects. But the display also conveys a pattern that is crucial to understanding the reversal. As we proceed from bottom to top through either column of site panels, the overall levels of the sites increase, except for Morris. Furthermore, the two patterns without Morris are roughly the same except that 1931 is shifted toward higher values. Finally, and most importantly, the visual impression is that if the years for Morris were interchanged, the Morris data would then fit the pattern.

The data are shown with the interchange in Figure 6.21. Now Morris does indeed fit the pattern. In other words, given the overall median of Morris, its 1932 values fit into the 1931 pattern of the other sites, and its 1931 values fit into the 1932 pattern. The interchange has produced greater harmony in the data. But this is a serious step, not to be taken lightly. We will persist in analyzing the altered data, assessing the effect of the alteration and studying further whether it is justified.

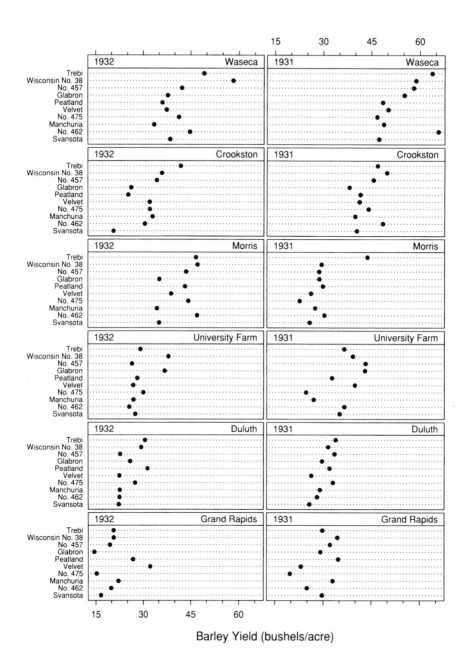

6.20 The multiway dot plot graphs barley yield at six sites for two years and ten varieties.

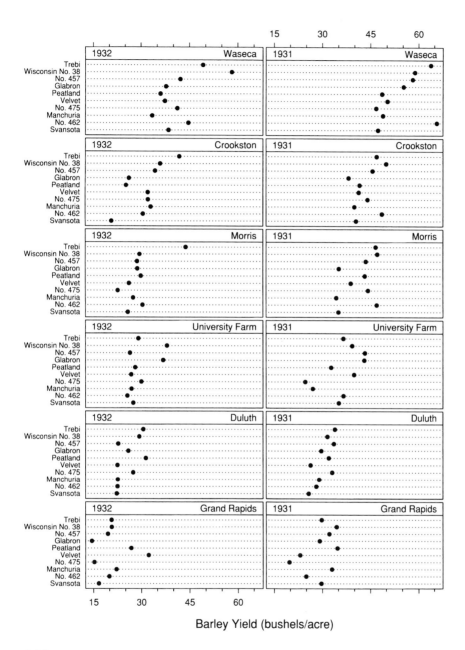

6.21 The barley data are displayed again with the 1931 and 1932 yields at Morris interchanged.

Visualizing the Altered Data

The chief issue at the moment is the year effect. The situation is similar to that of the previous section where the categorical variable targeted for study was the algorithm factor. Here, as there, we will take differences to focus on the targeted variable.

Figure 6.22 displays the 1931 yield minus the 1932 yield for each combination of site and variety. The order of the sites and varieties remains as in previous displays, so as we go from bottom to top through the panels, the median site yield increases, and as we go from bottom to top through the levels on each panel, the median variety yield increases. This allows us to assess whether there is a relationship between the differences and the site medians or between the differences and the variety medians. One noticeable effect on the display is that from bottom to top, the overall level of the differences at each site tends to increase. In other words, the effect of year at the different sites tends to increase as the overall site level increases. There is an interaction between site and year. The only site that appears to deviate from this pattern is Grand Rapids, not Morris. A similar interaction between variety and year does not appear to be present; no panel shows any tendency for the differences to increase.

An increase in the effect of one factor as the overall level of another factor increases is an exceedingly common form of interaction. Thus the interaction between site and year uncovered by Figure 6.22 is not surprising. Morris fits right into the pattern of this interaction. Thus the interchange of the years appears to be striking an even more harmonious chord than we previously expected.

But Figure 6.22 reveals new aberrant behavior. There is an unusually low value for Velvet at Grand Rapids, about −9 bushels/acre. In other words, the 1932 Velvet yield exceeds by a large margin the 1931 Velvet yield. We will resist the temptation to interchange the years, but the behavior of the two values makes it clear that for our fitting, coming next, we will need bisquare.

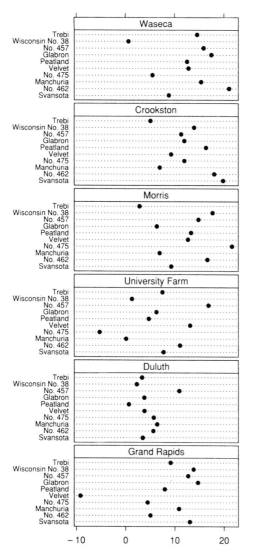

Differences of Barley Yield (bushels/acre)

6.22 The multiway dot plot displays the 1931 yields minus the 1932 yields for the altered data.

Fitting the Altered Data

The fit to the altered yields must account for the interaction between year and site. This is done by the function

$$b_{vys} = \mu + \alpha_v + \beta_{ys} \, ,$$

where v indexes the variety, y indexes the year, and s indexes the site. The 10 variety main effects, α_v, sum to zero and the 12 year-site interaction effects, β_{ys}, also sum to zero. Again, we will use bisquare to do the fitting. Figure 6.23 is an r-f spread plot; the fitted function accounts for much of the variation in the data.

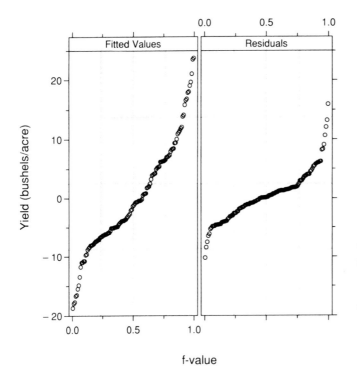

6.23 The r-f spread plot compares the spreads of the residuals and the fitted values minus their mean for the bisquare fit to the altered data.

The bisquare estimates of the year-site effects are shown in Figure 6.24. The pattern of the interaction between year and site, spotted in the data, is also evident here; as the mean of the two interaction effects for each location increases, the difference tends to increase. Figure 6.25 graphs the estimates of the variety effects. Amidst our interest in the Morris anomaly, it should not be forgotten that the original goal of the experiment was to investigate the performance of the different barley varieties. Trebi and Wisconsin No. 38 are the clear winners. Svansota is the loser. The range of the variety main effects, −3.4 bushels/acre to 4.5 bushels/acre, covers 7.9 bushels/acre. The range of the year-site interaction effects is considerably greater and covers 34.5 bushels/acre, which is a factor of about 4.5 greater. Thus, while selection of the best variety can improve yield, the changes in growing conditions that occur with changes in geography and time are clearly far more influential.

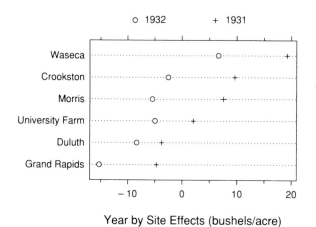

6.24 The dot plot graphs the bisquare estimates of the year-site interaction effects for the altered data.

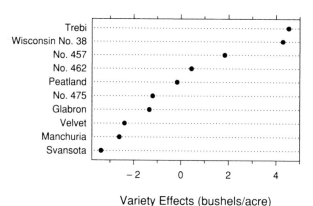

6.25 The dot plot graphs the bisquare estimates of the variety main effects for the altered data.

Figures 6.26 and 6.27 graph the residuals. We have not bothered to re-order the panels by the estimated effects, maintaining the category-median ordering of the exploratory visualization of the data. The reason is that no consistent pattern appears. The relatively simple fitted function appears to fit the data satisfactorily.

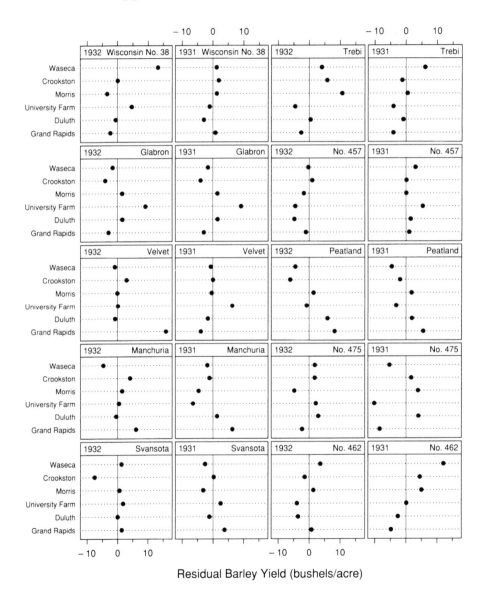

Residual Barley Yield (bushels/acre)

6.26 The multiway dot plot displays the residuals from the bisquare fit to the altered barley data.

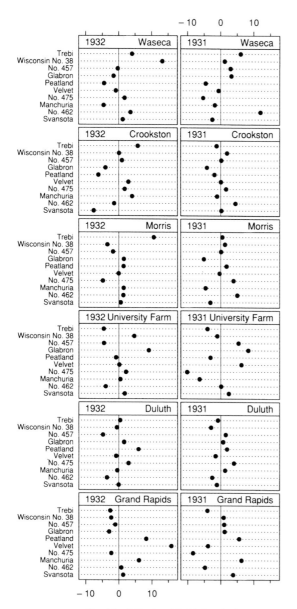

6.27 The multiway dot plot displays the residuals from the bisquare fit to the altered barley data.

Residual Barley Yield (bushels/acre)

Verdict

A simple function fits the altered data. No discordance has resulted from the Morris interchange. The harmony and simplicity that result from the alteration force us to entertain the possibility that the data are in error. The alternative is that an extraordinary natural phenomenon occurred — the yields at Morris happened to be reversed by nature in such a way that the negative of the Morris year effect just fits into the pattern of the year-site interaction at other sites. On the basis of the evidence, the mistake hypothesis would appear to be the more likely.

But there is other evidence, from the agronomists' report, that adds to the likelihood of the mistake hypothesis. This clue was discovered by Francis J. Anscombe [3]:

> There is one puzzle in the paper, namely that the crops are first
> described as having been grown in 1930 and 1931, but thereafter
> in all tables and discussion the years are referred to as 1931 and
> 1932. The same discrepancy occurs in Fisher's book. Presumably
> the later dates are correct. Barley in Minnesota is apparently
> always sown in the spring, so that the whole growing process
> occurs in one calendar year.

The incorrect specification of the years in the report evidences a carelessness that could easily infect other aspects of the specification of years.

What we need now is something akin to a motive. How could three agronomists analyzing data from the very state in which they lived overlook a blunder of this magnitude? The answer is provided by two sentences in their report:

> This paper is essentially a methodology study and illustrates the
> application of the analysis of variance to an endeavor to obtain
> answers to the above questions [statistically significant differences
> in the effects of the three categorical variables]. The statistical
> method used, known as the "analysis of variance," was developed
> by R. A. Fisher (1,2).

In other words, the agronomists were less interested in the agricultural conclusions of the paper than in brandishing the new method of analysis. Their allegiance was to the method, not to the data, providing fertile ground for overlooking a mistake, especially since they did not have the benefit of the powerful visualization methods now available.

The cumulative evidence, all of it circumstantial, is nevertheless convincing. The agronomists appear to be guilty of a missed finding.

6.5   *Visualization and Probabilistic Inference*

The barley example speaks forcefully to the importance of visualization as part of the process of data analysis. Data analysis without visualization, even with methods as brilliant as Fisher's, risks missing important happenings in data, and risks missing ways of simplifying the structure of data, and risks the use of probabilistic methods whose assumptions are not supported by the data. The agronomists, using rote data analysis, missed an important happening in the data — a mistake.

The barley data also teach us that tools matter. Two data analysts of exceptional acuity — Francis J. Anscombe [3, 4] and Cuthbert Daniel [29] — analyzed the data. In the 1960s and 1970s, both contributed pioneering methods for diagnosing the performance of fits to data and for judging how well data satisfy assumptions of probabilistic inference. Both were strong advocates of visualization well before it was fashionable, and established a legacy that continues into this book. Both had deep intuition for the processes of data analysis. Both missed the significance of the Morris reversal in their analyses. Tools matter, and many of the powerful visualization tools available to us today were not available at the time of their analyses, either as software or even as ideas.

Anscombe treated the years and sites as a single categorical variable with $6 \times 2 = 12$ categories — Waseca-1931, Waseca-1932, Morris-1931, Morris-1932, and so forth — giving up on distinguishing years since it appeared to him that year and site were less interesting than variety.

It also reduced the number of factors from three to two, which made the data more conducive to visualization given the tools Anscombe had available at the time. But this merging made it nearly impossible for the Morris anomaly to appear.

Daniel analyzed the barley data using tables but no graphs. He discovered the aberrant data for Velvet at Grand Rapids and suspected an error: "These facts suggest that the two entries [the 1931 and 1932 Velvet yields at Grand Rapids] have been interchanged in error." The immediate suspicion came from a vast experience in analyzing experimental data that had taught him blunders are common. But for Morris he missed the information that triggers suspicion. He did see that the 1932 year effect exceeded the 1931 year effect. But he failed to discover that the negative of the Morris year effect fits neatly into the pattern of the year-site interaction at the other sites. So his suspicious nature was not aroused, and he wrote simply, "The yearly differences were consistent for four locations but were reversed for location 2 [Morris]." The poverty of tabular presentation did not allow even an exceptional data analyst to see the pattern in the reversal that triggers suspicion.

Visualization is a necessary part of data analysis. Tools matter.

Bibliography

[1] E. Anderson. The Irises of the Gaspé Peninsula. *Bulletin of the American Iris Society*, 59, 2–5, 1935.

[2] D. F. Andrews, E. B. Fowlkes, and P. A. Tukey. Some Approaches to Interactive Statistical Graphics. In W. S. Cleveland and M. E. McGill, editors, *Dynamic Graphics for Statistics*, pages 73–90. Chapman and Hall, New York, 1988.

[3] F. J. Anscombe. *Computing in Statistical Science through APL*. Springer, New York, 1981.

[4] F. J. Anscombe. Looking at Two-Way Tables. Technical report, Department of Statistics, Yale University, New Haven, Connecticut, U.S.A., 1983.

[5] E. Bard, B. Hamelin, R. G. Fairbanks, and A. Zindler. Calibration of the ^{14}C Timescale Over the Past 30,000 Years Using Mass Spectrometric U-Th Ages from Barbados Corals. *Nature*, 345, 405–410, 1990.

[6] R. A. Becker and W. S. Cleveland. Brushing Scatterplots. *Technometrics*, 29, 127–142, 1987.

[7] C. Bellver. Influence of Particulate Pollution on the Positions of Neutral Points in the Sky in Seville (Spain). *Atmospheric Environment*, 21, 699–702, 1987.

[8] J. L. Bentley, D. S. Johnson, T. Leighton, and C. C. McGeoch. An Experimental Study of Bin Packing. In *Proceedings, Twenty-First Annual Allerton Conference on Communication, Control, and Computing*, pages 51–60. University of Illinois, Urbana-Champaign, Illinois, U.S.A., 1983.

[9] J. Berkson. Tests of Significance Considered as Evidence. *Journal of the American Statistical Association*, 37, 325–335, 1942.

[10] T. A. Boden, R. J. Sepanski, and F. W. Stoss. Trends '91: A Compendium of Data on Global Change — Highlights. Technical report, Carbon Dioxide Information Analysis Center, Oak Ridge National Laboratory, Oak Ridge, Tennessee, U.S.A., 1992.

[11] F. Briand and J. E. Cohen. Environmental Correlates of Food Chain Length. *Science*, 238, 956–960, 1987.

[12] N. D. Brinkman. Ethanol Fuel — A Single-Cylinder Engine Study of Efficiency and Exhaust Emissions. *SAE Transactions*, 80, 1410–1424, 1981.

[13] S. M. Bruntz, W. S. Cleveland, B. Kleiner, and J. L. Warner. The Dependence of Ambient Ozone on Solar Radiation, Wind, Temperature, and Mixing Height. In *Symposium on Atmospheric Diffusion and Air Pollution*, pages 125–128. American Meteorological Society, Boston, 1974.

[14] E. Buijsman, H. F. M. Maas, and W. A. H. Asman. Anthropogenic NH_3 Emissions in Europe. *Atmospheric Environment*, 21, 1009–1022, 1987.

[15] R. Buta. The Structure and Dynamics of Ringed Galaxies. III. Surface Photometry and Kinematics of the Ringed Nonbarred Spiral NGC 7531. *Astrophysical Journal Supplement Series*, 64, 1–37, 1987.

[16] J. M. Chambers, W. S. Cleveland, B. Kleiner, and P. A. Tukey. *Graphical Methods for Data Analysis*. Chapman and Hall, New York, 1983.

[17] G. Chong. Diagnostics for Nonparametric Regression Models with Additive Terms. *Journal of the American Statistical Association*, 87, 1051–1058, 1992.

[18] R. B. Cleveland, W. S. Cleveland, J. E. McRae, and I. Terpenning. STL: A Seasonal-Trend Decomposition Procedure Based on Loess. *Journal of Official Statistics*, 6, 3–73, 1990.

[19] W. S. Cleveland. Robust Locally Weighted Regression and Smoothing Scatterplots. *Journal of the American Statistical Association*, 74, 829–836, 1979.

[20] W. S. Cleveland. *The Elements of Graphing Data*. Hobart Press, Summit, New Jersey, U.S.A., 1985.

[21] W. S. Cleveland. A Model for Studying Display Methods of Statistical Graphics (with discussion). *Journal of Computational and Statistical Graphics*, 3, 1993.

[22] W. S. Cleveland, S. J. Devlin, and E. Grosse. Regression by Local Fitting: Methods, Properties, and Computational Algorithms. *Journal of Econometrics*, 37, 87–114, 1988.

[23] W. S Cleveland, E. Grosse, and W. M. Shyu. Local Regression Models. In J. M. Chambers and T. Hastie, editors, *Statistical Models in S*, pages 309–376. Chapman and Hall, New York, 1991.

[24] W. S. Cleveland and M. E. McGill, editors. *Dynamic Graphics for Statistics*. Chapman and Hall, New York, 1988.

[25] W. S. Cleveland, M. E. McGill, and R. McGill. The Shape Parameter of a Two-Variable Graph. *Journal of the American Statistical Association*, 83, 289–300, 1988.

[26] W. S. Cleveland and R. McGill. Graphical Perception: The Visual Decoding of Quantitative Information on Graphical Displays of Data. *Journal of the Royal Statistical Society, Series A*, 150, 192–229, 1987.

[27] W. S. Cleveland and I. J. Terpenning. Graphical Methods for Seasonal Adjustment. *Journal of the American Statistical Association*, 77, 52–62, 1982.

[28] P. Costigan-Eaves. *Data Graphics in the 20th Century: A Comparative and Analytic Survey*. PhD thesis, Rutgers University, New Brunswick, New Jersey, U.S.A., 1984.

[29] C. Daniel. *Applications of Statistics to Industrial Experimentation*. Wiley, New York, 1976.

[30] C. Daniel and F. Wood. *Fitting Equations to Data*. Wiley, New York, 1971.

[31] O. L. Davies, G. E. P. Box, W. R. Cousins, F. R. Himsworth, H. Kenney, M. Milbourn, W. Spendley, and W. L. Stevens. *Statistical Methods in Research and Production*. Hafner, New York, 3rd edition, 1957.

[32] J. C. Davis. Contour Mapping and SURFACE II. *Science*, 237, 669–672, 1987.

[33] W. E. Deming. Letter to William S. Cleveland, 1985.

[34] R. Descartes. *The Geometry of René Descartes*. Dover, New York, 1954.

[35] D. Draper, J. S. Hodges, C. L. Mallows, and D. Pregibon. Exchangeability and Data Analysis (with discussion). *Journal of the Royal Statistical Society, Series A*, 156, 9–37, 1993.

[36] J. Fan. Design-Adaptive Nonparametric Regression. *Journal of the American Statistical Association*, 87, 998–1004, 1992.

[37] R. A. Fisher. The Use of Multiple Measurements in Taxonomic Problems. *Annals of Eugenics*, 7, 179–188, 1936.

[38] R. A. Fisher. *Statistical Methods for Research Workers*. Hafner, New York, 13th edition, 1958.

[39] R. A. Fisher. *The Design of Experiments*. Hafner, New York, 9th edition, 1971.

[40] R. A. Fisher. *Collected Papers of R. A. Fisher*. University of Adelaide, Adelaide, Australia, 1971–1974.

[41] M. A. Fisherkeller, J. H. Friedman, and J. W. Tukey. Prim-9: An Interactive Multidimensional Data Display and Analysis System. In W. S. Cleveland and M. E. McGill, editors, *Dynamic Graphics for Statistics*, pages 91–109. Chapman and Hall, New York, 1988.

[42] J. D. Foley, A. van Dam, S. K. Feiner, and J. F. Hughes. *Computer Graphics: Principles and Practice*. Addison-Wesley, Reading, Massachusetts, U.S.A., 1990.

[43] E. B. Fowlkes. User's Manual for an On–Line Interactive System for Probability Plotting on the DDP–224 Computer. Technical report, AT&T Bell Laboratories, Murray Hill, New Jersey, U.S.A., 1971.

[44] J. P. Frisby and J. L. Clatworthy. Learning to See Complex Random-Dot Stereograms. *Perception*, 4, 173–178, 1975.

[45] H. G. Funkhouser. Historical Development of the Graphical Representation of Statistical Data. *Osiris*, 3, 269–404, 1937.

[46] E. H. Grosse. Approximation and Optimization of Electron Density Maps. Technical report, Computer Science Department, Stanford University, Stanford, California, U.S.A., 1980.

[47] A. Hald. *A History of Probability and Statistics and Their Applications Before 1750*. Wiley, New York, 1990.

[48] T. Hastie and C. Loader. Local Regression: Automatic Kernel Carpentry. *Statistical Science*, 8,120–143, 1993.

[49] T. Hastie and R. Tibshirani. *Generalized Additive Models*. Chapman and Hall, New York, 1990.

[50] A. H. Hersh. The Effect of Temperature upon the Heterozygotes in the Bar Series of Drosophila. *Journal of Experimental Zoölogy*, 39, 55–71, 1924.

[51] D. C. Hoaglin, F. Mosteller, and J. W. Tukey, editors. *Understanding Robust and Exploratory Data Analysis*. Wiley, New York, 1983.

[52] D. C. Hoaglin, F. Mosteller, and J. W. Tukey, editors. *Exploring Data Tables, Trends, and Shapes*. Wiley, New York, 1985.

[53] A. Houghton, E. W. Munster, and M. V. Viola. Increased Incidence of Malignant Melanoma After Peaks of Sunspot Activity. *The Lancet*, 8, 759–760, 1978.

[54] E. Imhof. *Cartographic Relief Presentation*. Walter de Gruyter, Berlin, 1982.

[55] F. R. Immer, H. K. Hayes, and Le Roy Powers. Statistical Determination of Barley Varietal Adaption. *Journal of the American Society of Agronomy*, 26, 403–419, 1934.

[56] B. Julesz. Texture in Visual Perception. *Scientific American*, 212(2), 38–48, 1965.

[57] B. Julesz. *Foundations of Cyclopean Perception*. University of Chicago Press, Chicago, 1971.

[58] C. D. Keeling, R. B. Bacastow, and T. P. Whorf. Measurements of the Concentration of Carbon Dioxide at Mauna Loa Observatory, Hawaii. In W. C. Clark, editor, *Carbon Dioxide Review: 1982*, pages 377–385. Oxford University Press, New York, 1982.

[59] R. A. Kerr. Fading El Niño Broadening Scientists' View. *Science*, 221, 940–941, 1983.

[60] B. Lia, R. W. Williams, and L. M. Chalupa. Formation of Retinal Ganglion Cell Topography During Prenatal Development. *Science*, 236, 848–851, 1987.

[61] D. Marr. *Vision*. Freeman, San Francisco, 1982.

[62] J. A. McDonald. Interactive Graphics for Data Analysis. Technical report, Department of Statistics, Stanford University, Stanford, California, U.S.A., 1982.

[63] D. H. McLain. Drawing Contours from Arbitrary Data Points. *Computer Journal*, 17, 318–324, 1972.

[64] R. Monastersky. Coral Corrects Carbon Dating Problems. *Science News*, 137, 356, 1990.

[65] F. Mosteller and J. W. Tukey. *Data Analysis and Regression: A Second Course in Statistics*. Addison-Wesley, Reading, Massachusetts, U.S.A., 1977.

[66] J. E. Ottenweller, W. N. Tapp, T. S. Chen, and B. H. Natelson. Cardiovascular Aging in Syrian Hamsters: Similarities Between Normal Aging and Disease. *Experimental Aging Research*, 13, 73–84, 1987.

[67] W. Playfair. *Statistical Breviary*. William Playfair, London, 1801.

[68] I. Rock. *Perception*. Scientific American Books, New York, 1984.

[69] R. N. Rodriguez. A Comparison of the ACE and MORALS Algorithms in an Application to Engine Exhaust Emissions Modeling. In L. Billard, editor, *Computer Science and Statistics: Proceedings of the Sixteenth Symposium on the Interface*, pages 159–167. North-Holland, New York, 1985.

[70] S. H. Schneider. *Global Warming: Are We Entering the Greenhouse Century?* Sierra Club Books, San Francisco, 1989.

[71] R. D. Snee. Experimenting with a Large Number of Variables. In R. D. Snee, editor, *Experiments in Industry*, pages 25–35. American Society for Quality Control, Milwaukee, Wisconsin, U.S.A., 1985.

[72] W. V. Snyder. Contour Plotting. *ACM Transactions on Mathematical Software*, 4, 290–294, 1978.

[73] W. Stuetzle. Plot Windows. *Journal of the American Statistical Association*, 82, 466–475, 1987.

[74] E. R. Tufte. *The Visual Display of Quantitative Information*. Graphics Press, Cheshire, Connecticut, U.S.A., 1983.

[75] E. R. Tufte. *Envisioning Information*. Graphics Press, Cheshire, Connecticut, U.S.A., 1990.

[76] J. W. Tukey. *Exploratory Data Analysis*. Addison-Wesley, Reading, Massachusetts, U.S.A., 1977.

[77] J. W. Tukey. Graphic Comparisons of Several Linked Aspects: Alternatives and Suggested Principles (with discussion). *Journal of Computational and Statistical Graphics*, 2, 1–49, 1993.

[78] P. A. Tukey and J. W. Tukey. Graphical Display of Data Sets in 3 or More Dimensions. In V. Barnett, editor, *Interpreting Multivariate Data*, pages 189–275. Wiley, Chichester, U. K., 1981.

[79] A. Watt. *Fundamentals of Three–Dimensional Computer Graphics*. Addison-Wesley, Reading, Massachusetts, U.S.A., 1990.

[80] M. B. Wilk and R. Gnanadesikan. Probability Plotting Methods for the Analysis of Data. *Biometrika*, 55, 1–17, 1968.

[81] F. Yates. The Design and Analysis of Factorial Experiments. *Imperial Bureau Soil Science Technical Committee*, 35,4–95, 1937.

[82] F. Yates and K. Mather. Ronald Aylmer Fisher. *Biographical Memoirs of Fellows of the Royal Society of London*, 9, 91–120, 1963.

[83] M. J. Zyda. A Decomposable Algorithm for Contour Surface Display Generation. *ACM Transactions on Graphics*, 7, 129–148, 1988.

Index

Colophon

Text and Graphics Layout

The layout of the book is unusual. There are two criteria that override everything else. First, a block of text discussing a graphical display needs to be as close as possible to the display, preferably on the same page or on a facing page. Second, it is vital to make content the master of design and not vice versa. Some approach text-display layout by writing to the design. This typically interferes with the coherence of the discussion. Throwing in a thought because space needs to be filled is not a good way to communicate. The design here solves the layout problem by giving up on filling and balancing pages, a convention thought to be inviolate by some. The spacing between paragraphs and the ragged-right text is meant to lessen the sense of visual order so that the lack of balance and fill is less salient.

Visualization Software Credits

The workhorse software of the book is S, the powerful system developed by Richard Becker, John Chambers, and Allan Wilks. The original visualizations of data that formed the basis of the writing were done in S. The only excursions out of S in the data analysis were to Geomview, the well designed software of Stuart Levy, Tamara Munzner, and Mark Phillips for direct manipulation 3-D graphics.

The final rendering of the displays for the first printing, however, used a number of systems. Except for the 3-D plots and the color level plot, all final rendering was done by proprietary software of MEM Research, Inc., written by Robert McGill. The software, which is based on S, enables very delicate control of the details of graphs so that graphical elements — such as labels, tick marks, and the positioning of the panels of multi-panel displays — can be placed precisely where they best serve the visualization. The placement was carried out by Marylyn McGill of MEM with enormous attention to detail. The final product was PostScript$^{\circledR}$ files.

The color level plot and the 3-D plot with shading traveled through a maze of software systems. Both started out in S as trivariate data sets. The color level plot was drawn by S and then moved to Abobe Photoshop for the assignment of CMYK colors to the levels. The information about the 3-D plot went to Geomview where rendering assignments were made — the lighting, the surface characteristics, and the orientation. Then it moved on to Renderman$^{\circledR}$ to improve the quality of the image, and finally, went to Quark XPress$^{\circledR}$ where the labels were added.

After the first printing, several displays were redrawn in Pictor, the exciting new graphics system developed by Allan Wilks.

Production

This book was typeset in LaTeX. The main text is set in palatino, figure legends in helvetica, italics in times, and mathematical symbols in computer modern. Camera-ready copy was produced at AT&T Bell Laboratories on a Linotronic 200 P with a resolution of 1270 dpi.

Edwards Brothers, Inc., of Ann Arbor, Michigan, U.S.A., printed the book. The paper is 70 pound Sterling Satin, the pages are Smythe sewn, and the book is covered with Arrestox$^{\circledR}$linen.